Brown v. Board of Education at Fifty

Brown v. Board of Education at Fifty

A Rhetorical Perspective

Edited by Clarke Rountree

LEXINGTON BOOKS

Lanham • Boulder • New York • Toronto • Oxford

LEXINGTON BOOKS

Published in the United States of America
by Lexington Books
An imprint of The Rowman & Littlefield Publishing Group, Inc.
4501 Forbes Boulevard, Suite 200, Lanham, Maryland 20706

PO Box 317
Oxford
OX2 9RU, UK

British Library Cataloguing in Publication Information Available

Library of Congress Cataloging-in-Publication Data

Brown v. Board of Education at fifty : a rhetorical perspective / edited by Clarke Rountree.
p. cm.
Includes bibliographical references and index.
ISBN 0-7391-0854-9 (cloth : alk. paper)
1. Segregation in education—Law and legislation—United States—History. 2. Discrimination in education—Law and legislation—United States. 3. Brown, Oliver, 1918– —Trials, litigation, etc. 4. Topeka (Kan.). Board of Education—Trials, litigation, etc. I. Title: Brown versus Board of Education at fifty. II. Rountree, Clarke, 1958–
KF4155.B7583 2004
344.73'0798—dc22

2004012557

Printed in the United States of America

∞™ The paper used in this publication meets the minimum requirements of American National Standard for Information Sciences—Permanence of Paper for Printed Library Materials, ANSI/NISO Z39.48–1992.

For my mother, who taught tolerance and understanding in the midst of ignorance and suspicion.

Contents

Acknowledgments

This volume is the product of a great deal of work by many hands. The editor thanks, first and foremost, the scholars whose chapter contributions made this book possible. Their insights provide an original contribution to our understanding of *Brown v. Board of Education*, its foundations, its contexts, and its outcomes, as well as our understanding of the rhetorical processes of law. Additionally, I thank the staff of Lexington Books for their help in copyediting this manuscript. Finally, I acknowledge timely and professional copyediting help from Kate Howard. I received additional last-minute copyediting advice from my permanent copyeditor and wife, Jennie Rountree, whose support and encouragement are a happy constant in my life.

Introduction

Clarke Rountree

Brown v. Board of Education is a half-century old now. It stands as a monument to many things: the defeat of Jim Crow and racial segregation in public life, particularly in schools. A repudiation of the "separate but equal" doctrine endorsed by the U.S. Supreme Court fifty-eight years earlier. The defeat of W.E.B. Du Bois's efforts to keep African American children in their own, less threatening schools and communities. The success of a decades-long campaign by the NAACP and its Legal Education and Defense Fund. The ascendancy of Thurgood Marshall, whose success in this case helped secure his eventual appointment as the first African American to serve on our nation's highest court. Given its monumental stature, the case has become a litmus test for rejecting judicial nominees who appear to question its outcome or its legal foundations.[1]

On the other hand, *Brown* has not prevented the resegregation of American schools through "white flight" to the suburbs and to private schools, nor has it prevented later Supreme Court decisions that undermined efforts to address this resegregation.[2] And, in its own day, it sparked the most serious challenge to the authority of the federal courts since *Dred Scott*'s contribution to the Civil War, with "massive resistance" movements in some southern states, antibusing movements in northern cities, and showdowns requiring the intervention of the president of the United States and the National Guard.

The story of *Brown* has been retold many times by historians, legal scholars, sociologists, and others. It typically begins with the passage of Jim Crow legislation in the post-Reconstruction South, where Louisiana's racial segregation laws for rail carriers gave rise to a missed opportunity for the U.S. Supreme Court to defend the goals of the post–Civil War amendments and early civil rights acts in *Plessy v. Ferguson*. Decades of struggle against the systematic subjugation of African Americans followed until Hitler showed the world the evil that is racism, and a more liberal Supreme Court found that there could be no equality in racial segregation. To be certain, this telling of the story has been qualified in numerous ways by scholars questioning the social science used to support *Brown*, the legal basis for arguments used throughout this period, and the historical roles played by the NAACP, by Chief Justice Warren and other judges, by various U.S. presidents, and others in this compelling drama.

What has not been systematically explored—and this is what this book seeks to add to our understanding of these pivotal events—is the role that *rhetoric* played in this sixty-year drama in establishing, defending, challenging, and overturning legalized educational segregation by race.[3] By "rhetoric" I do not mean the empty, bombastic, overstylized, nonsubstantive discourse to which the pejorative uses of this term refer. Instead, I refer to that ancient, full-bodied notion of rhetoric as discourse that is an engine of change in human history. This is the rhetoric that concerns itself with persuasion, with speakers (or writers) and their audiences, with situations and the constraints they place on communication, and with the processes "*of adjusting ideas to people and of people to ideas*."[4] Those who study rhetoric typically find their homes in communication studies departments, though scholars from law, philosophy, sociology, history, and other fields have adapted a rhetorical perspective to shed light on the common subjects of their fields.[5]

The rhetorical perspective is quite appropriate for analyzing legal discourse, since Western rhetoric first developed as a means to improve legal argument. As the story goes, a tyrant named Thrasybulus ruled Syracuse in Sicily in the fifth century B.C.E. until he was ousted, giving rise to competing property claims made without the benefit of now-destroyed deeds. An enterprising scholar named Corax developed a system of argument from probability, which he taught for a fee to some notable students, perhaps including the renowned speaker Gorgias of Leontini (given voice in the Platonic dialogue by the same name).[6] The Sophists carried this art to Greece, the Romans adapted it from the Greeks, it followed the Roman educational system into the Holy Roman Empire and became one of the seven liberal arts taught during the Middle Ages, and it has been a subject of theorizing through various permutations since then.

Contemporary rhetorical scholars have long been interested in courtroom advocacy, but widespread interest in legal argument outside of trial courts has been a more recent development, with the exception of First Amendment law.[7] The reason is obvious: While trial advocates appeal to juries of peers, whose knowledge of the law may be minimal, appellate advocates and legal scholars arguing about what the law is or ought to be speak to a more educated audience, which a rhetorical scholar must understand well. Only a handful of scholars from the 1960s through the 1980s have taken on the arduous task of becoming sufficiently conversant in law as well as rhetoric to analyze legal rhetoric outside the courtroom.[8]

Since the 1990s, however, this situation has changed dramatically. A cadre of rhetorical scholars has emerged to study judicial rhetoric, many of them sporting law degrees. In 1992, under the leadership of John Louis Lucaites and William Weithoff, Indiana University's Department of Speech and the Speech Communication Association cosponsored a Doctoral Honors Seminar titled "Rhetoric and the Law: History, Theory, and Criticism."[9] One outcome of the conference was a special issue of *Southern Communication Journal* on rhetoric and law two years later.[10] In that same year, the American Forensic Association published a special issue of *Argumentation & Advocacy* on the same topic.[11] Marouf Hasian, Jr., who authored the lead essay in this volume, has been the most prolific contributor to a growing body of studies in appellate rhetoric.[12]

The fiftieth anniversary of *Brown v. Board of Education* affords an opportunity to highlight the work of these scholars while offering a fresh perspective for analyzing the most important Supreme Court case of the twentieth century. The scholarly essays contained in the chapters of this volume run the gamut of the educational segregation issue, beginning with *Plessy*, considering the NAACP's development of a series of graduate school cases to challenge *Plessy*, analyzing the *Brown* decision itself (with particular focus on the controversial use of social scientific evidence), assessing the state responses to *Brown*, and critiquing the two Supreme Court decisions implementing the *Brown* decision. These essays use a variety of critical approaches, from traditional approaches to situation, style, arrangement, and argument, to postmodern concerns with broader cultural and ideological contexts. As a whole, they reflect much of the richness of the critical perspectives afforded by rhetorical theory.

These essays also provide fresh insight into law and educational segregation. Marouf Hasian Jr. begins with a reconstruction of the rhetorical context of *Plessy*, demonstrating the complexity of the social, political, and economic backdrop to arguments over segregation in public places. He challenges the traditional legal stories, suggesting that *Plessy* involved the simple choice between a "racist" majority position and Harlan's "enlightened" dissent presented in law school hornbooks.

Daniel Mangis looks particularly at the Harlan dissent in *Plessy*, explaining how this opinion was shaped by the Kentucky judge's religious convictions, the structural and stylistic choices he made working within the rhetorical constraints of the "dissent," and his use of the "color-blind" constitution metaphor. He concludes that Harlan's "argument was far more limited and introspective than what might appear from contemporary citations of his dissent," and that his dissent was canonized more for its repudiation of the *Plessy* majority than for its legal reasoning.

My own essay works with the largest swath of history here, looking at the NAACP's more than forty years of work to reverse *Plessy*'s support of educational segregation. I examine particularly the final twenty years of its work, involving a litigation campaign focused on graduate school cases. Applying theoretical work involving what I have dubbed "prospective argument," I look at the graduate school campaign as a strategic means for creating successive rhetorical situations conducive to the success of the ultimate argument in *Brown.*

David Droge looks at the *Brown* decision itself, focusing particularly on the social scientific evidence that supported the Court's finding that "[s]eparate educational facilities are inherently unequal."[13] Unfortunately, the Court misused this evidence, bringing criticism down on the social scientists whose work was cited. To craft an opinion less threatening to the southern audience, Droge argues, Chief Justice Warren left out evidence rejecting biological arguments about racial inferiority, and instead constructed African Americans as culturally deprived, and as objects of "contempt and pity." These rhetorical choices contributed to an unfortunate "liberal orthodoxy" that assured the American people that "the Negro problem" would be solved by lowering educational barriers and assimilating this group.

Ann E. Burnette considers the reaction to the *Brown* decision in the South, focusing particularly on Virginia's "massive resistance" movement. She notes the development of the movement's rhetorical vision, particularly in its reliance on historical arguments from eighteenth- and nineteenth-century philosophical debates, which supported constitutional and racial claims against school segregation and portrayed these dissenters as conservatives opposed to radical Supreme Court action. They did not change their arguments when addressing audiences outside of Virginia, but remained hopeful that historical arguments about state sovereignty and racial differences would resonate with a national audience. Yet, the "higher ground" of constitutional arguments on state sovereignty was tainted by unsavory, "low" appeals urging the racial inferiority of African Americans.

Ann M. Gill compares and contrasts two major Supreme Court decisions implementing the *Brown* decision: *Brown II* in 1955 and *Cooper v. Aaron* three years later. Each used a different strategy of legitimization, with different results. The first featured a rhetoric of partnership that demonstrated patience and was adapted to a hostile environment. The second, handed down in the face of Southern resistance following *Brown II*, used stronger strategies to invoke the authority of the Court and stress the inalienable and nonnegotiable nature of the rights and responsibilities at issue in the case.

Reading these essays side by side provides additional insights into *Brown* and its related cases. For example, Hasian's background on the cultural and discursive context within which Justice Harlan dissented sheds light on Mangis's portrait of that dissenter and his opinion. That background also provides a basis for understanding the context within which the NAACP declared war on *Plessy* and developed the campaign I describe. Droge elaborates on the NAACP legal team's development of social science evidence, filling out a portion of the long-term strategy which my essay describes only briefly. The concerns that Droge raises about *Brown*'s characterization of African Americans as "culturally deprived" are realized in Burnette's account of the use of "cultural inferiority" arguments in Virginia's "massive resistance" movement. Burnette's account of Virginia's "massive resistance" campaign, in turn, provides a good foundation for understanding what the Supreme Court faced after *Brown II*, and why they radically changed their rhetorical approach in *Cooper v. Aaron*, as Gill documents. And, jumping across the time span, Burnette's account of the state's arguments against segregation may fruitfully be read against *Plessy*-era arguments in favor of segregated passenger railroad cars.

Whether read separately or with each other, these essays provide valuable new insights into the rhetorical processes involved in creating, sustaining, challenging, and reversing educational segregation. They also demonstrate the value of the rhetorical perspective and provide encouragement to those who wish to help further develop this emerging field of judicial rhetoric.

Notes

1. A history of each of these achievements can be found in Richard Kluger, *Simple Justice* (New York: Alfred A. Knopf, 1976). On the litmus test for judicial nominees, the appointment of William Rehnquist as Associate Justice of the U.S. Supreme Court is an early example. See Kluger, 606-607.

2. For recent statistics on these trends and a history of legal and social developments that have led to resegregation, see Erica Frankenberg, Chungmei Lee, and Gary Orfield, "A Multiracial Society with Segregated Schools: Are We Losing the Dream?" (Cambridge, MA: The [Harvard] Civil Rights Project, January 2003) (www.civilrightsproject.harvard.edu; downloaded 9 July 2003).

3. The only studies related to the *Brown* decision published by rhetoric scholars, to my knowledge, are David B. Strother, "Polemics and the Reversal of the 'Separate but Equal' Doctrine," *Quarterly Journal of Speech* 49 (1963): 50-56; Milton Dickens and Ruth E. Schwartz, "Oral Argument before the Supreme Court: Marshall v. Davis in the School Segregation Cases," *Quarterly Journal of Speech* 57 (1971): 32-42; David M. Hunsaker, "The Rhetoric of Brown v. Board of Education: Paradigm for Contemporary Social Protest," *Southern Speech Communication Journal* 43 (1978): 91-109; Marouf Hasian, Jr., Celeste Michelle Condit, and John Louis Lucaites, "The Rhetorical Boundaries of 'The Law': A Consideration of the Rhetorical Culture of Legal Practice and the Case of the 'Separate but Equal' Doctrine," *Quarterly Journal of Speech* 82 (November 1996): 323-342; and Marouf Hasian, Jr. and Geoff Klinger, "Sarah Roberts and the Early History of the 'Separate but Equal' Doctrine: A Study in Rhetoric, Law, and Social Change," *Communication Studies* 53 (Fall 2002): 269-283. I am unaware of any studies of *Plessy*, of the graduate school cases that preceded *Brown*, of the Supreme Court's opinion in *Brown*, of the post-

Brown implementation decisions, or of the states' reactions to *Brown*, among other things.

4. Donald C. Bryant, "Rhetoric: Its Functions and Its Scope," *Quarterly Journal of Speech* 39 (December 1953): 413.

5. See, for example, John S. Nelson, Allan Megill, and Donald N. McCloskey, eds., *The Rhetoric of the Human Sciences: Language and Argument in Scholarship and Public Affairs* (Madison: University of Wisconsin Press, 1984).

6. See Thomas Cole, *The Origins of Rhetoric in Ancient Greece* (Baltimore: Johns Hopkins University Press, 1991).

7. Many works by communication scholars in legal advocacy are referenced in Richard D. Rieke and Randall K. Stutman, *Communication in Legal Advocacy* (Columbia: University of South Carolina Press, 1990). Work by communication scholars who study freedom of speech issues is featured annually in the *Free Speech Yearbook*, published by the National Communication Association, as well as journalism and mass communication journals. Here I am concerned with rhetorical scholars whose homes are in the communication field. There are a growing number of legal scholars who study rhetorical issues, often in ways similar to those used by communication scholars. See, for example, James Boyd White, *Heracles' Bow: Essays on the Rhetoric and Poetics of Law* (Madison: University of Wisconsin Press, 1985), among many others by White; Gerald B. Wetlaufer, "Rhetoric and Its Denial in Legal Discourse," *Virginia Law Review* 76 (1990): 1545-1597; Eileen A. Scallen, "Classical Rhetoric, Practical Reasoning, and the Law of Evidence," *American University Law Review* (Summer 1995): 1717-1815; and Gene R. Shreve, "Rhetoric, Pragmatism and the Interdisciplinary Turn in Legal Criticism: A Study of Altruistic Judicial Argument," *American Journal of Comparative Law* 46 (1998): 41-67. Much of the work of the Critical Legal Studies scholars reflects rhetorical concerns as well. See, for example, Robert Mangabeira Unger, *The Critical Legal Studies Movement* (Cambridge: Harvard University Press, 1983).

8. Some communication scholars who study argument have followed in the footsteps of philosophers Chaim Perelman and Stephen Toulmin in using law to shed light on argument theory, and vice versa. Perelman's key works in this area include *The Idea of Justice and the Problem of Argument*, trans. John Petrie (New York: Humanities Press, 1963); *The New Rhetoric: A Treatise on Argumentation*, trans. John Wilkinson and Purcell Weaver (Notre Dame, IN: University of Notre Dame Press, 1969) (with Lucie Olbrechts-Tyteca); and *The Realm of Rhetoric*, trans. William Kluback (Notre Dame, IN: University of Notre Dame Press, 1982). Toulmin's most important work in this area is *The Uses of Argument* (Cambridge: Cambridge University Press, 1958). Argument scholars from the communication field publishing on appellate rhetoric include

Richard E. Crable, "Models of Argumentation and Judicial Judgment," *Journal of the American Forensics Association* 12 (1976): 113-120; Stephen B. Jones, "Justification in Judicial Opinions: A Case Study," *Journal of the American Forensics Association* 12 (1976): 121-127; David A. Rabin, "Gottlieb's Model of Rule-Guided Reasoning: An Analysis of *Griswold v. Connecticut*," *Journal of the American Forensics Association* 15 (1978): 77-99; and Sara E. Newell and Richard D. Rieke, "A Practical Reasoning Approach to Legal Doctrine," *Journal of the American Forensic Association* 22 (Spring 1986): 212-222. Among the handful of communication scholars who have examined legal rhetoric outside the courtroom are Strother; Warren E. Wright, "Judicial Rhetoric: A Field for Research," *Speech Monographs* 31 (1964): 64-72; Dickens and Schwartz; Hunsaker; Michael R. Hagan, "*Roe v. Wade*: The Rhetoric of Fetal Life," *Central States Speech Journal* 27 (1976): 192-199; Gayle Lewis Levison, "The Rhetoric of the Oral Argument in '*The Regents of California v. Bakke*,'" *Western Journal of Speech Communication* 43 (Fall 1979): 271-277; Raymond S. Rodgers, "Absolutism and Natural Law Argument: William O. Douglas on Freedom of Expression," *Southern Speech Communication Journal* 48 (1982): 22-37 and "Generic Tendencies in Majority and Non-Majority Supreme Court Opinions: The Case of Justice Douglas," *Communication Quarterly* 30 (1982): 232-36; Josina M. Makau, "The Supreme Court and Reasonableness," *Quarterly Journal of Speech* 70 (1984): 379-396; A. Cheree Carlson, "John Quincy Adams' 'Amistad Address': Eloquence in a Generic Hybrid," *Western Journal of Speech Communication* 49 (Winter 1985): 14-26; Walter Ulrich, "The Creation of a Legacy: Brandeis' Concurring Opinion in *Whitney v. California*," *Southern Speech Communication Journal* 50 (Winter 1985): 143-155; Kristine M. Bartanen, "The Rhetoric of Dissent in Justice O'Connor's *Akron* Opinion," *Southern Speech Communication Journal* 52 (Spring 1987): 240-262; and William L. Benoit, "Attorney Argumentation and Supreme Court Opinions," *Argumentation and Advocacy* 26 (Summer 1989): 22-38.

9. Lucaites also has published a couple of essays in the area: John Louis Lucaites, "Between Rhetoric and 'The Law': Power, Legitimacy, and Social Change," *Quarterly Journal of Speech* 76 (1990): 435-49 and Hasian, Condit, and Lucaites.

10. The Fall 1994 issue of *Southern Communication Journal* (volume 60) featured the following essays: John Lucaites and William Weithoff, "Rhetoric and Law: History, Criticism and 'Praxis,'" 1-3; William Lewis, "Of Innocence, Exclusion, and the Burning of Flags: The Romantic Realism of the Law," 4-21; Per Fjelstad, "Legal Judgment and Cultural Motivation: Enthymematic Form in *Marbury v. Madison*," 22-32; Sean Patrick O'Rourke, "Cultivating the 'Higher Law' in American Jurisprudence: John Quincy Adams, Neo-classical Rhetoric, and the *Amistad* Case," 33-43; Marouf Hasian, Jr., "Critical Legal Rhetorics:

The Theory and Practice of Law in a Postmodern World," 44-56; Trevor Parry-Giles, "Property Rights, Human Rights and American Jurisprudence: The Rejection of John J. Parker's Nomination to the Supreme Court," 57-67; Eileen A. Scallen, "Judgment, Justification and Junctions in the Rhetorical Criticism of Legal Texts," 68-74; and Hanns Hohmann, "Judicial Legitimacy and Legal Interpretation in the Debate between *Brutus* and *Publius*," 75-86. Lucaites and Weithoff edited this special issue. A second special journal issue of *Legal Studies*—this one for the legal community—also grew out of the Indiana conference *Forum*. It also was published in 1994 (vol. 17, 341-436) and co-edited by Lucaites and Weithoff. It was titled "A Sampler for Legal Rhetoricians and Rhetorical Lawyers."

11. The Spring 1994 issue of *Argumentation & Advocacy* (volume 30) featured the following essays: Josina M. Makau and David Lawrence, "Administrative Judicial Rhetoric: The Supreme Court's New Thesis of Political Morality," 191-205; Doyle Srader, "Spanning Ideological Chasms: The Response to Conceptual Segregation in *Bowers v. Hardwick*," 206-219; John Bruschke, "A Critical Analysis of Objectivity in the Legal Sphere," 220-235; and Geoffrey D. Klinger, "Law as 'Communicative Praxis': Toward a Rhetorical Jurisprudence," 236-247.

12. Hasian's works include "Critical Legal Rhetorics: The Theory and Practice of Law in a Postmodern World," *Southern Communication Journal* 60 (Fall 1994): 44-56; "Narrative and the Invention of Legal Science: Oliver Wendell Holmes, Jr. and 'The Path of the Law,'" *Journal of Communication Studies* 13 (1994): 27-40; "'A Stranger to Its Laws': Freedom, Civil Rights, and the Legal Ambiguity of *Romer v. Evans* (1996)," *Argumentation and Advocacy* 34 (Summer 1997): 27-42 (with Trevor Parry-Giles); Hasian, Condit, and Lucaites; "Judicial Rhetoric in a Fragmentary World: 'Character,' and Storytelling in the Leo Frank Case," *Communication Monographs* 64 (September 1997): 250-269; "The Aesthetics of Legal Rhetoric: The Ambiguities of 'Race' in *Adarand v. Pena* and the Beginning of the End of 'Affirmative Action,'" *Howard Journal of Communication* 8 (January 1997): 113-27; "The Domestication of Legal Argumentation: A Case Study of the Formalism of the Legal Realists," *Communication Quarterly* 46 (Fall 1998): 430-45; *Legal Memories and Cultural Amnesias in Anglo-American Rhetorical Culture* (Boulder, CO: Westview Press, 2000); Hasian and Klinger; Marouf Hasian Jr., *Colonial Legacies in Post Colonial Contexts: A Critical Rhetorical Examination of Legal Histories* (New York: Peter Lang Publications, 2002); and "Holocaust Denial Debates: The Symbolic Significance of *Irving v. Penguin & Lipstadt*," *Communication Studies* 53 (Summer 2002): 129-145. Additionally, Hasian has other works on the relationship between law and culture, among other things. Other contributors to the study of judicial rhetoric include William L. Benoit, "Argumentation in *Miranda v. Arizona*," *Communication Studies* 42

(Summer 1991): 129-140; William L. Benoit and J. Michael D'Agostine, "'The Case of the Midnight Judges' and Multiple Audience Discourse: Chief Justice Marshall and *Marbury v. Madison*," *Southern Communication Journal* 59 (Winter 1994): 89-96; Clarke Rountree, "On the Rhetorical Analysis of Judicial Discourse and More: A Response to Lewis," *Southern Communication Journal* 61 (Winter 1995): 166-173 and "Instantiating 'The Law' and Its Dissents in *Korematsu v. United States*: A Dramatistic Analysis of Judicial Discourse, " *Quarterly Journal of Speech* 87 (February 2001): 1-24; Carrie Crenshaw, "The Normality of Man and Female Otherness: (Re)Producing Patriarchal Lines of Argument in the Law and the News," *Argumentation and Advocacy* 32 (Spring 1996): 170-184 and "Colorblind Rhetoric," *Southern Communication Journal* 63 (Spring 1998): 244-256; Todd F. McDorman, "Challenging Constitutional Authority: African American Responses to *Scott v. Sandford*," *Quarterly Journal of Speech* 83 (May 1997): 192-209; Theodore O. Prosise and Craig R. Smith, "The Supreme Court's Ruling in *Bush v. Gore*: A Rhetoric of Inconsistency," *Rhetoric & Public Affairs* 4 (Winter 2001): 605-632; and Steve Schwarze, "Rhetorical Traction: Definitions and Institutional Arguments in Judicial Opinions about Wilderness Access," *Argumentation & Advocacy* 38 (Winter 2002): 131-150.

13. *Brown v. Board of Education*, 345 U.S. 483, 495 (1958).

1

Revisiting the Case of *Plessy v. Ferguson*

Marouf Hasian Jr.

Justice Henry Billings Brown's 1896 opinion in *Plessy v. Ferguson*[1] is often considered to be one of those landmark cases, an aberrant decision that allowed for the "reconstitution of aspects of chattel slavery in a system of segregation."[2] In that year, it was the U.S. Supreme Court that "gave official sanction to the 'separate but equal doctrine,'" and "Arkansas, Alabama, Virginia, North Carolina, and Florida all adopted more stringent Jim Crow laws."[3] In some of the traditional legal stories that have been told about this infamous target of *Brown v. Board of Education*,[4] this was a case that involved the "constitutionality of a Louisiana law, passed in 1890, which mandated" that the state provide "equal but separate accommodations for white and colored races" on all passenger railways.[5] N. Lee Cooper, in a 1997 article in the *American Bar Association Journal*, told readers that Homer Plessy, "because of his one-eighth's African ancestry," was "required to ride in a separate train car from full blooded white passengers."[6] Formalists have argued that Brown's opinion deviated from both the letter and the spirit of the Thirteenth, Fourteenth, and Fifteenth Amendments.[7] Cooper, for example, argued that the "deciding factor" in Brown's *Plessy* opinion was the "accepted custom of the day, not consistent constitutional principles of state power or individual liberty."[8] Within this orthodox narration of events, the progress that had been achieved between *Plessy* and *Brown* "all started with a single voice of dissent."[9] Legal realists contend that after "Reconstruction," some of the Southern states took "control of local politics," and used "conservative strains in American constitutional law" so that they could "recreate the dynamics of slavery."[10] The confluence of these factors supposedly created a situation where the American judicial system had the opportunity to comment on the "reasonableness" of certain police powers, while at the same time addressing the "broader question of constitutive rhetoric and collective identity: who belongs to the American polity and on what conditions?"[11]

In many of these scholarly commentaries on the case, it would be Justice John Harlan's dissent in *Plessy* that would preserve the principle of equal treatment before the law, and the "voice crying in the wilderness"[12] would be vindicated with the arrival of the 1954 *Brown* decision. The *Plessy* case could therefore be viewed as just one of many "temporary setbacks"[13] that stood in the way of the progress of American law.

These generally accepted contextualizations of the *Plessy* case help us to understand why select U.S. Supreme Court opinions appear in law school hornbooks, but they often have to be told in ways that hide some of the uncertainties, contingencies, and selectivities that are involved in particular legislative and judicial contests. As Charles Lofgren explains, legal historicizing "is seldom so neat and often more cunning. A case can be made that it was Justice Brown and the *Plessy* majority who stood vindicated by the last decades of the twentieth century." Lofgren went on to explain that Chief Justice Warren's *Brown* opinion never explicitly overruled *Plessy*, that courts did not reject the reliance on racial facts in their decisions, and the Chief Justice seemed to imply "that some classifications based on race might be legitimate."[14]

In this particular chapter, I will revisit and recontextualize the *Plessy* case, so that we can see some of the arguments, debates, and characterizations that influenced the trajectory of this controversial decision. While Lofgren and other scholars have done a fine job of explaining how previous court cases and Social Darwinian ideas influenced the trajectory of this seminal case, we also need to understand that there were many other religious, political, and economic factors that impacted these complex debates. Not everyone shared either Brown's or Harlan's vision of the Constitution, and there were a whole host of extrajudicial factors that are often left out of many orthodox accounts of the *Plessy* decision. As I will argue later in the chapter, the participants in some of these contentious debates were worried about the social climbing of "mulattoes" such as Plessy,[15] the political power of the Bourbons, possible federal intervention, the purportedly radicalism (and agnosticism) of the "carpetbagger" Albion Tourgée, and the violation of natural laws of scientific racism. An analysis of the vernacular and elite discourse of the times will show that Justice Brown was not the only social agent who could come up with plausible defenses for the "separate but equal" doctrine.

In order to carry out my rhetorical recontextualization of the *Plessy* case, this chapter has been divided into four major segments. In the first section of the essay, I provide a brief overview of some of the civil rights arguments that circulated during the Reconstruction years and post-Reconstruction years (1870-1889). I then extend this work in the second portion of the chapter, where I show that between 1890 and 1895, both supporters and critics of Louisiana's "Separate Car Bill" engaged in some heated disputation over the meanings of "civil rights," "separate," and "equal." In the third portion of the chapter I compare these arguments to the ones that circulated after the public announcement of Justice Brown's opinion in *Plessy*. Finally, in the concluding section, I explain what this critical rhetorical approach tells us about legal discourse, and I speculate on some of the reasons why we have forgotten some of the rhetorical histories that were associated with this infamous decision.

"Civil Rights" and the Local and National Debates over Public Accommodations during the Reconstruction Years and Post-Reconstruction Years, 1870-1889

In the aftermath of the Civil War, many of the supporters of civil rights causes realized that the gains that had been won on the battlefield would not automatically bring needed social, political, or economic reform. At the same time that radical Republicans were battling in Congress for benefits and legal protection for African Americans, many Southern states retaliated by passing vagrancy laws and other restrictive acts. One observer noted in March of 1866 that it seemed as though "no single Southern Legislature has yet recognized the right of Blacks to the civil rights accorded to every White alien," and that an army of some "20,000" might have to "compel the planters to give justice to the freedmen."[16] A dozen years later, D. H. Chamberlain was still complaining that despite the passage of the post–Civil War amendments, the South still had communities that had the "same oligarchical power," that was "crushing the colored race under its feet." In states such as South Carolina, Mississippi, and Louisiana, "a system of deliberate, organized violence" had been built "with bloody and rapacious hands," and these same groups were now trying to "grasp the national power" so that they could extend and perpetuate the "practice of caste and oppression."[17] As Kirt Wilson explains, the abolitionists and radical Republicans—Reconstruction's "equalitarians"—now did battle with those who believed that "blacks deserved no rights."[18]

Many former slaves and their allies worked to ensure that all citizens had at least some basic political or civil rights—often defined as the ownership of small tracts of land, securing the ballot, or gaining elected office. When Frederick Douglass visited a "Colored National Convention" in the spring of 1872, he couldn't help but notice that the Radical Republicans had helped put several people of color into high offices in several of the Gulf States—Henry Cardoza was the Secretary of State of South Carolina, Alonzo Ransier was the Lieutenant Governor of South Carolina, and Pickney Pinchback was the Lieutenant Governor in Louisiana. The famous orator knew that it was the federal government's troops that were helping blacks deal with the "local injustice and barbarism," and he was realistic enough to realize that their present political power came from the "abnormal condition of things in the South."[19] Douglass told readers that decades before, he had been at the slave auction at a New Orleans market, and he marveled at the progress that had been made by a nation that now treated "enlightened colored citizens" as "free American" citizens. Yet he also commented on the fact that the "spirit of bondage" still created difficulties for African American travelers: "No matter how intelligent, how refined and gentlemanly a black man may be, he is compelled to ride in a second-class car, amid filth and smoke, and virtually denied the right to purchase refreshments at railroad inns and restaurants."[20]

Obviously this discursive war for civil rights was going to be waged on many fronts, and some of the most visible and vitriolic battles were fought over what would be called "separate but equal accommodations for white and negro passengers."[21] During 1865 and 1866, there was a brief period of time when Mississippi, Florida, and Texas tried to pass statutory Jim Crow laws that segregated their railroads, but all these laws were "quickly aborted during Reconstruction."[22] This however, was just the opening salvo in a very protracted legal battle.

While abolitionists, radical Republicans, and other egalitarians viewed unfettered travel as a natural or "civil" right, their critics responded by arguing that this was an arena that touched on "social" rights. The opponents of the egalitarians were arguing that the recently freed slaves hadn't yet earned this extension of rights, and that travel restrictions and accommodation regulations were private matters. The same state legislatures that regulated interracial marriage or the prevention of "social amalgamation"[23] also had the duty to pass legislation that would be rationally related to the protection of public safety, health, and welfare. The "usual arrangement" at this time was for blacks to be able to sit with whites in second-class "smokers' cars," but they had a much more difficult time trying to sit in the first class, or "ladies' cars."[24]

During these post–Civil War struggles, many travelers found that there was little uniformity in either the formal or informal laws that governed interstate travel,[25] and indignant African Americans often had to make agonizing decisions about whether they were going to object to the total exclusion from the railways, the empirical equality of the facilities,[26] or the more popular separate provisions of these laws. At the same time, the railroads found themselves caught in federal and state battles over the status of interstate transportation, which impacted the ways that courts thought about racial seating arrangements on private and public carriers. In 1878, for example, the U.S. Supreme Court in *Hall v. De Cuir* unanimously struck down a provision that had been passed by the Louisiana Reconstructionists that had tried to give "equal rights and privileges" to all passengers on public conveyances.[27] The segregation of passengers was considered to be a reasonable regulation that helped provide comfort for passengers.

What often gets forgotten in our orthodox attacks on Justice Brown's decision in *Plessy* is that many African Americans may have strategically accepted some of these rationales in order to advance their own interpretations of civil rights advances, and that many whites took full advantage of these choices. By the mid-1870s, moderate Southerners were praising the efforts of blacks who appreciated the chasm that separated social from civil rights. "C. L. B.," for example, would write in the *New York Times* in June of 1875 that a "colored preacher" by the name of J. P. Weaver had some sage advice for the people of color who frequented particular inns and public conveyances. As the nation approached the end of the Reconstruction years, many assumed that the best choices that blacks could make involved the patronizing of their own "race," as far as comfortable accommodations are "practicable."[28] This implied that they would avoid racial friction and keep the rule of law by appreciating the importance of maintaining separate accommodations. As long as they acceded to the demands of conductors who couldn't automatically exclude them from the trains, then they would be protected by beneficent and paternalistic whites who wanted to help elevate their inferior and less fortunate neighbors.

The harder choices came when people of color wanted to use public facilities that were frequented by whites. Weaver, a preacher and graduate of Hampton, made this prudential suggestion:

> if you can find no place kept for the accommodation of colored people, then go where you can find such accommodation rather than be left in the cold. It is your privilege to do so, provided that you are a fit subject in every other way, except race, color, or previous condition of servitude. If first-class accommodations are furnished you in a separate coach or cabin on public conveyance, I would prefer a seat in such a car or cabin. . . . But if there is no such accommodation set apart for you, and you are crowded upon by base and reckless beings, depriving you of all that tends to your happiness . . . excuse yourself for being colored, and walk in another car and cabin (taking your lady along, if you have one). If you are deprived of such privileges for no other reasons than race, color, &c., you will have the law in your favor.[29]

This type of approach appeared to be both moderate and pragmatic because it recognized the popularity of more restricted interpretations of the privilege and immunities clause of the Fourteenth Amendment. "C. L. B." was fairly certain that this type of reasoning represented the "general tone of the intelligent negro populations," and it provided another illustrative example of how African Americans could defend their "civil rights" without worrying about "merely social privileges."[30]

When Ulysses S. Grant's federal troops left the South, many blacks and whites began renegotiating the definitions of "equal rights" in debates over the meaning of the post–Civil War amendments in the areas of trade and travel. An editorialist for the *New York Times* noted that by this time there were many who believed that the "Civil Rights laws" were those "complex series of enactments" that included the "important laws which bear upon ordinary business, and the hotels, saloons, theaters, cars, and steamboats." The Acts of Congress of 1866 and 1870 had declared that "all persons within the United States shall have the same right in every state and territory to make and enforce contracts," and that this should mean that there shouldn't be any place in the Union where the "disability to property" was incurred because of doing "business founded on color."[31] In theory, the 1875 Civil Rights Act extended these rights so that "all persons" were entitled to the "free and equal enjoyment of inns, public conveyances on land or water, theaters, and other places of public amusement."[32]

Yet when these laws were put into practice, it became abundantly clear that not everyone held the same views on what constituted "free and equal" enjoyment. Given the "ethnological laws" of the times, there were those who believed that the study of census statistics or differential birth rates for the races showed the "futility of egalitarian or even traditionally paternalistic approaches to black economic, social, and political participation."[33] When one of the Louisiana State legislatures had tried to pass a law that prohibited the segregation of passengers in the cars and cabins of the state, reporters noted that the U.S. Supreme Court had stepped in and said that this was an impermissible state regulation of commerce.[34] Justice Joseph P. Bradley, who wrote one of the key opinions in *The Civil Rights Cases* (1883),[35] typified the feelings of those who were fed up with the egalitarian rhetorics of the radical Republicans when he averred that it "would be running the slavery argument into the ground"[36] to believe that "private" acts of discrimination were badges of slavery. Some members of the Court intoned that legislatures could only deal with state, and not private action.

In the state of Louisiana, many black communities had been engaged in civil rights battles since the passage of the Civil Rights amendments, and they realized that the ebb and flow of national political change often influenced the amount of support that they received from the federal government or their white allies. The public commentaries on the enforcement debates of the 1870s,[37] and the judicial remarks that appeared in the Civil Rights decisions of 1883,[38] illustrated some of the constraints that stood in the way of those who sought stable meanings for words like "equality" and "civil" rights. As the relatively egalitarian interpretations lost their political persuasiveness in the 1880s and 1890s, Louisiana activists realized that local organizations had to take a more active role in campaigns that were aimed at the preservation or enforcement of existing civil liberties. This often meant that they had to band together and performatively engage in acts that showed that they deserved unfettered travel, which they believed to be one the paramount rights of all U.S. citizens. When the Florida legislature passed some new Jim Crow laws (1887) that required that railroads put blacks in separate cars or in separate compartments, some civil rights activists in Louisiana must have realized that the handwriting was on the wall.

The Louisiana Legal and Public Commentaries on "Civil Rights," "Equality," and the Separate Car Bill, 1890-1895

Between 1889 and 1892, several Southern states, including Mississippi, Texas, Alabama, Arkansas, Georgia, Tennessee, and Kentucky, passed Jim Crow "car" laws. Benno Schmidt has argued that the promoters of these statutory provisions where "riding the crest of Democratic radicalism,"[39] and critics of these laws realized that this legislation threatened to eviscerate the gains that had been made during the post–Civil War years. In Louisiana, many New Orleans residents joined groups such as the American Citizens' Equal Rights Association so that they could take up "the cudgel in defense" of their rights.[40] *The [Indianapolis] Freeman* told readers in May of 1890 that there were "bills pouring in from the North Louisiana" region that were trying to make people of color "travel in Jim Crow cars," branding them "as social outcasts."[41]

Some strange alliances were created when representatives from Louisiana's railroads joined forces with the leaders of various New Orleans committees so that they could challenge the constitutionality of an "Act to promote the comfort of passengers" by providing "equal but separate accommodations for the white and colored races."[42] The subsections of this legislation indicated that any railway company that did not provide separate coaches for blacks and whites could be fined $500, and that except for "nurses attending children of the other race," individual whites and blacks would be forbidden to ride together. Violations of this act were treated as misdemeanors, where a person could receive a $25 fine or 20 days in jail.[43]

Given the creole histories of Louisiana's past,[44] establishing one's racial identity—and discovering potential violators of this law—were no easy matters. This region's legal inheritance was filled with Spanish and French laws about various racial divisions and ranks, and these complex racial hierarchies often confounded those Americans who believed in competing black-white racial binary systems. Keith Weldon Medley, for example, argues that those activists who challenged the constitutionality of Louisiana's Separate Car laws were "black Republicans" who engaged in acts of "civil disobedience,"[45] but this was not necessarily the way that French-speaking members of the Comitè des Citoyens viewed their racialized identities. The calculated choice of having Homer Plessy as a litigant—an "octoroon"—signaled the fact that only some blacks deserved to be given equal rights.

Yet regardless of whether we think that Plessy and his supporters represented some or all blacks in Louisiana, there is little question that between 1890 and 1895, they fought a valiant fight in the name of equality and fairness. With the aid of a local newspaper, *The [New Orleans] Crusader*, six black state senators, the Comitè des Citoyens, and their allies all tried to combat what they considered to be the virulent racism of their opponents. L. A. Martinet and other activists sent letters to Governor Nicholls, and they hoped that he would consider vetoing this controversial measure. The "staunch Young Republican," R. L. Desdunes, was praised for having suggested that blacks protest by the avoidance of unnecessary railroad travel, and an editorial writer for *The Crusader* implored his readers to think about the need for the gathering of funds so that local communities could "test the constitutionality" of the separate car law.[46]

When the Separate Car Bill was first debated in the Louisiana legislature in May of 1890, one of the few speakers who spoke out against the measure was Henry Demas. He worried that this bill made "no distinction"[47] between the different social or economic classes of blacks, and placed "the entire Negro race upon one common level."[48] Given their vast understanding of the habits of the "negro race," didn't his colleagues realize that they needed to differentiate between those who were "ignorant and illiterate" and those who were more refined and educated? Lumping together all blacks was considered by Demas to be an "evil" form of "class legislation," that destroyed the "harmony" of the races and the economic development of the state. This Louisiana legislator was not going to deny that the "white people of Louisiana" controlled the wealth of the state, but he wanted to underscore the fact that within their "humble" capacities, blacks had elevated themselves in the previous twenty-five years and had dealt with insurmountable obstacles. At this point in his address, Demas hinted at one of the arguments that would resurface in the legal and public commentaries of the *Plessy* case:

> Mr. President, this State is peopled by a far larger number of cultured and wealthy colored people than is conjectured, and, owing to the intermingling of the races, it is not frequently a difficult matter to determine—from a standpoint of color—the white from the Negro. Would it not be unjust, I ask, to relegate this class to a coach occupied by those much inferior to them in life, and by thus doing humiliate a people accustomed to better surroundings. It would be forcing them to associate with the worst class of the Negro element, and would be an unmerited rebuke upon the colored man of finer sensibilities.[49]

We can readily appreciate why this type of argument does not appear in our traditional legal histories of the *Plessy* era, but it has much to tell us about the rhetoric of the times. This kind of remark might resonate with several different Louisiana audiences: the white patricians who were worried about the growing power of the state's "lower" classes, the listeners who were interested in the agrarian and industrial growth of the "New South," the social reformers who understood the importance of recognizing the achievements of the upper classes, and anyone else who welcomed the possibility of forming alliances across racial lines. This type of approach also could be viewed as a moderate stance that served as an alternative avenue for change: Now legislators didn't have to follow the ideas of the radicals who confused social with civil equality, and they didn't have to listen to the clarion call of the white supremacists who refused to acknowledge that any gains had been made in the post–Civil war years.

Demas, like many of the other critics of Louisiana's 1890 Separate Car Bill, understood that he was fighting an uphill battle because he was speaking at a time when many other Southern states were considering similar segregationist measures. In Mississippi, for example, legislators had passed a law that "compelled railroads" to "haul" a "'Jim Crow' car in which the colored people are indiscriminately packed, without the slightest regard for their social or moral status, or their mental or educational attainments." Demas told his fellow legislators that he knew that there were those who believed that this "innovation" of "separating the races" was "progressive," but that he felt that these measures only brought a breach of the peace as well as disharmony. Intelligent blacks, who had broken the "yoke of slavery," couldn't be held back by "arbitrary laws" that stood in the way of "a higher plane of citizenship and civilization."[50]

Interestingly enough, Demas was willing to name names in the apportionment of political blame, and he was sure that the Separate Car Bill came from the ranks of the Democratic Senators who pandered to the needs of the lower classes. As far as Demas was concerned, the "enemies of the colored people" were not the "educated and refined white" people, but those whites who had no "social or moral standing in the community." This was the group that supposedly felt a keen sense of their own "inferiority," and resorted to anti-black measures that were "unholy" and "hellish." These Democratic Senators and their supporters were characterized as innovative "restless spirits" who were "never satisfied with the present order of things," and Demas made it clear that he had a personal stake in the outcome of these Separate Car debates:

> Mr. President . . . you have inflicted upon us every oppression known to your race, and we have borne it with a patience unknown to other races without a single word of resentment, because we desired the security of peace, prosperity and happiness for all. But the time will and must come in our case, as it has in the history of other races, when we will rise and strike for our liberties, let the chips fly where they may or consequences be what they will. . . . There is nothing left for us to do now but to wait and see if you gentlemen will carry out your promises sacredly made to us.[51]

Despite these efforts, the Separate Car Act passed the Louisiana Senate by a vote of 23 to 6.[52]

In many of our collective memories of the *Plessy* case, we have forgotten the name of Demas, and some of his arguments have passed into oblivion, but his contemporaries viewed him as a leading civil rights activist and as a savvy political leader. R. L. Desdunes, who would later be a part of the group that hired Tourgée, would write in *The Crusader* that the "language of Senator Demas" showed how the Democrats were passing the bill as "a punishment to the colored people" who had supported an earlier Republican lottery measure. This contributor was obviously enraged because he warned the "majority" that had passed this "Jim Crow business" that the "colored people" of the state would "rise in the majesty of their offended pride." These marginalized critics of "race prejudice" would use "every legal means in their power to oppose that monster of immorality which wants to suck the life blood of Louisiana."[53]

Desdune's ideas about the nature of this legal redress are interesting, in that they are a blend of elitist and egalitarian arguments. On the one hand, it would be "Louisiana's most talented sons [sic]" who would lead the fight against this type of legislation, but on they other hand they also needed the support of those who stood on the lower rungs of the racial, social, and political ladder—the "colored people to a man" who might feel these indignities.[54] Desdune believed that these groups needed to think about "boycotting" segregated railroad lines, and he wanted to make sure that his colleagues kept track of the senators who voted for the Separate Car Bill so that they could vote against them in future political elections.

Other African American critics of the Louisiana's Separate Car Bill focused on the measure's "impracticability." Paul Trevigne, for example, was convinced that this type of "force class legislation" would prove to be "abortive in the near future" because it flew in the face of the realities of living in "cosmopolitan" Louisiana. He told his readers that in this modern age, it was sometimes "difficult" to "tell who is who or which is which," and he predicted that future generations would be ashamed when they looked back and found this segregation law in their "Statute-Books." Trevigne thought that the majority of the legislators who voted for the Separate Car Bill, and the governor who approved it, knew that the measure was not advancing the "public good." This writer harkened back to the Reconstruction days when "the Louisiana Constitution was once free from class legislation," but now his opponents were engaging in acts of "futility" as they stood in the way of the "laws of progress."[55]

After losing the deliberative battle in the Louisiana legislature, *The Crusader* staff and the Comitè des Cotiyens began making plans for judicial challenges to the Separate Car Bill. They solicited funds from local social groups and religious societies, and they collected thousands of dollars from former abolitionists so that they could launch several test cases, including one that challenged segregation on intrastate conveyances. One Comitè statement indicated that they were willing to appeal their case all the way up to the U.S. Supreme Court because they felt that without "recourse to it," they would "sink into a state of helpless inferiority."[56]

In many of the traditional histories that have been written about the *Plessy* era, it is often assumed that most of the people of color who lived during these turbulent times shared Tourgée's ideological views[57]—he was, after all, a former Republican "carpetbagger"—but there were many African American civic leaders who worried about the radicalism of what was going on in these Louisiana courtrooms. For example, one contributor to the Indianapolis *Freeman* was highly critical of "Judge Tourgée," who had attacked "colored ministers" for supposedly being "depleted laxatives" who counseled submission, apathy, and indifference in the battles for civil rights.[58] This African American writer was convinced that there were times when "apparent submission accomplishes more than ill-timed resistance," and that the "Judge" was forgetting that it was much easier for "a white man to be brave"—he, after all, was "surrounded by all the appliances of civilization, wealth and education." Tourgée was vilified for having circulated untruths in the form of "the elegant froth that comes from the pen of a famous ex-carpet bagger [sic]."[59]

For many African Americans, Plessy and his supporters were on a new "fool's errand,"[60] and these Louisiana litigants were excoriated for having abandoned the more moderate stance of incremental legal change and racial accommodation. Tourgée was sometimes characterized as a demagogue, a writer who "seems desirous to become the oracle of ten millions of Negroes in America."

These critics often recognized that the "Judge" might be sincere, but they were worried that his "vicious and mischievous reflections" were only "inflamable [sic] suggestions" that did little to advance the progress of people of color.[61]

These African American critiques of the Plessy/Tourgée position were being advanced at the same time that whites were defending both the efficacy and desirability of Louisiana's Separate Car Bill. An editorialist for *The [New Orleans] Daily Picayune* was convinced that there was "almost unanimous demand on the part of the White people of the State for the enactment of the law," and that the passage of the Bill would "increase the comfort of the traveling public and put Louisiana in line with the other Southern States." This writer was bothered by the fact that the railways seemed to be some of the prime movers in this debate, and that these "powerful corporations" had forgotten about Louisiana's "liberality" and laws. Moreover, he went on to argue that the notions of civil equality needed to be based on a symmetrical view of racial rights and duties:

> The arguments of the colored members of the Legislature that such a law would amount to oppression of their people and would humiliate and degrade them does not hold, as it is not proposed to deprive them of the enjoyment of the same accommodations that white people enjoy for the payment of an equal fare, the law distinctly providing for separate accommodations, but otherwise equal in all respects. In fact the proposed measure prevents as strictly the whites from occupying the accommodations set apart for the colored people as it prohibits the latter from using those reserved for the former.[62]

In many of these Anglo-American reviews of these separate car debates, the radicals were confusing civil with social rights, and vociferous demands for egalitarian treatment were treated as positions that blurred the lines between government and society. One of the key points of contention in these Plessy debates involved the issue of whether alterations in positive laws could change the "social" attitudes of the various "races" who sat in various public accommodations, and the vast majority of observers who wrote on this topic during the first half of the 1890s were convinced that the radical egalitarians were confusing cause and effect. When one Pennsylvania judge tried to hand down a decision that attempted to mitigate some of the discrimination that he observed in his state, he was accused of believing in the myth that "prejudice should be removed and social conditions be equal for transportation." This particular judicial opinion was said to have been handed down by a jurist who obviously had "little social relations with the colored race," and who didn't understand that people of color might be equal under the law, but "socially, the inferior to the white."[63]

In sum, by the summer of 1892, there were a wide range of arguments that were being presented in these Louisiana "Separate Car" debates, and the local rhetorical cultures were filled with many permutations of these arguments. The supporters of the Bill underscored the importance of keeping the peace, the need for incremental change, states' rights and the regulation of railroads, the symmetry of the laws, and observance of the scientific laws on the sources of race prejudice,[64] while critics claimed that these laws were socially harmful and constitutionally problematic. By now, many Louisiana residents were familiar with many of these arguments, and they probably weren't surprised when *The [New Orleans] Daily Picayune* announced in June that "a negro named Adolph Plessy was arrested" by "Private Detective Cain" for having violated section 2 of act 111 of the 1890 "separate coaches" act.[65] In this particular chronicling of events, this "negro traveler" had "persisted" in demanding that he ride with "white people," and when he was asked by the conductor if he was "colored," he said that "he was," and he would not "go into the car set aside for colored people." This confrontation gets coded as a criminal matter, and readers are told that Plessy was arrested and sent to criminal court.[66]

Plessy's legal representatives, and the Comitè des Cotiyens, tried to underscore the constitutional issues that were at stake in this legal contest, and they used a number of different rationales in their challenges. At Plessy's arraignment in front of John Howard Ferguson, James Walker argued that neither the state nor any railroad conductor had any right to deny Plessy's Fourteenth Amendment "liberty" interest on the basis of race, but the judge determined that the railroad had only "deprived" him of the "liberty of doing as he pleased, and of violating a penal statute with impunity."[67] Ferguson's decision reiterated the point that the Louisiana legislature had been making about the rationality of the Bill. When the case was appealed to the Louisiana Supreme Court, Justice Charles Fenner also upheld the constitutionality of the Separate Car Bill, and he quoted from an 1867 Pennsylvania decision which noted that, "following the order of Divine Providence, human authority ought not compel these widely separated races to intermix."[68]

At the same time that Plessy's lawyers attacked the discretion that was given to railroad conductors (the supposed autocrats "of taste"[69]), they also implied that the Separate Car Bill violated their client's equal protection rights or privileges and immunities. Albion Tourgée, for example, tried to convince Justice Brown and the other members of the U.S. Supreme Court that the law was designed to debase the "inferior race," to gratify the "sentiment of white superiority and white supremacy of right and power."[70] Moreover, he insisted that Louisiana's segregation law was depriving Plessy of some of his proprietary rights, in that his client deserved the "reputation of being white."[71] The former Union carpetbagger would write in his Supreme Court appellate brief that:

> The exemption of nurses shows that the real evil lies not in the color of the skin but in the relation the colored person sustains to the white. If he is a dependent, it may be endured; if he is not, his presence is insufferable. Instead of being intended to promote the general comfort and moral well-being, this act is plainly and evidently intended to promote the happiness of one class by asserting its supremacy and the inferiority of another class. Justice is pictured blind, and her daughter, the Law, ought at least to be color-blind.[72]

Justice Henry Billings Brown, who wrote the majority opinion in *Plessy v. Ferguson* (1896), disagreed. He was convinced that the American legislators who passed the Fourteenth amendment had not prohibited racial segregation, and that each state had the discretion to decide who was black, and who was white. He argued that while that amendment did try to abolish racial distinctions that were based on "political equality," these Congressional leaders were not trying to "enforce social" equality, and they were not trying to advocate the "commingling of the two races upon terms unsatisfactory to either."[73] Given the fact that state legislatures were supposed to pass "reasonable" laws, the Court couldn't ignore the pragmatics of the situation: If the "two races" were going to meet upon "terms of social equality," this had to be based on "natural affinities." At this point, Justice Brown provided an infamous passage that encapsulated some of the Social Darwinian maxims that circulated during this period:

> Legislation is powerless to eradicate racial instincts or to abolish distinctions based on physical differences, and the attempt to do so can only result in accentuating the difficulties of the present situation. If the civil and political rights of both races be equal one cannot be inferior to the other civilly or politically. If one race is inferior to the other socially, the Constitution of the United States cannot put them on the same plane.[74]

The lone dissenter, Justice Harlan, was said to have left us with an address that was meant to appeal to the "conscience of posterity."[75] He characterized the majority's commentaries about "equal" accommodations as a "thin disguise" for laws that would protect the "dominant ruling class of citizens." Like Tourgée before him, Harlan was convinced that the Constitution "is color-blind."[76] The purported legality of the Separate Car Bill could now be used as precedent for the segregation of streets, jury boxes, legislative halls, and public gatherings. It would be years before the "nation's conscience had reached the point where the specified kind of injustice" would no longer be considered "tolerable."[77]

The Public and Legal Responses to Brown's Decision in *Plessy*, 1896

Some of the leading experts on the *Plessy* case have often claimed that decision was met with silence and general acceptance,[78] but this underestimates the amount of symbolic power that this type of decision had in the local and state communities who were battling over the meaning of racial "discrimination," "equality," and permissible segregation. Both defenders and detractors enjoyed quoting parts of the decision. For many whites who lived in Louisiana and other Southern states, the U.S. Supreme Court decision in *Plessy* certainly represented the common sense wisdom of most Americans, regardless of color. Both Ferguson and Brown had underscored the importance of segregation for racial harmony, and they highlighted the reasonableness of Louisiana's criminal laws. Moreover, conservative ministers could lobby for the "equality" of the races without having to adopt the coercive tactics of radicals like Plessy's supporters, and, at various times, the participants in these debates wrote about the importance of racial harmony, incremental social change, state control of railroads, and the end of the Reconstruction. When one New Orleans newspaper reported on decision no. 210—"Homer Plessy, plaintiff in error, vs. J. H. Ferguson, judge, etc., from the Louisiana state court"—it characterized this as a "Jim Crow car case." After telling readers that Justice Brown had authored the opinion, this news writer averred that the appellant had been represented by Ex-Solicitor General Phillips and "Judge Albion W. Tourgée, the author of several books attacking the [s]outh." This summary also noted in passing that Justice Harlan gave a dissenting opinion that followed his "course in the civil rights" cases, but it quickly moved toward a defense of Justice Brown's commentaries on the Separate Car Bill:

> It provides equal privileges to all on all the railroads engaged in interstate transit. It does not discriminate unfairly between citizens of the United States or between citizens of the state, of whatever color or race. It was legislation which it was competent for the state to enact as within the police power . . . which extends to the protection of the lives, limbs, health, comfort, morals, and quiet of society, private interests being subservient to the public. Plessy was proceeding against [the Bill] in the criminal district court for the parish of Orleans for violating the act in question in June, 1892, on a train of the East Louisiana Railroad. The pleas of the defendant was [sic] overruled by Judge Ferguson, and Plessy filed application in the [S]upreme [C]ourt [sic] for writs of prohibition and certiorari, which were refused. He then took a writ of error to the United States [S]upreme [C]ourt.[79]

On that same day, an editorial columnist explained that what Plessy was arguing for was "absolute socialism," where the "equality of rights" was being merged with "community of rights." This type of framework would erase the protections that were afforded to those who needed "private property, private life, or social distinctions." In Tourgée's potentially chaotic world, the "individual would be extinguished in the vast mass of human being [sic]," a "condition repugnant to every principle of enlightened democracy."[80]

By the 1900s, the *Plessy* case was considered to be an illustration of how police regulations became the means by which state and federal laws impacted both intrastate and interstate travel, and Brown's decision was often characterized as a popular and progressive opinion. For example, J. Newton Baker, a member of the District of Columbia Bar, argued in the *Yale Law Journal* that "where the colored population is large, public sentiment demands and requires a separation of the races, to prevent the breach of the peace."[81] An editorialist for the *Richmond Dispatch* explained in January of 1900 that if Virginia decided to pass a "Separate Cars" law, there would be "no discrimination or hardship for the colored race," and the "law will be better for the colored race as well as the whites."[82]

In many of these commentaries, there was little discussion of Plessy's constitutional rights or Tourgée's allegations, and there were even some legal summaries that claimed that the *Plessy* decision protected the rights of the conductors and other representatives of common carriers. These social agents were said to have needed the right "to separate passengers" because of the "public interest" and the "right of private property in the resources of conveyance." In the absence of Congressional legislation, a state could make "reasonable regulations to secure the safety of the passengers," and this sometimes meant that under "the commerce act [sic], carriers may place white and colored passengers in separate cars, but they cannot discriminate in the accommodations that they furnish each, which must be substantially equal in quality and convenience."[83] This particular "rule of law" could be justified on a number of apparently rational-related grounds, including the "comfort and safety of the passengers," the "preservation of order by reason of numbers," or the "feelings between the races" that made it "desirable to keep them separated." The carriers were supposedly given the complete authority to establish and adopt those regulations that were needed to "relieve them of all the danger and inconvenience that may arise on account of the two races traveling together."[84]

These types of arguments may have represented some of the dominant interpretations of the *Plessy* decision, but there were also many regional and national communities who still maintained that the Louisiana Separate Car Bill was unconstitutional. Justice Harlan's dissenting opinion was reprinted or commented on in many newspapers and journals.[85] For example, a writer for the Cleveland *Gazette* supported his position, and underscored the fact that he was arguing that it would be "just as reasonable and proper" for "states to pass laws requiring separate cars to be furnished for Catholics and Protestants," or for "the descendants of those of the Teutonic race and those of the Latin race."[86] In Kansas, Parson's *Weekly Blade* told readers that "the Democratic majority of the Supreme Court" had "wantonly" disgraced the land by "declaring that the 'Jim Crow' car laws of the South" were constitutional. Justice Harlan was described as the only "one on the bench with grit enough in him to utter a protest against this damnable outrage upon a race that for more than 275 years labored [under] the yoke of bondage."[87] Hundreds of miles away, a Harrisburg, Virginia newspaper ridiculed the notion that that state needed to pass any novel separate car legislation because for years, whites and blacks had been riding in the same railroad trains, and all these travelers seemed to be "well-behaved."[88]

For many extrajudicial commentators on the case, the members of the *Plessy* majority were forgetting about the spirit of American constitutional governance. In May of 1896, an editorial writer for New York's *Independent* had this to say about the decision:

> We cannot argue law with the Supreme Court of the United States, but we can argue morals. That court has decided that the Louisiana Jim Crow law is not unconstitutional, which requires railroad companies to provide separate coaches for whites and Negroes. But the law is a crime before God, no matter

> whether it does or does not contradict the Constitution of the United States. The Constitution is not as broad as the Golden Rule, and the justices of that court have narrower jurisdiction than God has; nay, a narrower jurisdiction than any man's conscience.[89]

Yet despite these admonitions, more than half a century would pass before the American judicial system would take up the challenge of abandoning some of the principles that were embedded in the *Plessy* decision. Part of the tragedy of this situation is that Brown's arguments may have resonated with the vast majority of whites and people of color, and that Tourgée's heretical arguments fell on deaf ears.

Conclusion

By looking at some of the legal and public discourse that prefigured and followed the *Plessy* case, we gain an appreciation of some of the complexities of this case, as various communities grappled with the political, social, and economic aspects of the Louisiana race "problems" of these Jim Crow years. Scholars today tend to think of Justice Harlan's dissent in *Plessy* as a direct precedent for educational desegregation in *Brown v. Board of Education*, but Plessy's contemporaries contextualized the decision as one that touched on the rights of carriers, the private rights of passengers, states' rights, police powers, and local discretion. As long as the state lawyers could come up with rational reasons for legitimating these "Separate Car" bills, then these acts could be treated as criminal regulations that withstood constitutional scrutiny. Within these scenarios, Plessy was the interloper, the villain who was asking the state to take away the rights of peaceful blacks and whites who didn't share his "social" opinions. In theory, blacks and other people of color had already been given their political and civil rights, and as the "separate" races evolved, then perhaps prejudice would naturally be reduced. Louisiana Democrats could play on populist fears of racial amalgamation, the return of the Republican Reconstruction, or societal degeneration as they crafted laws that could be interpreted as progressive measures. The state's separate car bill could be justified as a measure that reflected both the will of the people and the natural laws of racial antipathy.

Today's scholars and activists may like to quote Harlan's dissent or talk about Tourgée's prescient arguments, but their contemporaries considered them to be idealists who didn't understand the realities of their era. In this Social Darwinian world, the term "separate but equal" served as a condensation symbol for many different gradation systems, where human beings were ranked according to "class," racial superiority, culture, racial ability, laboring ability, etc. Within "Louisiana's triracial system,"[90] Plessy represented the "man in the middle," the "proactive citizen who took revolutionary ideas seriously."[91]

One of the many ironies of this case is that, at times, it appeared that Demas, Tourgée, or Harlan weren't always interested in the total elimination of some of these racial or class hierarchies—they were simply arguing that various citizens or immigrants needed to be placed on different rungs of the mythic evolutionary ladders.[92] While there were some communities who believed that Plessy's efforts would help all people of color, there were other participants in this debate who had a more limited agenda. These conservatives and moderates worked for incremental change, accepting some forms of "separateness" in order to prevent total "exclusion." Lofgren may be right when he notes that the losers in the *Plessy* case have provided us with some of the "records" that would be needed to "instruct later generations,"[93] but communication scholars have the obligation of illustrating some of the complexities of this tragic affair.

Notes

The author thanks Bryan Hubbard, who collected this primary information while providing research assistance for me when we were both in the Department of Communication at Arizona State University.

1. *Plessy v. Ferguson*, 163 U.S. 537 (1896).

2. Eric J. Sundquist, "Mark Twain and Homer Plessy," *Representations* 24 (Fall 1988): 105. For some of the best general overviews of the *Plessy* decision, see Richard Kluger, *Simple Justice: The History of Brown v. Board and Black America's Struggle for Equality* (New York: Vintage Books, 1975); Paul Oberst, "The Strange Career of *Plessy v. Ferguson*," *Arizona Law Review* 15 (1973): 389-418; C. Vann Woodward, *The Strange Career of Jim Crow* (New York: Oxford University Press, 1955).

3. Kirt H. Wilson, *The Reconstruction Desegregation Debate: The Politics of Equality and the Rhetoric of Place, 1870-1875* (East Lansing: Michigan State University Press, 2002), 44.

4. *Brown v. Board of Education*, 347 U.S. 483 (1954).

5. Charles A. Lofgren, *The Plessy Case: A Legal-Historical Interpretation* (New York: Oxford University Press, 1987), 3.

6. N. Lee Cooper, "The Harlan Standard," *American Bar Association Journal* 83 (June 1997): 8.

7. The Thirteenth Amendment, section one, reads as follows:

> Neither slavery nor involuntary servitude, except as a punishment for crime whereof the party shall have been duly convicted, shall exist within the United States, or any other place subject to their jurisdiction.

The Fourteenth Amendment, section one, contains this language:

> All persons born or naturalized in the United States and subject to the jurisdiction, thereof, are citizens of the United States and of the State wherein they re-

> side. No State shall make or enforce the law which shall abridge the privileges or immunities of citizens of the United States; nor shall any State deprive any person of life, liberty, or equal protection of the laws.

The Fifteenth Amendment, section one, reads:

> The right of citizens of the United States to vote shall not be denied or abridged by the United States or by any State on account of race, color, or previous conditions of servitude. The Congress shall have power to enforce this article by appropriate legislation.

8. Cooper, "The Harlan Standard," 8.

9. Ibid.

10. Simeon C. R. McIntosh, "Reading *Dred Scott*, *Plessy*, and *Brown*: Toward a Constitutional Hermeneutics," *Howard Law Journal* 38 (1994): 67-68.

11. Ibid., 67.

12. For example, an editorial in the *New York Times*, which was written after the *Brown* decision, contained these words:

> Justice Harlan said: "Our Constitution is color-blind and neither knows nor tolerates classes among citizens. . . ." There was not one word in Chief Justice Warren's opinion that was inconsistent with the earlier views of Justice Harlan. This is an instance in which the voice crying in the wilderness finally becomes the expression of a people's will and in which justice overtakes and thrusts aside a timorous expediency.

"Justice Harlan Concurring," *New York Times*, 23 May 1954, sec. 4, 10.

13. Glenda E. Gilmore, *Gender and Jim Crow: Women and the Politics of White Supremacy in North Carolina, 1896-1920* (Chapel Hill: The University of North Carolina Press, 1996), 20.

14. Lofgren, *The Plessy Case*, 204, 205.

15. For an excellent analysis of the roles that privacy and racial identity played in the *Plessy* affair, see Amy Robinson, "Forms of Appearance of Value: Homer Plessy and the Politics of Privacy," in Elin Diamond, ed., *Performance and Cultural Politics* (New York: Routledge, 1996), 237-261.

16. "Civil Rights," *New York Daily Tribune*, 1 March 1866, 4.

17. D. H. Chamberlain, "Reconstruction and the Negro," *The North American Review* 128 (February 1879): 173.

18. Wilson, *The Reconstruction*, 10.

19. Frederick Douglass, "Colored National Convention at New Orleans," *The [New York] Independent*, 2 May 1872, editorial page.

20. Ibid.

21. "Equality, but Not Socialism," *The [New Orleans] Daily Picayune*, 19 May 1896, 4.

22. Benno C. Schmidt, "Principle and Prejudice: The Supreme Court and Race in the Progressive Era. Part I: The Heyday of Jim Crow," *Columbia Law Review* 82 (1982): 463.

23. *Berea College v. Commonwealth*, 123 Ky. 225-226 (1906).

24. Schmidt, "Principle," 463.

25. For an extended discussion that explains some of the reasons for this lack of uniformity, see Michael J. Klarman, "The Plessy Era," *1998 Supreme Court Review* (1999): 327-336.

26. For example, there were times when the Interstate Commerce Commission was asked to step in and decide about the substantial equality of accommodations on railroads, and they sometimes ruled that unequal accommodations violated the Interstate Commerce Act. See *Council v. Western & A. R.R.* 1 I.C.C. 339 (1887); *Heard v. Georgia R.R.*, 1 I.C.C. 428 (1888); *Heard v. Georgia R. R.* 3 I.C.C. 111 (1889).

27. *Hall v. De Cuir*, 95 U.S. 485 (1878).

28. J. P. Weaver, quoted in C. L. B., "Civil Rights, The New Law in the South," *New York Times*, 21 June 1875, 2.

29. Weaver, quoted in ibid.

30. Ibid.

31. "Equal Rights in Trade and Travel," *New York Times*, 29 November 1879, 4.

32. Civil Rights Act of 1 March 1875, *United States Statutes at Large*, vol. 18, p. 335.

33. Schmidt, "Principle," 453.

34. "Equal Rights in Trade," 4. This is probably a commentary on the *Hall* (1878) decision.

35. *The Civil Rights Cases*, 109 U.S. 3 (1883).

36. Justice Joseph Bradley, *The Civil Rights Cases*, 109 U.S. at 24.

37. Note, for example, how some writers were talking about some of the problematics of the Civil Rights Bill, which theoretically didn't take into account the fact that "blacks themselves" didn't want "social equality," or the mixing of schools, hotels, cemeteries, inns, or "common carriers." "The Civil Rights Bill," *The Nation* 481 (17 September 1874): 180-181.

38. "Civil Rights Decision," *The [Cleveland] Gazette*, 27 October 1883, 1.

39. Schmidt, "Principle," 453.

40. "The Separate Car Bill," *The [New Orleans] Crusader*, 19 July 1890, 2.

41. "Finalists and Literary Folks," *The [Indianapolis] Freeman*, 31 May 1890, 6.

42. 1890 La. Acts, no. 111.

43. Keith Weldon Medley, "The Sad Story of How 'Separate' but 'Equal' Was Born," *Smithsonian* 24 (February 1994): 108-109.

44. See Carlyn C. Bell, *Revolution, Romanticism, and the Afro-Creole Protest Tradition in Louisiana, 1718-1868* (Baton Rouge: Louisiana State University Press, 1997).

45. Medley, "The Sad," 105. Interestingly enough, in another section of his essay, Medley also notes that:

> In a city that had for so long seen so much racial mixing, railway conductors would now have to decide who was white and who was black—a touchy business, especially since some wives and husbands would not be allowed to ride together. One of the reasons that Homer Plessy was picked for the job was that he had fair skin. Had it been left to chance, he probably could have ridden the train in the "whites only" section unnoticed. But by prearrangement between the Comitè and the East Louisiana Railroad, everything was ready for him when he came. (112)

46. "The Separate Car Bill," 2.

47. The term "distinction" was a popular word during this period, and it could be used in a number of different ways. Sometimes it was used to explain the unique power of the "white race" and the need for the "separation of the races." See "Senator McEnery," 27 January 1900, *The Republic Courier*, 1.

48. "Speech of Hon. Henry Demas, on the Separate Car Bill, Delivered in the Senate, at Baton Rouge, La, July 8, '90," *The [New Orleans] Crusader*, 19 July 1890, 4.

49. Ibid.

50. Ibid.

51. Ibid.

52. Medley, "The Sad," 109.

53. R. L. Desdunes, "Was It a Measure of Revenge?" *The [New Orleans] Crusader*, 19 July 1890, 1.

54. Ibid.

55. Paul Trevigne, "The World Will Move," *The [New Orleans] Crusader*, 19 July 1890, 1.

56. Medley, "The Sad," 111.

57. Tourgée was a popular figure in some Northern and Southern communities because many Americans considered him to be one of the few whites who was willing to face the problematics associated with the politics and economics of slavery. For an overview of Tourgée's work, see Otto H. Olsen, *The Carpetbagger's Crusade: A Life of Albion Winegar Tourgée* (Baltimore: John Hopkins University Press, 1965). As David Blight explains, Tourgée would write in 1888 that blacks faced a past filled with "only darkness replete with unimaginable horrors," and this "only echoed a discourse well under way among blacks themselves." However, in an "age that exalted self-made business titans, when Christianity stressed personal responsibility, and in a culture riven by theories of inherent racial characteristics, blacks carried the stigma of bondage." David W.

Blight, *Race and Reunion: The Civil War in American Memory* (Cambridge, MA: Harvard University Press, 2001), 313. The difficulties came when these communities disagreed on the policies that needed to be implemented in erasing this stigma.

58. "The Colored Ministry," *The [Indianapolis] Freeman*, 31 October 1891, 4.

59. Ibid.

60. The "older" novel, Tourgée's *A Fool's Errand*, sold somewhere between 100,000 and 200,000 copies. It was a story that explained the trials and tribulations of the author in North Carolina during the Reconstruction years. See George J. Becker, "Albion W. Tourgée: A Pioneer in Social Criticism," *American Literature* 19 (1947): 59-72.

61. "Judge Tourgée's Ill-Seasoned Vaporings," *The [Indianapolis] Freeman*, 25 June 1892, 4.

62. "The Separate Cars Bill," *The [New Orleans] Daily Picayne*, 10 July 1890, 4.

63. Baker, "The Segregation," 451.

64. On the role that scientific racism played in this controversy, see Lofgren, *The Plessy Case*, 93-115.

65. "Another Jim Crow Car Case: Arrest of a Negro Traveler Who Persisted in Riding with the White People," *The [New Orleans] Daily Picayune*, 9 June 1892, 3.

66. Ibid.

67. John Howard Ferguson, quoted in Medley, "The Sad," 113-114.

68. Justice Charles Fenner, quoted in Sundquist, "Mark Twain," 107.

69. Tourgée brief, quoted in Otto H. Olsen, *The Thin Disguise: Plessy v. Ferguson, A Documentary Presentation* (New York: Humanities Press, 1967), 103.

70. Albion Tourgée, quoted in Schmidt, "Principle," 466.

71. Sundquist, "Mark Twain," 114.

72. Albion Tourgée, appellant Supreme Court brief in *Plessy*, quoted in Woodward, *The Strange Career*, 152-153; Schmidt, "Principle," 466.

73. Justice Henry Billings Brown, *Plessy*, 537, 545.

74. Justice Henry Billings Brown, *Plessy*, 551-552.

75. Schmidt, "Principle," 467.

76. Justice Harlan, dissent in *Plessy*, 557-563.

77. "Justice Harlan Concurring," *New York Times*, 23 May 1954, sec. 4: 10.

78. Schmidt, for example, has argued that the "country hardly noticed" the decision. "Principle," 466.

79. "News Gathered at the Capital: The 'Jim Crow' Car Bill Declared Constitutional," *The [New Orleans] Daily Picayune*, 19 May 1896, p. 8.

80. "Equality, but Not Socialism," *The [New Orleans] Daily Picayune*, 10 May 1896, 4.

81. J. Newton Baker, "The Segregation of White and Colored Passengers on Interstate Trains," *Yale Law Journal* 19 (1910): 445.

82. "Separate Cars," *The Richmond Dispatch*, 12 January 1900, 4.

83. Ibid., 449.

84. Baker, "The Segregation," 451.

85. See, for example, "Black Laws in Louisiana," *The [Indianapolis] Freeman*, 27 June 1896, 1.

86. "That 'Decision': The Constitutionality of the Louisiana 'Jim Crow' Car Law Sustained by the Supreme Court," *The [Cleveland] Gazette*, 30 May 1896, 2.

87. "The Democratic Majority," *Parson's Weekly Blade*, 30 May 1896, 2.

88. *The Spirit of the Valley*, quoted in "Separate Cars," *The Richmond Dispatch*, 12 January 1900, 4.

89. "Editorial Notes," *The [New York] Independent*, 26 May 1896, 12.

90. This "triracial" system was purportedly made up of "whites," "blacks," and "creoles."

91. Gary B. Mills, "Book Review: *Revolution, Romanticism, and the Afro-Creole Tradition in Louisiana*," *The American Historical Review* 104 (1999): 1303.

92. As Sundquist has insightfully observed, some of the arguments that were used by Plessy's lawyers seemed to "protect only those who could pass—the mulatto elite," and they defined "equal protection just as restrictively and negatively as the Court already had, only locating it at a different mark on the color line" ("Mark Twain," 114).

93. Lofgren, *The Plessy Case*, 208.

2

Dissent as Prophecy: Justice John Marshall Harlan's Dissent in *Plessy v. Ferguson* as the Religious Rhetoric of Law

Daniel Mangis

If the Old Testament is an appropriate metaphoric framework for understanding the struggle for racial justice and equality in the United States, then Justice John Marshall Harlan is surely the prophet Isaiah. Like the Book of Isaiah, Harlan's dissent in *Plessy v. Ferguson* can be read as an indictment of a nation blind and deaf, and devoid of justice and righteousness.[1] Arguably, Harlan's dissent is the first of the three most important rhetorical texts of the civil rights movement, preceding *Brown v. Board of Education* and Martin Luther King's "I Have a Dream Speech." Despite never becoming positive law, the dissent has been nominated for inclusion in so-called canon of American constitutional law. Moreover, Harlan's dissent remains a powerful rhetorical force in contemporary legal arguments over racial discrimination, with both conservatives and liberals invoking the text.[2]

Literally cited thousands of times in legal decisions and scholarship, Harlan's dissent clearly has staying power, but perhaps more as a matter of rhetoric than as a matter of law. Indeed, the leading legal-historical account of the *Plessy* decision concludes that the majority opinion "had a firmer grounding in current law," but that Harlan's dissent "was better rooted in republican truths" and arguably history.[3] Thus, in his *Plessy* dissent, Harlan is more like Isaiah than Moses, a deliverer of prophecy rather than of law.[4] The rhetorical appeal of the decision also might explain why both liberals and conservatives cite Harlan's *Plessy* dissent as a favorite and trusted legal authority.[5]

Developing a better understanding of the rhetorical dimensions of Harlan's *Plessy* dissent is important for both legal and rhetorical scholars as well as people generally concerned with civil rights in this country. In general, dissents arguably improve judicial decisions, guide future interpretation of the law, and give substantive expression to disfavored groups and minorities. The central legal argument of Harlan's dissent has been enormously influential, especially in the legal efforts to end segregation.[6] Legal scholars join rhetorical scholars with their interest in the dissent's continuing influence on contemporary constitutional law.[7] Most important, Harlan's "color-blind" Constitution metaphor continues to hold sway over contemporary efforts to deal with racial inequities—a matter of universal interest.

Because of the dissent's continuing importance as a rhetorical tool, Harlan's comment deserves more scrutiny. This chapter explores both the memorable and largely forgotten rhetorical characteristics of Harlan's dissent in an attempt to better understand the primary text. First, this chapter details the background of the author and then describes the contemporary debate over the proper reproduction of Harlan's argument. A closer examination of the structure and stylistic features of Harlan's dissent, especially the "color-blind" Constitution metaphor, suggest that his argument was far more limited and introspective than what might appear from contemporary citations of his dissent.

The Worldview of Dissenter Harlan

The quick biography of Justice John Marshall Harlan is invariably accompanied by the following adjectives: Republican, Kentuckian, named after Chief Justice John Marshall, former slave owner, half-brother to a mulatto, and racist. There is an undeniable urge to point out the contradictions in Harlan's personality and jurisprudence that make the *Plessy* dissent so surprising, if only because these details add some color to an otherwise dull and complicated story about Louisiana state railroad statutes and federal court jurisdiction doctrines. However, the story of Harlan's dissent need not be melodramatic to be engaging. The bare facts of the case are enough.

The Republican from Kentucky should not be confused with his grandson, also a Republican named John Marshall Harlan, but from New York, who was appointed to the Court by President Eisenhower in 1955. The legal pedigree should not be surprising. The original Justice Harlan was named for Chief Justice John Marshall, whom Harlan's father admired to no end. Harlan's father was an attorney, as were his three brothers. In addition, Harlan's mulatto half-brother was also a distinguished and well-respected attorney. Harlan was an accomplished attorney and politician in his own right, serving as attorney general of Kentucky prior to his appointment to the Supreme Court in 1877. Harlan served until his death on the bench in 1911, evading calls for his nomination as a presidential candidate. His colleague Justice Oliver Wendell Holmes would later (both fondly and derisively) label Harlan a "tobacco spittin' judge," but if the term was intended to reveal some intellectual or political inadequacies, it surely missed the mark. Harlan was no simpleton stumbling upon a higher truth in spite of himself, but a nimble-minded and powerful intellect with a long track record of protecting the civil rights of African Americans.[8]

Along with Holmes, Justice William Brennan, Justice William Johnson, Justice Roger B. Taney, and Justice William O. Douglas, Harlan is often regarded as one of the Great Dissenters of the Supreme Court. Anita Krishnakumar notes that the "canonization" of the *Plessy* dissent in the 1960s transformed Harlan in legal scholarship from a judge poorly regarded in his own time to inclusion among the list of "great" Supreme Court Justices and even a "judicial saint." However, Harlan's reputation for dissent would likely have been secured even without *Plessy*. Harlan also memorably dissented in the *Civil Rights Cases*, *Hurtado v. California*, *Pollack v. Farmers' Loan & Trust Co.*, and *Lochner v. New York*, all cases in which the majority position was eventually overturned, overridden by constitutional amendment, or abandoned.[9]

During Harlan's 33 years on the Court, he dissented in 380 cases. When he dissented, he was usually the only dissenter. In every case in which the Court upheld the rights of African Americans, Harlan wrote the majority opinion. In every case in which the Court declared federal civil rights legislation to be unconstitutional, he dissented. In every case in which the Court denied African American rights under the Civil War Amendments, he dissented.[10] This judicial record must be understood within the context of his worldview formed by a brand of late nineteenth-century Presbyterian Constitutionalism, and a vision of color blindness that was steeped in white paternalism and Republican federalism.[11]

First, Harlan's practice of dissent, particularly when the controversy involved the application of the Thirteenth and Fourteenth Amendments, was more than merely an academic exercise in counterpoint. Instead, Harlan's dissents are an exercise in faith, reflecting the spirit of religious dissidents. Clearly, the most important influence was Harlan's Presbyterian upbringing. From grammar school to college to law school, Harlan attended Presbyterian educational institutions. Harlan was a self-made expert on the Bible, reading it daily and teaching Sunday school classes most of his adult life.

Harlan's personal worldview, and consequently his dissent, cannot be completely understood without some understanding of his religious background. James W. Gordon's analysis of Harlan's professed religious beliefs suggests that Harlan's faith in the Constitution and the Bible were identical. Harlan's conscience called for obedience to both textual authorities. Indeed, Harlan was reputed to sleep with a copy of the Constitution and the Bible nearby on his nightstand. Understanding Harlan's devotion to constitutional and biblical principles explains away many of the apparent contradictions of his personal beliefs and judicial opinions.[12] For an example of Harlan's dual commitment, religion partially explains the contradiction between Harlan's treatment of African Americans and the Chinese in his powerful dissent (561). The Chinese, being heathens to Christianity, did not merit the same protections as the Christian African Americans.

Nevertheless, Harlan was a racist, even if only because he was a man of his times.[13] It seems clear that Harlan's personal view of African Americans, at best, paralleled the image of African Americans as "happy simple folk devoted to the whites they served" common to whites.[14] Many of the African American contemporaries that Harlan held in esteem were likely understood by him as exceptions to the traditional Southern stereotype. Of course, Harlan's judicial views on race seem clear as well. In his *Plessy* dissent, he stated: "The white race deems itself to be the dominant race in this country. And so it is, in prestige, in achievements, in education, in wealth, and in power" (449).

A closer examination of Harlan's personal beliefs on race and the *Plessy* dissent reveal a more sophisticated view of race that is mediated by his adherence to the Constitution. As a Whig nationalist and Republican, Harlan vigorously advocated the goals of Reconstruction, unpopular as they were in Kentucky. Harlan had a close relationship with Fredrick Douglass, both as a fellow Republican politician and also a friend.[15] Harlan's political views seem to have allowed him to bridge racial divides. Indeed, even in his infamous assertion of white superiority in *Plessy*, Harlan adds that the white race's success depends on "if it remains true to its great heritage, and *holds fast to the principles of constitutional liberty*" (559, emphasis added).

Although other broad historical forces shaped his *Plessy* opinion, Harlan's great dissent was comparatively far more influenced by his strong religious and federalist beliefs than any prophetic understanding of American race relations. Such a view explains why Harlan would likely have tolerated some degree of social racism, which would not have offended his basic federalist beliefs. Indeed, in the *Plessy* dissent, Harlan speaks disparagingly of the "Chinaman," suggesting that the Chinese immigrants could never integrate into American social and political culture (561). In most cases involving the civil rights of Asian litigants, Harlan voted against them. Properly understood as noncitizens with no religious connections to Harlan's beloved Presbyterian faith, his apparent hypocritical prejudice against the Chinese seems explicable.[16]

The Limited Argument in Harlan's *Plessy* Dissent

At the end of the Civil War, the Republican-controlled Congress forced the passage of the Thirteenth, Fourteenth, and Fifteenth Amendments, which purported to grant African Americans the same rights, privileges, and immunities as white citizens of the United States. In hindsight, the three so-called Civil War

Amendments were clearly intended to apply to all American citizens and to a broad range of rights and privileges of citizenship. However, the federal judiciary initially relied on rather narrow definitions of the scope of the Amendments.[17]

Aside from a grant of civil rights, the Civil War Amendments also could be understood as an effort to provide a foundation for the rise of federalism. Southern resistance to the Amendments, while no doubt motivated by antipathy toward African Americans, was also an effort to stem the political losses of the states' rights movement. For whites, property rights in the Reconstruction South were associated with citizenship rights. While whites could maintain positions of economic privilege in commercial settings, the commingling of races in public settings threatened perceptions of white privilege. Jim Crow laws might then also be understood not only as a reflection of the South and race relations, but also the development of the modern American state. In that sense, Jim Crow laws were a modern exercise of state power using space to mark status.[18]

Into this mix walked Homer Plessy, a railroad passenger denied access to a whites-only rail car under an 1890 Louisiana statute that required "separate but equal" accommodations based on race. With a light complexion and a claim to mixed ethnic heritage that was indiscernible, Plessy agreed to initiate a test case against the constitutionality of the Louisiana separate but equal statute. He purchased a rail ticket inside Louisiana borders to avoid jurisdictional conflicts, informed the rail conductor of his mixed heritage, sat in a section reserved for white passengers, and refused to move to the "coloreds only" rail car. He was forcibly removed, arrested, and placed on trial.[19]

The trial was delayed pending appellate review of the constitutionality of the Louisiana statute, and after state courts denied review, the U.S. Supreme Court heard Plessy's case and denied relief, with only Harlan dissenting. The basic thrust of the majority's decision, authored by Justice Henry Brown, was that the separate but equal accommodation requirement did not violate the Thirteenth Amendment's abolishment of slavery and involuntary servitude or the Fourteenth Amendment's call for legal equality. The Thirteenth Amendment argument failed when the majority rejected the analogy of reserved seating to slavery. The Fourteenth Amendment argument failed when the majority adopted a distinction between legal and social/political equality.

The central argument in Harlan's dissent is that legally mandated racial separation is always unconstitutional under the Thirteenth and Fourteenth Amendments to the U.S. Constitution. While this is a broad claim, it is not nearly as broad as one might contemplate. For example, Harlan's dissent is not much of an argument for the unfairness or injustice of state-sanctioned racial segregation. As Harlan explains at the outset of his dissent: "However apparent the injustice of such legislation may be, we have only to consider whether it is consistent with the constitution of the United States" (553).

In that constitutional spirit, Harlan's argument explicitly rejects the notion that state-sanctioned mandatory racial segregation might be sometimes justified, if supported by reasonable objectives. Harlan used the metaphor of a color-blind Constitution to make his point that the Constitution can never use race as a distinction when providing for the protection of civil rights:

> But in view of the constitution, in the eye of the law, there is in this country no superior, dominant, ruling class of citizens. There is no caste here. *Our Constitution is color-blind*, and neither knows nor tolerates classes among citizens. In respect of civil rights, all citizens are equal before the law. The humblest is the peer of the most powerful. The law regards man as man, and takes no account of his surroundings or of his color when his civil rights as guaranteed by the supreme law of the land are involved. (559, emphasis added)

Harlan's dissent offered a very limited counterargument to the majority's holding. Harlan only sought to answer the constitutional problem of mandatory racial separation. He did not address the wisdom of segregation, whether public or private.[20] Neither did Harlan engage in a technical analysis of the merits of the Louisiana law authorizing train conductors to segregate on the basis of race. Additionally, *Plessy* dealt with transportation, a limitation noted by Chief Justice Earl Warren in *Brown v. Board of Education*. Harlan also did not attempt to answer the broader question of when the Constitution might allow state-mandated racial integration.[21] While the dissent may hold clues to Harlan's broader views, he hardly intended for it to be the final word on those views.

A final limitation of Harlan's argument is that he is expressly concerned with individual civil rights granted to citizens under the Fourteenth Amendment. Throughout his dissent, Harlan consistently frames his legal arguments in terms of the protection of civil rights, using the term "civil rights" eleven times in his dissent (554-556, 560, 562-563, 559). "Civil rights" limit Harlan's dissents because of their narrow historical interpretation. As Richard Primus explains, "civil rights" in the nineteenth century is not an "umbrella term coextensive with 'constitutional rights' in the way that it largely is today." Instead, the term only refers to a subclass of rights that allow people to act as "private individuals in civil society, capable of personal independence and self-sufficiency." For example, Primus notes that the Civil Rights Act of 1866 guaranteed African Americans the rights to "make and enforce contracts, to sue, be parties, and give evidence, to inherit, purchase, lease, sell, hold, and convey real and personal property." Civil rights are contrasted with social and political rights, and the distinctions between the three categories of rights were hotly contested. Thus, while Harlan was more progressive than his brethren in his willingness to view public transportation as a "civil right," he certainly was not arguing for anything approaching absolute equality between African Americans and whites.[22]

The limited scope of Harlan's argument has not prevented subsequent scholars, advocates, and courts from citing Harlan for the proposition that racial discrimination can be unconstitutional or is always unconstitutional. Dissents are never binding, without some formal adoption of the dissent by a subsequent court. Harlan's dissent has never formally been adopted by a court as anything more than a description of an underlying constitutional principle. In other words, Harlan's dissent is not universally accepted as binding constitutional authority, and it may not be persuasive authority.[23]

The Structure of Harlan's Dissent

On first reading, Harlan's dissent might seem like a rambling series of unconnected paragraphs. However, Harlan's argumentative structure reflected the organizational style of the day and is as tightly structured as any latter-day Supreme Court opinion. Additionally, his argument is fashioned as an embryonic majority position, proposing a color-blind government as an alternative to the majority's position that a government can be race-conscious.

It is helpful to understand that Supreme Court dissents are organized along a spectrum of rhetorical concerns. On one end is a wholly organized dissent, capable of standing on its own as an alternative majority opinion. On the other end of the spectrum is the less organic partial or point dissent, which merely takes exception to particular claims in the majority's position, but does not offer any alternative judgment or rule. Harlan's dissent exists somewhere between these two poles, such that he only offers a partial critique of the majority position, within which exists the components of an embryonic majority position.

The term "embryonic majority position" is used here to identify arguments provided by dissenters for the benefit of future courts.[24] By providing counterarguments to the majority position, the dissenter arms future litigants with potentially persuasive arguments. In addition, the dissenter's misgivings about a majority position also might be understood as establishing a predicate for a subsequent reexamination of the majority's holding. Thus, Harlan's dissent arguably is directed as much at Thurgood Marshall and the other legal strategists for the NAACP as future members of the Court.

The term "embryonic" is appropriate because the argument is not yet fully formed, for lack of an illustrative set of facts or pattern of case law. Harlan's dissent is merely "an attack, not on the use of racial classifications, but on a social system based on an ideology of white supremacy." However ambitious Harlan's dissent may have been, it surely does not complete the task of providing a fully formed theory of a "color-blind" Constitution. Instead, Harlan provides a colorful metaphor useful in illustrating the antithesis of the majority's color-conscious government. Harlan's dissent has properly been labeled a jeremiad. The label fits not only for its religious connotations, but also for Harlan's political effort to weaken the legal and political foundations of the majority's argument.[25]

The unfinished character of Harlan's dissent becomes clear when the argument the dissent is popularly represented to contain is contrasted with the actual text. The popularized version suggests the following syllogism:

> The Equal Protection Clause forbids the use of racial classifications by states;
> The Louisiana statute draws a racial classification;
> Therefore, the statute is unconstitutional.
> (Furthermore, such racial lines maintain a race-consciousness that is harmful to society.)

But nowhere in the dissent does Harlan make these claims. Instead, his dissent is best understood as a commentary "about the meaning of freedom embodied in the Thirteenth Amendment and the nature and scope of rights inhering in national citizenship as embodied in the Fourteenth Amendment." Since those rights of citizenship may very well predate the Constitution, Harlan's argument need not rest on the Fourteenth Amendment.[26]

Instead of trying to reduce Harlan's dissenting argument to a logical syllogism, it may be more helpful to understand Harlan's organizational scheme as a proposal for a "color-blind" constitutional principle. From that perspective, Harlan's dissent has four basic argument sections: First, he establishes the factual and legal predicate for looking at the Louisiana statute as a broad attack on the Civil War amendments; second, Harlan's color-blind government constitutional analysis contemplates the Civil War amendments more broadly than the majority; third, the majority's position counteracts the purpose of the Civil War amendments where a color-blind government would serve those purposes; and fourth, that the majority position would cause more harm to the civil liberties and personal freedom of whites and blacks than Harlan's proposed principle of a color-blind government. Harlan introduces his proposed principle of a color-blind Constitution in the second section and explains its benefits in the third and fourth sections.

First, Harlan lays the factual premises necessary for understanding the case as a pure constitutional question of the disparate treatment of citizens (552-53). Harlan restates the facts of the case from the outset of his dissent, but avoids citing the specific language of the statute and focuses on its limitations. This effort in painting the case in more general terms is crucial in order for Harlan to lay the argumentative predicate necessary for understanding the matter as a problem of equal protection. Equal protection violations require that two similarly situated groups be treated differently. Initially, he notes that the social division between the races is clear. Then, he notes that the rail managers completely lack discretion and can face criminal punishment for resisting. Finally, Harlan notes that the statute's only exception (permitting African American nurses of white children to remain in the whites-only rail car) did not apply to the case of an African American nurse with an adult patient.

Harlan wants to address the problem as a matter of citizens being treated differently. Only after establishing that the only difference between the otherwise similarly situated African Americans and whites is the racial classification does Harlan discuss the issue in terms of citizenship. While the statute applies to all rail passengers, citizens and noncitizens alike, Harlan focuses on the fact that the statute establishes as "a crime for a citizen of either race to enter a coach that has been assigned to citizens of the other race" (553).

Harlan's next argumentative move is to offer two alternative approaches to examining the Louisiana statute (553). Harlan frames the issue within the context of a constitutional question, not one of fairness or justice. This maneuver allows him to suggest that the best constitutional analysis should be preferred. Clearly, however, Harlan is not interested in performing the same sort of constitutional analysis as the majority opinion. Justice Brown simply asked whether the Thirteenth or Fourteenth Amendments prevented the state from crafting the law. Harlan is interested in asking whether the law itself violates the citizen's rights under the Amendments.

Harlan describes the railroad as a public highway (553-54). Recasting the railroad as a public highway is important to implicate the state in the discrimination. This link is critical because the Fourteenth Amendment is limited to state actors by its language. Having established the railroad as a proxy for the state, Harlan previews his constitutional arguments by noting that governments cannot take into account the race of citizens without harming their civil rights and their basic claims to liberty.

After this rather lengthy buildup, Harlan finally addresses the constitutional amendments cited by the *Plessy* majority. Responding to the majority's determination that the Thirteenth Amendment only applies to slavery, Harlan asserts instead that the Amendment also "prevents the imposition of any burdens or disabilities that constitute badges of slavery or servitude" (555). Where the majority argued that the Fourteenth Amendment only stood for legal equality among blacks and whites, Harlan explains that the Fourteenth Amendment was intended to extend protections unavailable under the Thirteenth. Harlan argues that combining the two amendments "if enforced according to their true intent and meaning, will protect all the civil rights that pertain to freedom and citizenship" (555). Finally, Harlan recasts the Fifteenth Amendment from the right to vote into the right to participate in the political process of the country (555).

Having attacked the majority's analysis regarding the Amendments, he introduces his alternative standard for evaluating the constitutionality of racial discrimination. In the next paragraph, Harlan argues that the Amendments "removed the race line from our governmental systems" (556). As support for this broad scope of the Amendments' collective force, he cites the Court's opinions involving jury pool discrimination cases, in which the Court prohibited the states from barring African Americans from jury service. Where the majority opinion dealt with the Thirteenth and Fourteenth Amendments separately, Harlan crafts a narrative about the purposes underlying all the Civil War amendments that supports a standard of color blindness.

The most memorable section of Harlan's dissent comes when Harlan tests the majority's position against the standard implicated by the purposes of the Civil War amendment. First, Harlan notes that the majority position detracts from every passenger's enjoyment of civil rights (557). By noting that the underlying purpose of the statute was to make the races keep to themselves and not to provide the most comfortable traveling arrangements for each race, Harlan reveals the state's efforts discriminate on the basis of race as an affront to the personal liberty of each person, regardless of race, to choose to sit with a person of another race.

Harlan next attacks the majority's claim that separate but equal is a reasonable regulation (558-559). First, he questions the limits of the policy's application to city streets or in government buildings, and then to religion. The State's response is that the line between Harlan's purportedly absurd examples would be a judicial determination of reasonableness. Here exists a portion of Harlan's dissent that is neglected. Harlan engages in a discussion about whether a court should be involved in determining the reasonableness of a legislative act. It is a precursor to Harlan's less famous dissent in *Lochner v. New York*.[27] Harlan's federalist roots reveal themselves as he expresses his lack of trust in the state legislatures to provide for the protection of civil liberties. Because Harlan does not believe that courts provide a limit to the application of the separate but equal doctrine, he fears its unchecked use to the deprivation of personal liberties of all citizens.

Only after establishing that no other protections exist for the extension of the doctrine does Harlan begin discussing his vision of a "color-blind" Constitution requiring that legislatures take no account of race (559). At this point, Harlan clearly directs his comments to those fearful that a race-blind government would be harmful to whites. Harlan builds his argument that the white race's superiority is based in part on its heritage and its adherence to civil rights. Harlan seems to suggest that whites will dominate the nation in culture, religion, politics, and business even if civil rights are accorded to citizens of all races.

The next most often quoted passage of the dissent appears when Harlan prophecies that the majority's opinions will one day be as unpopular as its infamous decision in *Sanford v. Dred Scott* (559). In that decision, the Court held that freed slaves born in the United States nevertheless did not have the rights and privileges of citizenship. Harlan notes that the passage of the Civil War amendments was partially in response to that case as well as the Union victory in the war. Harlan's distaste for *Dred Scott* seems to have more to do with that decision's departure from the aims of the Civil War, rather than the apparent unfairness of the treatment of newly freed slaves.

Harlan then worries that by allowing the states to avoid the obvious purpose of the Amendments, hateful actions toward the African Americans will also harm whites (560-563). Harlan finds mutual security for both races in equality before the law. He disregards the majority's distinction between legal and social equality as meaningless. As an example of the illogical nature of the Louisiana statute, Harlan notes that the statute would permit Chinese immigrants to sit with whites, rather than black citizens of the United States who might have been veterans of the war. Harlan uses this example to justify the African American resistance to segregation laws, in contradiction to the majority's apparent suggestion that African Americans have no real complaints. Instead, Harlan labels the condition a "badge of servitude" that offends the Thirteenth Amendment. In another neglected passage, Harlan's federalist roots are revealed again when he weighs the evils of racial mixing against the loss of rights to African American citizens. Harlan draws up the image of a mixed-race jury attempting to deliberate a verdict through a partition designed to separate the different races.

In his conclusion, Harlan dismisses the case law cited by the majority for either predating the Civil War amendments or being affected by prejudicial public opinion (563-564). In doing so, he reaffirms that the passage of the Civil War amendments began a new era that

> established universal civil freedom, gave citizenship to all born or naturalized in the United States, and residing here, obliterated the race line from our systems of governments, national and state, and placed our free institutions upon the broad and sure foundation of the equality of all men before the law. (563)

Harlan continues to note his concern for the "mischievous" effect of many states replicating Louisiana's efforts to evade the Constitution's requirements for equal protection of the law. Harlan's concern is not just for African Americans, but also the rights of whites. His final sentence supports his claim that both Congress and the federal courts have the constitutional authority to strike down such "sinister legislation" by the states.

Stylistic Features of Harlan's Dissent

Judge Benjamin Cardozo argued that because dissenting opinions are not law, the dissenter-author is liberated to write less cautious, more stylized opinions. Primus notes that "[p]art of the reason why we think of dissents as being well written is that we only read the good ones." In terms of style, Harlan's dissent is a good one. Primus would argue that Harlan's writing style lacked literary precision, but style is more than just a proper use of language. The effect generated by Harlan's stylistic choices in crafting his opinion continue to make the dissent powerful reading today.[28]

Harlan's dissent in *Plessy* is enhanced by several interesting stylistic features common to U.S. Supreme Court dissents as well as individual marks of his personality. Ray notes that prior to Holmes and Brandeis's celebration of the dissent as a mode for personal judicial expression, Supreme Court dissenters were apologetic about having to disrupt the Court's unanimity.[29] Harlan's closing, while perhaps going overboard with judicial civility, reveals a tone of regret for his inability to join the majority: "For the reason stated, I am *constrained* to *withhold* my assent from the opinion and judgment of the majority" (564, emphasis added). It is the old-fashioned notion of a duty to dissent that Harlan shares with modern Justices like Brennan.[30]

From the outset, it should not be taken for granted that Harlan chose to write a dissenting opinion. Writing and researching opinions was arduous work, and Harlan was hardly the Court's most prolific or efficient draftsman. He could have dissented without comment. At the turn of the century, it was more common for Justices to simply dissent without issuing any sort of opinion.[31] Instead, Harlan openly challenged the majority position with a dissent nearly the same length as the majority opinion. In addition, it should not be overlooked that Harlan wrote his dissent in the first person. Harlan's decision to use a personal tone in his opinion is significant. Many judicial dissents written in Harlan's era were drafted as abstracted statements of law, instead of personalized expressions of disagreement.[32] Harlan's decision to write in the first person is a crucial part of his dissent's canonization and his posthumous elevation to "sainthood."[33] Harlan's use of the first person signals that he is rejecting the traditional rhetorical characteristic of judicial objectivity by "speaking directly to the people, Congress, and the lawyers of the future, speaking against closure, and seeking to cause people to identify with his position and to change what is now the law."[34] In what James Boyd White calls the "double voice" of the judiciary, Harlan speaks with both legal and personal authority.[35]

Despite the characterization of Harlan as a lonely prophet, many of the legal points expressed in the dissent would have been agreeable to the majority. When Harlan writes that "[i]n respect of civil rights, all citizens are equal before the law" (559), his statement is not a revolutionary opposition to the majority, but actually a point of agreement. It is important to understand that Harlan's discussion of equality is only stated within the nineteenth-century meaning of "civil rights." The disagreement between Harlan and the majority is on the relatively narrow point of whether or not riding in public transportation was, in fact, a civil right. Expressing points of agreement, such as these, allow the dissenter to bridge argumentative gaps with the majority position, which is important if the dissent is to be helpful in correcting the majority's error. It cannot be forgotten that the Court operates as a deliberative democracy and that the Justices must interact, even when they disagree.[36]

A final common feature of the Supreme Court dissent genre is projection of future consequences that give many dissents the similar qualities of a prophecy. Many scholars have noted the similarity between legal interpretation and scriptural interpretation.[37] In many ways, Harlan's dissent in *Plessy* is much like a religious text of prophecy. The rhetorical genre of legal dissent is similar to the genre of religious dissent long associated with resistance to an established religious order. A legal dissenter may be described as either a "heretic whose heresy may not stand the rays of established thought or the spectrum of time"; yet he may also be a "prophet whose heresy of today becomes the dogma of tomorrow."[38] In descriptions of his dissent, Harlan becomes a modern-day version of John the Baptist, prophesizing as a lonely voice in the wilderness, speaking to the future in an effort to warn against repeating past mistakes.[39]

The loss of an institutional voice is key to understanding the stylistic characteristics of a dissent. The dissenter is removed from the majority, much as a disciple who is critical of his religious elders would be separated from his church. The language of legal dissent reflects that sense of institutional separation in the dissenter's use of the first person. My own review of dissenting opinions of the U.S. Supreme Court reveals that dissenters write in the first person, while the majority opinions, *per curium* (unsigned, "by the court") opinions, and concurring opinions are written in the plural voice.[40] Even when other justices sign onto a dissent, the dissenter speaks in the first person. In contrast, an author of concurring opinion joined by other justices uses the plural voice.

Another religious-oriented stylistic feature of Supreme Court dissents that is found in Harlan's dissent is the passing of judgment on the Court's mistake. First, Harlan's language suggests emotions lacking in the majority opinion. Harlan had an apoplectic temper, so it is fitting that his writing reflects his temperament.[41] Another way in which dissenters often explain the depth of a majority's lapse is by pointing to prior errors of the Court. Harlan follows suit in pointing to one of the Court's most egregious rulings in *Dred Scott v. Sandford*: "In my opinion, the judgment this day rendered will, in time, prove to be quite as pernicious as the decision made by this tribunal in the *Dred Scott* case" (559). As Primus explains, the backward-looking notion of prophecy may be appropriate:

> Prophecy, however, comes in a backward-looking form as well as a forward-looking one. One kind of prophet announces a vision of the future, and the other recalls a people to its foundations, chastising them for having strayed from the true path where they or their ancestors once walked.[42]

Harlan's stylistic choices in writing his dissent help in understanding the dissent as a prophecy. Harlan's willingness to use the first person, to pass judgment on his peers, and invoke the Court's prior sin in *Dred Scott* are hallmarks of a calling to redemption. Perhaps the most interesting stylistic choice made by Harlan was his decision to use the "color-blind" Constitution metaphor.

Harlan's Use of the "Color-Blind" Constitution Metaphor

Harlan's use of the "color-blind" Constitution metaphor is easily the most memorable aspect of his dissent, freely quoted by courts and scholars. Invariably, law students studying the *Plessy* dissent in case books read the excerpt from the dissent containing that metaphor. Oddly, mainstream legal commentators rarely unpack the metaphor, commenting only on the subsequent judicial application of "color-blind Constitution." However, Harlan's expression remains a metaphor and not a literal statement of law. In this section, I attempt to unpack the elements of the metaphor and better situate Harlan's rhetorical use of the device in his dissent.[43]

Metaphors, as understood by Perelman, posit a similarity between two relationships existing in different realms. While an analogy might explain that "old age is to life what the evening is to the day," metaphors tend reduce the comparison between the two different relationships into statements like "the old age of the day," "evening of life," or "old age is an evening." Metaphors are worthy of close scrutiny because they go beyond ordinary examples, illustrations, models, and comparisons. Perelman's understanding of metaphor is particularly applicable in analyzing legal metaphors, given his background and interest in jurisprudence. Sooner or later, Perelman claims, metaphors provide ground for counterargumentation because the comparison is limited. Kuusisto suggests that metaphors can rarely be regarded merely as "individual poetic words"; instead, they usually imply a whole way of thinking and a concrete plan of action.[44]

In reviewing Harlan's "color-blind Constitution" metaphor, credit must first be given where credit is due. Harlan freely lifted the metaphor from the court brief submitted by Plessy's counsel, Albion Tourgée. Tourgée's original reference is: "Justice is pictured as blind and her daughter, the Law, ought at least to be colorblind."[45] Harlan's use of the color-blind metaphor is similar to Tourgée's in at least two significant ways. First, Harlan is using the metaphor in conjunction with "the eye of the law" to personify the Constitution just as Tourgée personifies the Law. The Constitution can see things, but not discern the colors that distinguish the races. Because of this color blindness, Harlan claims that the Constitution "neither knows nor tolerates classes among citizens" (559).

However, Harlan's version of the metaphor is also somewhat different. While Tourgée describes the personifications of the ideals of Justice and Law, Harlan is discussing the Constitution as a tangible textual source and the principles that flow from it. While Tourgée celebrates the ideal of color blindness of law, Harlan's conceit is framed as a declaration: "Our Constitution is color-blind" (559).

In addition, Tourgée's use of the color-blind metaphor is a playful evocation of the maxim that "Justice Is Blind," whereas Harlan's purpose is to declare the limits of race-consciousness in applying the Constitution. One might understand Harlan's version of color blindness as really a metaphor for an "absence of race." A strict color blindness would never allow the government to take race into account.[46] However, when Harlan's reference to the "color-blind Constitution" is fully read, there is little doubt that race was clearly on Harlan's mind.

> The white race deems itself to be the dominant race in this country. And so it is, in prestige, in achievements, in education, in wealth, and in power. So, I doubt not, it will continue to be for all time, if it remains true to its great heritage, and holds fast to the principles of constitutional liberty. But in view of the constitution, in the eye of the law, there is in this country no superior, dominant, ruling class of citizens. There is no caste here. Our constitution is color-blind, and neither knows nor tolerates classes among citizens. In respect of civil rights, all citizens are equal before the law. The humblest is the peer of the most powerful. The law regards man as man, and takes no account of his surroundings or of his color when his civil rights as guaranteed by the supreme law of the land are involved. It is therefore to be regretted that this high tribunal, the final expositor of the fundamental law of the land, has reached the conclusion that it is competent for a state to regulate the enjoyment by citizens of their civil rights solely upon the basis of race. (559)

This passage, read in its entirety, suggests three points about Harlan's understanding of the metaphor. First, Harlan understands color blindness to relate to social classes, not individual citizens. Indeed, he declares that "all citizens are equal before the law" only in respect of civil rights. As Aleinikoff notes, if the "evil of the challenged statute is that it is based on a racial classification (thereby violating the norm of color blindness)," Harlan would not have needed to comment on the underlying purpose of the law.[47]

Second, Harlan only requires the Constitution and the law to be color-blind, but clearly allows society and history to celebrate the accomplishments of a race. His use of the "color-blind Constitution" metaphor is in contrast to his lauding of the white race. His lament is not that the Court recognized the superiority of whites, but that the majority reached that position as "this high tribunal, the final expositor of the fundamental law of the land" (559).

A third and most compelling point in this excerpt is that a strict, literalist understanding of Harlan's "color-blind Constitution" metaphor is betrayed by the final statement in the excerpt. Harlan's complaint is that the Court has reached the conclusion that "it is competent for a state to regulate the enjoyment of citizens of their civil rights solely upon the basis of race" (559). Strictly applied, Harlan's color-blind Constitution metaphor would never allow state regulation on the basis of race. This is the preferred interpretation of the metaphor by some modern conservative legal commentators and jurists. For example, after reviewing the jurisprudence of Justice Thomas and Justice Scalia, Lundin argues that governmental race-based action should never be permissible. Lundin views Harlan's dissent as supporting this claim, constructing the opposing view as "tolerance of benign race-conscious law."[48] Like many modern conservative legal commentators, Lundin suggests that the only difference between equal protection in the 1890s and today is the broader scope of racial equality, so the metaphor can still be strictly applied.

The irony of modern conservatives using Harlan's color-blind Constitution metaphor to strike down affirmative action programs designed to improve education opportunities for minorities "is a normal product of a process by which the redemption and canonization of dissent is a function not of the dissenting Justice or of the opinion he wrote but of the rereadings that later courts conduct when they [reverse precedent] and revise the constitutional canon." In that sense, a color-blind interpretation of the Constitution "legitimates, and thereby maintains, the social, economic, and political advantages that whites hold over other Americans." Even if that were not the case, Lundin would find it difficult to find consensus on what constitutes a proper scope of racial equality, given the multiple definitions available.[49]

Lundin's position that Harlan's metaphor was limited to civil rights because that was the dominant view of his contemporaries is misplaced. Clearly, Harlan's use of a color-blind Constitution also encompassed a far narrower, less intrusive legal authority than the modern Constitution. However, Harlan's understanding of governmental color blindness does take into account the historical treatment of African Americans, yet allows for private, nongovernmental discrimination for the advantage of whites. Harlan saw the larger impact of the majority's position as a separation of the races. In fact, Jim Crow laws eventually applied to whites as well, often to their surprise. Several whites sued rail companies premised on the "insult of being asked to move because the space was assigned to or needed for black passengers."[50] Accordingly, Harlan was aware of a broader application of that metaphor, but chose to limit it by his inclusion of the terms "civil rights" and "solely" (559). Just four sentences after Harlan uses the color-blind Constitution metaphor, he suggests that it would be limited in cases involving the regulation of civil rights exclusively on the basis of race (559).

Conclusion

The majority's position in *Plessy* is lamentable largely for its passivity. For the majority, deliberative democracy, in all of its potential, could not rectify what seemed to be natural inequalities between the races. As the *Plessy* Court explained, "If the civil and political rights of both races be equal one cannot be inferior to the other civilly or politically. If one race be inferior to the other socially, the Constitution of the United States cannot put them upon the same plane" (551-52). In contrast, Harlan's Isaiah-like repudiation of the majority is most notable for its optimism. While Harlan likely shared with his brethren a lack of faith that African Americans could ever become the social or political equal of whites, Harlan did believe that the Constitution could provide a foundation for civic equality.

The question of whether the *Plessy* dissent has ever become law relies in many senses on an understanding of law as a "product of what we, as a culture, want law to be." While *Plessy* has never been explicitly overturned, the core holding that a state's provision of separate but equal accommodations to different races is constitutional clearly no longer is useful in any general sense. After *Brown*, the Court has struck down laws requiring segregated accommodations at beaches, municipal golf courses, public buses, parks, stadiums, and courtrooms. However, the Court has never directly cited Harlan's dissent in *Plessy* as positive law. Yet, Harlan's dissent remains squarely in the canon of American constitutional law, as if we should want it to be good law.[51]

Primus posits that dissents are redeemed for "holdings" reconstructed by later courts. "The possibility that a dissent will become canonical is limited by the canon's structural need, or lack of need, for a canonical text." In order for a dissent to be helpful, the dissenter must be "reimagined" as a contemporary legal thinker and his "holding" created retrospectively. Primus thus argues that Harlan "was reimagined as a racial egalitarian so that his *Plessy* dissent could be redeemed for the holding that the Constitution is "color-blind." Primus may be correct, but I believe the rhetorical characteristics of Harlan's dissent make it a candidate for canonization. Substantively, Harlan's argumentative structure reinforces a central, unifying argument based in civil rights. Stylistically, Harlan's prophetic voice reflects an effort at institutional separation. These features make Harlan's dissent readable in the first instance, and thus capable of reimagination by subsequent legal scholars.[52]

Yet there is more to the canonization of Saint Harlan and his prophecy than his rhetorical skill. Modern "canonization" of dissents arguably occurs for two reasons: first, the dissent is memorialized as a judicial entrenchment of the repudiation of a hated precedent; or second, the dissent is a source as a vehicle for the judicial expansion of a constitutional right. Krishnakumar notes that the first judicial citation to the *Plessy* dissent did not occur until 1961, and frequent quotation of the dissent did not begin until the 1980s. Krishnakumar concludes that this citation pattern suggests that "the lionization of the *Plessy* dissent occurred as a memorial, rather than a source, for the demonization of the *Plessy* decision and the racist doctrine it propounded." Krishnakumar also notes that modern courts have used the *Plessy* dissent in two distinct ways. Initially, the citations of the 1960s focused on the wisdom of Harlan's dissent. However, the courts of the 1980s most frequently cited the dissent "almost exclusively as a warning not to repeat the mistakes of the past."[53]

Krishnakumar's analysis, combined with this chapter's review of the rhetorical features of the dissent, reveals two possible findings. First, modern judicial usage of the *Plessy* dissent's language, particularly the color-blind metaphor, strongly suggests that modern courts have canonized the *Plessy* dissent for its repudiation of the precedent in *Plessy*, not for its argument. Harlan's understanding of the distinction between civil, social, and political rights is not helpful to modern jurists, but his skillful rebuttal of the *Plessy* majority opinion offers a strong model. James Boyd White argues that the meaning of an opinion lies in its performance rather that its message: "The truest meaning of the opinion is not its message, but the experience of mind that it holds out as a model of legal thought."[54] Harlan's performance of his dissent carries an ethos of endless goodwill and wisdom. Second, dissents are powerful for their rhetorical authority, rather than just their legalistic authority. Casebook editors present two claims about the *Plessy* dissent: first, that the superficiality of the "equality" of the Louisiana statute could not mask the racist underpinnings of the law; and second, that the Constitution is colorblind.[55] However, even a broad reading of the entire *Plessy* dissent reveals that the legal holdings are quite different. Instead, it seems more accurate to say that casebook editors present the two claims that Harlan's dissent have since come to stand for in contemporary times.

White encourages scholars to understand law as a branch of rhetoric, instead of a system of rules. In that regard, law "might be the particular set of resources made available by a culture for speech and argument on those occasions, and by those speakers, we think of as legal."[56] The strength of a legal argument may not be in the particular argumentative tools, for the best advocates make the best of what rhetorical resources that are available. Instead, Harlan's *Plessy* dissent is a reminder that strong advocacy can reflect a wisdom in seeking a worthwhile goal. Judicial dissent, like religious prophecy, is most powerful when it gives audiences a new way of seeing its surrounding circumstances. In that sense, Harlan's dissent is timeless not for the precision of its legal argument, but for his willingness to see a world unfettered by racial prejudice.

Notes

1. *Plessy v. Ferguson*, 163 U.S. 537, 559 (J. Harlan dissenting). (Additional references to the *Plessy* decision will be made in the text.) Demonstrating something of a sarcastic bent, God commissions Isaiah to tell His people "Be ever hearing but never understanding; be ever seeing, but never perceiving. Make the heart of this people calloused; make their ears dull and close their eyes. Otherwise they might see with their eyes, hear with their ears, understand with their hearts, and turn and be healed." Isa. 6:9-10. Isaiah's mission of prophecy was by lawlessness of God's people: "And he looked for justice, but saw bloodshed; for righteousness, but heard cries of distress." Isa. 5:7.

2. Gabriel J. Chin argues that "[e]ven today, the symbolic power of Harlan's rejection of segregation of African Americans and whites . . . is rivaled only by the Reverend Martin Luther King's *I Have a Dream* speech and *Brown v. Board of Education* itself" ("The *Plessy* Myth: Justice Harlan and the Chinese Cases,"

Iowa Law Review 82 [1996]: 151). Although hundreds of court opinions have cited to the *Plessy* dissent, it has never been expressly adopted as a formal statement of law. Whether the general principle of constitutional color blindness, if one exists in the opinion at all, reflects a statement of American constitutional law remains open to debate. Richard A. Primus describes the canon of constitutional law as "a set of greatly authoritative texts that above all others shape the nature and development of constitutional law" ("Canon, Anti-Canon, and Judicial Dissent," *Duke Law Journal* 48 [1998]: 243). However, if a canon of law exists, then it must be undisputed that the dissent is of canonical statute. For a further discussion of the nature and importance of canonical legal texts, see J. M. Balkin and Sanford Levinson, "The Canons of Constitutional Law," *Harvard Law Review* 111 (1998): 963-1024; Anita S. Krishnakumar, "On the Evolution of the Canonical Dissent," *Rutgers Law Review* 52 (2000): 781-826.

3. Charles A. Lofgren, *The Plessy Case: A Legal-Historical Interpretation* (Oxford: Oxford University Press, 1987), 195.

4. In the Pentateuch, the first five books of the Old Testament, God delivers to Moses the laws and regulations for Israel. In contrast, the Book of Isaiah offers only warnings of repentance for those violating God's commandments.

5. Harlan's dissent in *Plessy* has been admired by the ideological polar opposites of Justice William Brennan and Justice Clarence Thomas. Hunter R. Clark, *Justice Brennan: The Great Conciliator* (New York: Birch Lane, 1995), 256; Clarence Thomas, "Toward a 'Plain Reading' of the Constitution—The Declaration of Independence in Constitutional Interpretation," *Howard Law Journal* 30 (1987): 983-995. In fact, Thomas criticizes *Brown v. Board of Education* for its failure to rely on his interpretation of Harlan's *Plessy* dissent. Ibid., 990. Other members of the Supreme Court bench are also fans of the dissent. In the gay-rights case, *Romer v. Evans*, 517 U.S. 620 (1996), Justice Anthony Kennedy begins the majority opinion by quoting Harlan's admonition that the Constitution "neither knows nor tolerates classes among citizens." *Romer*, 517 U.S. 620, 623. Meanwhile, Justice Antonin Scalia quotes the same language in his dissenting opinion. *Romer*, 517 U.S. 620, 650.

6. Meredith Kolsky, "Justice William Johnson and the History of the Supreme Court Dissent," *Georgetown Law Review* 83 (1995): 2082. The NAACP legal team that battled segregation under the direction of Thurgood Marshall turned the phrase into both a creed and a standard legal response. Constance Baker Motley, "In Memory of Thurgood Marshall," *New York University Law Review* 68 (1993): 210. The NAACP's brief in *Brown* stated a preference for the primacy of Harlan's dissent: "It is the dissenting opinion of Justice Harlan, rather than the majority opinion in *Plessy v. Ferguson*, that is in keeping with the scope and meaning of the Fourteenth Amendment as consistently defined by this Court both before and after *Plessy v. Ferguson*." "Brief for Appellants in Nos. 1, 2, and 4 and for Respondents in No. 10 on Reargument, *Brown v. Board*

of Education, 347 U.S. 483 (1954)," in *Landmark Briefs and Arguments of the Supreme Court of the United States: Constitutional Law*, eds. Philip B. Kurland and Gerhard Casper (Washington, D.C.: University Publications of America, 1975), 49:554.

7. For example, Primus is interested in how the *Plessy* dissent is canonized or "redeemed" by subsequent courts interested in the substantive merits of the dissenting argument ("Canon, Anti-Canon, and Judicial Dissent," 247-248). In addition, several critical scholars in law and rhetoric have focused on the history and rhetoric of equal protection law and the civil rights movement. See Marouf Hasian, Jr., "Critical Legal Rhetorics: The Theory and Practice of Law in a Postmodern World," *Southern Communications Journal* 60 (Fall 1994): 44-56; Marouf Hasian, Jr., "Judicial Rhetoric in a Fragmentary World: 'Character' and Storytelling in the Leo Frank Case," *Communication Monographs* 64 (September 1997): 250-269; John Louis Lucaites, "Between Rhetoric and 'The Law,'" *Quarterly Journal of Speech* 76 (1990): 435-449.

8. Tinsley E. Yarbrough, *Judicial Enigma: The First Justice Harlan* (New York: Oxford Press, 1995), 10. Interestingly, one descendent of John Harlan's stepbrother, James Nabrit, was a member of the NAACP legal team that prevailed in ending the separate but equal doctrine's application to education in *Brown*. Ibid., 11. For a less scholarly account of the relationship between Harlan and Holmes, see Frank B. Latham, *The Great Dissenter: John Marshall Harlan* (New York: Cowles, 1970), 114.

9. Krishnakumar, "On the Evolution of the Canonical Dissent," 802. *Civil Rights Cases*, 109 U.S. 3 (1883); *Hurtado v. California*, 110 U.S. 516 (1884); *Pollack v. Farmers' Loan & Trust Co.*, 157 U.S. 429 (1895); *Lochner v. New York*, 198 U.S. 45 (1905).

10. Dissent statistics were taken from Latham, *The Great Dissenter*, 161.

11. Molly Townes O'Brien, "Justice John Marshall Harlan as Prophet: The *Plessy* Dissenter's Color-Blind Constitution," *William & Mary Bill of Rights Journal* 6 (1998): 755. For a general account of Harlan's religious background and beliefs, see James W. Gordon, "Religion and the First Justice Harlan: A Case Study in Late Nineteenth Century Presbyterian Constitutionalism," *Marquette Law Review* 85 (2001): 317-422.

12. Gordon, "Religion and the First Justice Harlan," 363. The notion of law as faith is not merely limited to religious-minded jurists. Steven D. Smith argues that law is an expression of faith, and all lawyers and jurists act as believers. "Believing Like a Lawyer," *Boston College Law Review* 40 (1999): 1047-1048.

13. After reviewing Harlan's jurisprudential treatment of African Americans, Native Americans, and the Chinese, Earl M. Maltz suggests that Harlan's sympathy for minority rights was limited to African Americans and a narrow range of civil rights. "Only Partially Color-Blind: John Marshall Harlan's View of Race and the Constitution," *Georgia State University Law Review* 12 (1996): 973-1016.

14. Yarborough, *Judicial Enigma*,139.

15. Yarborough reports that among other intimate connections, Harlan attended Douglass's funeral. Ibid., 142

16. For a succinct review of the historical era surround the *Plessy* case, see Michael J. Klarman, "The *Plessy* Era," *Supreme Court Review* 303 (1998): 303-414; James C. Cobb, "Segregating the New South: The Origins and Legacy of *Plessy v. Ferguson*," *Georgia State University Law Review* 12 (1996): 1017-1036. For more analysis of Harlan's view of Asians, see Gabriel J. Chin, "The First Justice Harlan by the Numbers: Just How Great Was 'The Great Dissenter'?" *Akron Law Review* 32 (1999): 633; Chin, "The *Plessy* Myth"; Gordon, "Believing Like a Lawyer," 396.

17. *Slaughter-House Cases*, 83 U.S. 36 (1872); *Civil Rights Cases*, 109 U.S. 3 (1883).

18. Melissa Cole, "The Color-Blind Constitution, Civil Rights-Talk, and a Multicultural Discourse for a Post-Reparations World," *New York University Review of Law & Social Change* 25 (1999): 131, 135-36; Barbara Y. Welke, "Beyond *Plessy*: Space, Status, and Race in the Era of Jim Crow," *Utah Law Review* 267 (2000): 268-269.

19. Plessy claimed a seven-eighths Caucasian and one-eighth African American mix in his blood line, which was described by the *Plessy* majority as "not discernible in him" (538). See also, Yarborough, *Judicial Enigma*, 158. However, for the definitive account of Plessy, his challenge of the statute, and the legal support he received, see Lofgren, *The Plessy Case*.

20. Harlan's opinions in subsequent cases suggest that Harlan might have supported segregation in more personally intimate settings than public transportation, voting booths, places of public amusement, or the jury box. Yarborough, *Judicial Enigma*, 160. In fact, Justice Felix Frankfurter and Justice John Harlan (Harlan's grandson) privately debated for years whether the elder Harlan would have supported school segregation. James F. Simon, *The Antagonists: Hugo Black, Felix Frankfurter and Civil Liberties in Modern America* (New York: Touchstone, 1989), 239.

21. 347 U.S. 483, 494 (1954). The *Brown* court clearly emphasized the critical role of education in determining a child's success, devaluing transportation by implicit comparison. See Mark Strasser, "*Plessy*, *Brown* and HBCUs: On the Imposition of Stigma and the Court's Mechanical Equal Protection Jurisprudence," *Washburn Law Journal* 40 (2000): 50. For further analysis of Harlan's missing arguments, see John C. Duncan, Jr., "The American 'Legal' Dilemma: Colorblind I/Colorblind II—The Rules Have Changed: A Semantic Apothegmatic Permutation," *Virginia Journal of Social Policy and the Law* 7 (2000): 390.

22. Jeffrey Rosen, "The Color-Blind Court," *American University Law Review* 45 (1996): 793. Primus, "Canon, Anti-Canon, and Judicial Dissent," 289-290. Citing from the Civil Rights Act of 1866, 14 Stat. 27, 27 (1866), Primus

also suggests that "social rights" included rights of private association and possibly access to public transportation while political rights denoted suffrage and the right to hold office. Primus, "Canon, Anti-Canon, and Judicial Dissent," 290. For further reference, Akhil Reed Amar offers a comprehensive and approachable dissection of the Reconstruction theory of rights. See "The Fifteenth Amendment and 'Political Rights'," *Cardozo Law Review* 17 (1996): 2225-2229; "The Bill of Rights and the Fourteenth Amendment," *Yale Law Journal* 101 (1992): 1193-1284; and "The Bill of Rights as a Constitution," *Yale Law Journal* 100 (1991): 1131-1210.

23. For a scholarly dismissal of segregation, see Alexander Bickel, *The Morality of Consent* (New Haven: Yale University Press, 1975). The U.S. Supreme Court has demonstrated the flexible uses of Harlan's dissent. As Chin notes, the Harlan dissent was cited in the introductory epitaph of the Court's majority decision in *Romer v. Evans*, 517 U.S. 620, 623 (1996). Aside from its rhetorical use in striking down the Colorado anti-gay-rights initiative in *Romer*, Harlan's dissent has never been treated as positive law (Chin, "The Plessy Myth," 155 n. 24). Much debate remains over whether the majority position in *Plessy v. Ferguson* remains good law, such that a state-sponsored "separate but equal" system of racial discrimination might be constitutional. *Brown* hardly resolves the question definitively because it only overrules *Plessy* by implication. Even if *Brown* does effectively overrule *Plessy*, *Brown* does not clearly take up Harlan's dissent. Although Harlan's dissent must have weighed heavily on the Warren Court's decision-making process, Chief Justice Warren (1977) never mentions Harlan's dissent in his discussion of the case in his memoirs.

24. LaValley similarly describes the concept of "embryonic" future decisions as dissents in the "true tradition" (1422). Whether those dissents do influence future courts is an important question. LaValley's article contains an empirical study of New York appellate dissenters that merits further scrutiny and replication at the level of federal circuits and the U.S. Supreme Court. Harlan's dissent functionally differs from the majority opinion in that Harlan's purpose is not to embody and characterize actions of the Court, which remains the rhetorical work of the majority. For a fuller discussion of a court's opinions and orders as communicative acts, see Clarke Rountree, "Instantiating 'The Law' and Its Dissents in *Korematsu v. United States*: A Dramatistic Analysis of Judicial Discourse," *Quarterly Journal of Speech* 87 (2001): 1-24.

25. T. Alexander Aleinikoff, "Re-reading Justice Harlan's Dissent in *Plessy v. Ferguson*: Freedom, Antiracism, and Citizenship," *University of Illinois Law Review* 1992 (1992): 961-997; Robert G. Flanders, Jr., "The Utility of Separate Judicial Opinions in Appellate Courts of Last Resort: Why Dissents Are Valuable," *Roger Williams University Law Review* 4 (1999): 401-424; Kurt W. Ritter, "American Political Rhetoric and the Jeremiad Tradition: Presidential Nomination Acceptance Addresses, 1960-1976," *Southern Speech Communication Journal* 31 (1980): 153-171.

26. Aleinikoff, "Re-reading," 963-964. Aleinikoff's reading of the dissent suggests the following argument:

1) the Civil War Amendments defined national citizenship and protected the rights associated with citizenship from unreasonable burdens;
2) although courts should defer to the legislature on issues of policy, "reasonable review" demanded that the state identify a legitimate purpose; and
3) at least when fundamental rights are at stake, judges must disregard state justifications for statutes if they are but a "thin disguise" for an impermissible purpose.

Ibid., 970. See also Simeon C. R. Mcintosh, "Reading *Dred Scott*, *Plessy* and *Brown*: Toward a Constitutional Hermeneutics," *Howard Law Journal* 38 (1994): 70.

27. 198 U.S. 45, 65 (1905). In *Lochner*, Harlan dissented from the majority's decision not to grant deference to a New York state regulation limiting the number of hours a baker might work. Harlan's dissent was premised on deference to the superior fact-finding capacities of the state legislature. Justice Holmes' briefer and more colorful dissent is the more famous of the *Lochner* dissents, but Harlan's reasoning best reflects the position adopted by the Court when it abandoned its position in *Lochner*. For a comparison of the Holmes and Harlan dissents in *Lochner*, see Krishnakumar, "On the Evolution of the Canonical Dissent," 788-790.

28. Benjamin N. Cardozo, *Selected Writings of Benjamin Nathan Cardozo*, ed. Margaret E. Hall (New York: Fallon, 1947); Primus, "Canon Anti-Canon, and Judicial Dissent," 267.

29. Laura Krugman Ray, "Justice Brennan and the Jurisprudence of Dissent," *Temple Law Review* 61 (1988): 312-314.

30. Justice Brennan argues that "[n]o one has any duty simply to make noise," however, "where significant and deeply held disagreement exists, members of the Court have a responsibility to articulate it." William J. Brennan, Jr., "In Defense of Dissents," *Hastings Law Journal* 37 (1986): 437.

31. Of the 16 dissents noted in Volume 163 of the U.S. Reporter, seven offered no explanation or reasoning.

32. For a discussion of voice and emotion in judicial opinions, see Laura Krugman Ray, "Judicial Personality: Rhetoric and Emotion in Supreme Court Opinions," *Washington & Lee Law Review* 59 (2002): 193-234.

33. Krishnakumar theorizes that Harlan is a "saint" in the eye of the modern public looking back on the "constitutional sins" of Harlan's contemporaries. "On the Evolution of the Canonical Dissent," 781-782.

34. Gerald Wetlaufer, "Rhetoric and Its Denial in Legal Discourse," *Virginia Law Review* 76 (1990): 1564.

35. James Boyd White explains that a "good judge thus speaks in a double voice, as one who has brought to bear as well as he can the sources of authority

external to himself, and as one who makes a choice for which he is responsible." *When Words Lose Their Meaning: Constitutions and Reconstitutions of Language, Character, and Community* (Chicago: University of Chicago Press, 1984), 269.

36. Primus, "Canon, Anti-Canon, and Judicial Dissent," 292; Ray, "Justice Brennan and the Jurisprudence of Dissent," 351; Kevin M. Stack, "The Practice of Dissent in the Supreme Court," *Yale Law Journal* 105 (1996): 2259.

37. Sanford Levinson, *Constitutional Faith* (Princeton, NJ: Princeton University Press, 1988); Thomas C. Grey, "The Constitution as Scripture," *Stanford Law Review* 37 (1984): 1-25; Samuel J. Levine, "Unenumerated Constitutional Rights and Unenumerated Biblical Obligations: A Preliminary Study in Comparative Hermeneutics," *Constitutional Commentary* 15 (1998): 511-527.

38. Percival E. Jackson, *Dissent in the Supreme Court* (Norman: University of Oklahoma Press, 1969), 3.

39. Noting the etymologic relationship between "dissenter" and "dissidents," Jackson suggests that "[t]he American dissenter" wears the dissident mantles of Galileo and Luther. Ibid. Harlan's dissent is described as the "lone prophetic dissent in *Plessy*" by Clark, *Justice Brennan: The Great Conciliator*, 75. Dean Jefferies describes Harlan's dissent as words that "leapt across the decades to rebuke race-consciousness and warn the Court of repeating past mistakes." John C. Jefferies, Jr., *Justice Lewis F. Powell, Jr.: A Biography* (New York: Scribner's, 1994), 463.

40. Daniel E. Mangis, "Today's Dissents and Tomorrow's Law: A Generic Analysis of U.S. Supreme Court Dissenting Opinions in Equal Protection Clause Cases, 1872-2002," paper presented at the annual meeting of the National Communication Association, New Orleans, November 2002.

41. Sheldon M. Novick, *Honorable Justice: The Life of Oliver Wendell Holmes* (Boston: Little, Brown and Co., 1989), 254.

42. Primus, "Canon Anti-Canon, and Judicial Dissent," 278.

43. My review of *Shepard's Citations* indicated that at least 500 court decisions and 3,100 law review articles have cited the color-blind language from Harlan's dissent. There are undoubtedly just as many indirect references to the metaphor. For a discussion of law students' exposure to the *Plessy* dissent, see Aleinikoff, "Re-reading," 962.

44. Chaim Perelman, *The Realm of Rhetoric* (Notre Dame, Ind.: University of Notre Dame Press, 1984), 114-125. For Perelman, analogies spell out the two relationships being compared (the analogy's theme and phoros), but a metaphor fuses the two relationships by condensing the analogy. Ibid., 120. For a concise summary of Perelman's view of metaphors, as well as those of Kenneth Burke and Perelman and Olbrechts-Tyteca, see Riikka Kuusisto, "Heroic Tale, Game, and Business Deal? Western Metaphors in Action in Kosovo," *Quarterly Journal of Speech* 88 (2002): 50-68.

45. Brook Thomas, "*Plessy v. Ferguson* and the Literary Imagination," *Cardozo Studies in Law and Literature* 9 (1997): 62. Tourgée's brief is reprinted in *The Thin Disguise*, ed. Otto H. Olsen (New York: Humanities Press, 1967). Thomas notes that Tourgée had previously used the color-blind metaphor in a novel, but in a derogatory sense ("Literary Imagination," 62). In Tourgée's 1880 novel, *Bricks without Straw*, the attorney-cum-novelist writes that the newly freed slaves had rights only in the abstract: "Justice would not hear his voice. The law was still color-blinded by the past." *Bricks without Straw* (New York: Fords, Howard & Hulbert, 1880), 35. The difference between the two metaphors is telling: Tourgée describes Law as being blinded by color, where Harlan views Law as incapable of distinguishing colors.

46. O'Brien, "Justice John Marshall Harlan as Prophet," 757. A review of federal district court opinions reveals that modern federal district courts regularly apply color-conscious standards in supporting affirmative action programs. See John Cocchi Day, "Retelling the Story of Affirmative Action: Reflections on a Decade of Federal Jurisprudence in the Public Workplace," *California Law Review* 89 (2001): 59-127.

47. Aleinikoff, "Re-reading," 963.

48. Marquez Lundin, "The Call for a Color-Blind Law," *Columbia Journal of Law and Social Problems*, 30 (1997): 426. For a review of the conservative treatment of color blindness, see Brad Snyder, "How the Conservatives Canonized *Brown v. Board of Education*," *Rutgers Law Review* 52 (2000): 383-494.

49. Lundin, 426. For a discussion of judicial "rereadings," see Primus, "Canon Anti-Canon, and Judicial Dissent," 293; Randall Kennedy, "Race Relations Law in the Canon of Legal Academia," *Fordham Law Review* 68 (2000): 1985-2010. Kennedy further asserts that

> [p]eople differ over what they mean by racial justice. Some mean preventing all forms of private or public racial discrimination. Some mean preventing all forms of invidious racial discrimination. Some mean preventing all forms of invidious racial discrimination and redressing the discernible vestiges of racial wrongs done in the past. On the other hand, some mean merely prohibiting governments from engaging in invidious racial discrimination, while expressly permitting private parties to do so. (2010)

50. Neil Gotanda, "A Critique of 'Our Constitution Is Color-blind,'" *Stanford Law Review* 44 (1991): 39; Welke, "Beyond *Plessy*, 296.

51. Jane B. Baron, "Law, Literature, and the Problems of Interdisciplinarity," *Yale Law Journal* 108 (1999): 1085. There may be no difference between the Court's treatment of *Plessy* after the *Brown* decision and formally overruling *Plessy*. See Albert P. Blaustein and Andrew H. Field, "Overruling Opinions in the Supreme Court," *Michigan Law Review* 57 (1958): 51 (arguing that *Plessy* was overturned by inference in *Gayle v. Browder*, 352 U.S. 903 [1956], a per

curiam decision that simply cited *Brown* and its progeny). Cases in which "separate but equal" racial segregation was not permitted include *Mayor of Baltimore v. Dawson*, 350 U.S. 877 (1955); *Holmes v. City of Atlanta*, 350 U.S. 879 (1955); *Gayle*, 352 U.S. 903 (1956); *New Orleans City Park Improvement Association v. Detiege*, 358 U.S. 54 (1958); *State Athletic Commission v. Dorsey*, 359 U.S. 533 (1959); *Johnson v. Virginia*, 373 U.S. 61 (1963).

52. "Redeeming and canonizing a dissent involves the misreading, or reimagining, of the author as well as the text." Primus, "Canon Anti-Canon, and Judicial Dissent," 285. Harlan's dissent was "redeemed for its 'holding' that the constitution is 'color-blind.'" Ibid., 280. But Primus understands the "holding" to be "the proposition for which later courts cite the original case." Ibid., 283. The "greatness" of the dissenter is also retrospectively constructed. "Harlan's status as a great Justice relies on the fact that his *Plessy* dissent has been redeemed." For a broader discussion on dissents and judicial reimagining, see ibid., 281-285.

53. Krishnakumar, "On the Evolution of the Canonical Dissent," 801, 819.

54. James Boyd White, "The Judicial Opinion and the Poem: Ways of Reading, Ways of Life," *Michigan Law Review* 82 (1984): 1679-1680, 1681.

55. Aleinikoff, "Re-reading," 962.

56. James Boyd White; "Law as Rhetoric, Rhetoric as Law: The Arts of Cultural and Communal Life," *University of Chicago Law Review* 52 (1985): 684, 689.

3

Setting the Stage for *Brown v. Board of Education*: The NAACP's Litigation Campaign against the "Separate but Equal" Doctrine

Clarke Rountree

In the 1896 case of *Plessy v. Ferguson*, the U.S. Supreme Court decided that Louisiana's law requiring the segregation of white and black passengers into "separate but equal" accommodations on intrastate railroads was constitutional and did not violate the Fourteenth Amendment, relying in part on the accepted practice of segregating public schools.[1] Fifty-eight years later, the same court ruled in *Brown v. Board of Education* that "[s]eparate educational facilities are inherently unequal" and that such inequality constituted a deprivation of equal protection of the laws under the Fourteenth Amendment.[2] This about-face was not accomplished in one fell swoop, but was the product of decades of constant work by the NAACP in the first long-term litigation campaign undertaken in this country.

This chapter examines this litigation campaign from the perspective of rhetorical theory. Specifically, I consider the NAACP's campaign as a particular form of what I have called "prospective argument,"[3] which seeks not simply successful persuasion in "a given case" (as Aristotle taught), but to create the grounds for successful argument over the long term. I begin with a consideration of what prospective argument is and how it functions. Next, I consider the particular context of the litigation campaign as a unique form of prospective argument, sketching a model of what ideally it would encompass. Finally, I turn to the litigation campaign to overturn *Plessy*, focusing particularly on the strategy of the NAACP and its Legal Defense and Education Fund (hereinafter LDF) in litigating graduate school cases.

Prospective Argument

Conceiving of argument as "prospective" challenges the idea that students of argument should be concerned primarily with the strategic adaptation of the available means of persuasion to the "given case" that was Aristotle's focus.[4] Rather, we should be paying more attention to those advocates who respond to and manipulate larger rhetorical situations—those spanning time and opening up the possibility of long-term strategies. Notably, speakers often adapt arguments not simply for the exigencies of the present, but with an eye to future argument. Obvious examples include those involved in campaigns or social movements, long-serving politicians, and appellate judges (who write binding opinions). Prospective argument looks to social movements, not just as events or phenomena, but as contexts for shaping future arguments.[5] It looks to individual court decisions, not as completed arguments, but as strategically anticipated stepping stones toward future arguments. And it considers how material interventions can be undertaken specifically for subsequent incorporation into rhetorical strategy.

Two considerations are paramount in this orientation toward the future. First, advocates want to avoid unfavorably constraining what they can subsequently argue and do. Second, they want to set the stage for effective argument in the future. This dual objective leads to the development of "constraint avoidance" strategies and "stage-setting" strategies. Although these two types of strategies can be described independently, good prospective argument usually requires that they be carefully co-articulated.

Constraint avoidance strategies attempt to anticipate and ward off possible criticisms that might limit argumentative strategy in the future, especially those charging inconsistency. For example, advocates must beware of making claims about "appropriate" conduct, which they may find themselves violating in the future (i.e., not "practicing what one preaches"). I have catalogued a number of constraint avoidance strategies that are used to avoid future inconsistencies and thereby protect the future credibility or oneself or one's allies.[6]

Stage-setting strategies, by contrast, involve positively building the groundwork for effective future argument. These provide a "productive" complement to constraint avoidance, notwithstanding the fact that such strategies are also often aimed at constraining what one's likely opponents may argue in the future.[7] Prospective rhetorical strategies of this sort take advantage of symbolic and material interventions made possible by an expanded time horizon. They typically concentrate on manipulating the intimate relationship between texts and contexts, as well as shaping the interplay between symbolic and non-symbolic factors.

Classic rhetorical situations have involved the marshalling of symbolic resources immediately available within a prescribed and relatively narrow time frame. For example, a speech introducing a speaker uses symbolic means (a speech) to reach a symbolic end (enhancing an audience's view of the speaker); it seeks to give the speaker more credibility, to raise interest in what he or she has to say, to connect him or her to the audience, and so forth. In short, the introductory speech serves to build the groundwork for an effective speech by the introduced speaker. In an expanded temporal horizon, as one finds in the case of prospective argument, other strategies become available:

(1) One important means of stage setting in prospective argument is to alter the discursive context, for example, the publication of research as a means of changing discursive conditions for anticipated future arguments. The Atkins Foundation, for instance, recently sponsored a study demonstrating the health benefits of Dr. Atkins' low-carbohydrate diet, thereby setting the stage for his appeal to those wishing to lose weight to buy his book and follow his diet.[8] Published medical research often serves as a prospective argument strategy in this way. In the *Brown* case, social science research served the same prospective function, as David Droge's chapter in this volume illustrates.

(2) Other prospective strategies use discursive means to change the nondiscursive contexts within which future arguments are made. The pro-life legal advocacy group, Americans United for Life, provides a good example of this.[9] To support their long-term goal of reversing *Roe v. Wade* (the 1973 Supreme Court decision that legalized abortion), this group appealed to Congress and the President to appoint conservative federal judges likely to support reversing the decision. While these appeals were symbolic, the overall strategy encompassed means that were not just symbolic: They wanted conservative judges sitting as the audience they needed to persuade in the future when they defended a state law banning abortion. Similarly, those attempting to overturn *Plessy* sought to seat judges favorable to their position, and to prevent the appointment of those not favoring their position, as I explain below.

(3) A third type of strategy uses nondiscursive intervention to shape the possibilities of future persuasion. This use of "extra-argumentative" means to reframe argument is illustrated by President George Bush's 1990 strategy in opposing Saddam Hussein's occupation of Kuwait.[10] A large contingent of American and Allied troops had been deployed for Operation Desert Shield to protect Saudi Arabia from Iraqi incursions across the border from occupied Kuwait. The United Nations had placed sanctions against Iraq, and Senate Armed Services Committee Chairman Senator Sam Nunn and others were calling for the President to give sanctions time to work. Bush waited until Congress recessed for the holidays in November and then ordered a doubling of troops in the Persian Gulf region "to ensure that the coalition has an adequate offensive military option should that be necessary to achieve our common goals."[11] This military action changed the context within which a congressional debate on whether to give

Bush approval to use military force would be made. For example, it steered the debate away from issues such as the cost of such a deployment since that was a fait accompli. It also put American credibility on the line, as former Secretary of Defense James Schlesinger testified in considering our "vital interest" in liberating Kuwait: "I do not think that it was a vital interest on the 2nd of August when it [the occupation] took place. But the investment of American prestige, the investment of the prestige of the President of the United States, now makes it vital for Iraq to withdraw from Kuwait."[12] Thus, a material action (doubling the number of troops) served the strategy of persuasion (making the approval of military action appear necessary to maintain U.S. prestige), promoting Bush's long-term strategy of winning approval to make war against Iraq.

The NAACP and the LDF used nondiscursive intervention to shape future persuasion when they encouraged financial contributions from black communities to directly support black litigants who lost their livelihoods when the white establishment took revenge on them for challenging the status quo.[13] Such tangible support allowed litigants to stay the course and have their constitutional challenges heard.

The Litigation Campaign as a Form of Prospective Argument

Litigation campaigns, which have proliferated since the success of the NAACP's efforts to overturn *Plessy*,[14] are a form of prospective argument. They seek to persuade courts to change the law over the long run, assuming that litigation in a single case will not accomplish all their purposes. Although they seek to win individual decisions, they are most concerned with how winning those decisions contributes to achieving their overall ends. Because they are long-term efforts, they typically rely upon an organization to lead them. Those organizations seek to maintain their credibility over the long run (avoiding rhetorical constraints) and to lay the groundwork for successful argument on behalf of their causes in the future.

The ideal litigation campaign would shape every facet of a future rhetorical situation, whereby a final successful litigation effort could fulfill the overall purposes of the litigation campaign. Theoretically, that means that the speaker, audience, message, and occasion would all carry the imprint of those conducting the campaign. Developing these elements requires both symbolic and nonsymbolic prospective means and ends which are adapted to the particular needs of legal discourse.

Developing a "speaker" in a litigation effort involves two distinct efforts. The first is the development of litigants with standing to bring suits that challenge the law. Symbolic means (such as persuasive pitches) may be used to encourage prospective litigants to come forward (as symbolic means lead to nonsymbolic ends—literally getting a living, breathing client to stand and challenge a law). Nonsymbolic means (such as monetary support for poor litigants whose lives are disrupted) may be required to sustain them for the long run. And, of course, these living, breathing nonsymbolic creatures are valuable to litigation efforts for their symbolic value as well, representing, as they do, other similarly situated people.[15]

The second effort regarding a "speaker" has to do with the lawyers who literally speak for the litigants and the organizations they represent. Nonprofit organizations leading litigation campaigns often rely on the commitment of lawyers to the goals of the litigation effort, rather than big salaries, to attract their legal talent. Fostering a cadre of lawyers ready to respond to opportunities to advance the cause is partly a symbolic effort, partly a nonsymbolic effort. Lawyers must be persuaded to join the cause, but there must be a cadre of trained lawyers (preferably, specially trained) from which to draw. In the NAACP case, the development of a civil rights law course at Howard University was invaluable.[16]

Long-term litigation efforts may attempt to shape the audiences of their arguments, notably the judges who decide their cases. This is achieved in two ways: first, by shopping for courts thought to be most conducive to long-term success. For constitutional issues such as educational segregation, decisions must be made whether to bring suits in federal or state court, in one state or jurisdiction or another. Of course, choices such as the state within which to bring a suit depends upon which clients are available and willing to have suits brought in their names, though long-term strategies may "shop" for jurisdictions by fostering the development of clients in particular places or, alternatively, simply waiting until a suitable client appears.

A second way the audience is adapted to the rhetorical purposes of long-term litigation efforts is by influencing judicial appointments and elections.[17] Obviously, such efforts are made easier if the organization spearheading the litigation effort has a great deal of political clout. Organizations like the NAACP, which relied on legal strategies to force change *because it lacked the clout to make changes through political means*, exercised limited influence over such appointments.

Prospective strategies with respect to the message involve developing arguments and evidence in support of litigation. For a long-term campaign, this involves much more than merely collecting available evidence and coming up with new lines of argument; there is the opportunity to actively develop the evidence to be used later and to refine or extend earlier arguments. As David Droge explains in his chapter in this volume, the LDF worked closely with social scientists to develop studies supportive of the claim that segregated education was harmful to black schoolchildren.[18]

Of course, the strongest evidence one can bring to bear in a legal argument is a precedent. Here, cases decided beforehand provide the groundwork for supporting cases that follow the "trajectory" of those cases. Instead of asking for large changes in the law in a single case, long-term litigation campaigns can eat away at existing law, incrementally extending law in a new direction and offering the weight of precedent for continuing such extensions.[19] As this chapter demonstrates, the development of precedents in several graduate school cases was invaluable for setting the stage for *Brown.*

The occasion for a rhetorical effort encompasses concerns such as the place or setting and time or timing of litigation. Place and setting have been covered somewhat in the previous discussion of audiences, whereby the "Supreme Court of Maryland" or the "First Circuit Court of the United States" may be chosen as a place to make a rhetorical stand and address a particular audience. Setting may address more specific concerns as well, such as whether a litigating party wishes to avail itself of a particular state-sanctioned legal procedure.

Timing is one of the most important strategic choices in a litigation campaign. This is the concern with *kairos* (effective rhetorical timing) identified by classical rhetorical theorists. In the case of legal argument, several issues of timing are critical: Arguing a constitutional issue before it is "ripe" can lead to failure.[20] Arguing for too big a change in law, rather than eating away at existing law first, can do more harm than good.[21] Changes in the political climate, in ideas about jurisprudence, and in the standing of the litigating organization, among other things, make some arguments more salient, palatable, or compelling than at other times.[22]

These lawyers would be supported or hindered by the reputation of the organizations that sponsored them. It is important that organizations sponsoring long-term litigation campaigns develop a reputation that puts them in good stead before the judges who hear them. Incoherent litigation efforts that appear to argue opportunistically rather than consistently (from a legal, political, or ideological perspective) may hurt the reputations of the organizations that underwrite them.[23]

In shaping this ultimate rhetorical situation, whereby a litigation effort's purposes might be met (e.g., overturning *Plessy* or overturning *Roe*), a great deal of secondary prospective work must be performed. Organizations supporting long-term litigation efforts require resources such as money, volunteers, and staff. To get such resources, groups or communities must be motivated to support the cause. Membership drives, conferences, marches, newsletters, and other means typically have been employed to aid such efforts. Such needs take a litigation campaign far beyond simply arguing in court.

Fortunately for the opponents of racial segregation, the NAACP and LDF stepped forward to take on the complicated organizational tasks required for a successful long-term litigation effort. The next section reviews the situation faced by the NAACP at the beginning of the litigation effort. Following that, I provide an overall review of their prospective strategy before examining more closely their particular strategy of attacking segregation at the graduate school level as a prelude to attacking elementary and secondary school segregation in *Brown*.

Plessy v. Ferguson and Its Aftermath

In a political agreement culminating in the controversial election of Rutherford B. Hayes in 1876, federal troops were withdrawn from the Reconstruction South, initiating the return of "home rule" to the former Confederate states. After a brief period of continued protection of minority rights by Northern politicians and of political alliances between Southern blacks and key Southern Democrats, the era of Jim Crow began. The reasons for this change are complicated, but the result was the widespread use of legal and extra-legal means to achieve the political, social, and economic subjugation of African Americans throughout the South. Central to this subjugation were efforts to segregate blacks and whites in public places.[24]

With a few early exceptions, the United States Supreme Court's decisions did not prevent this regression, but exacerbated it.[25] In 1873, the Court limited the reach of the Fourteenth Amendment's protections in the *Slaughterhouse Cases*.[26] Ten years later, it struck down the Civil Rights Act of 1875, which sought to prohibit racial discrimination in inns, public conveyances, and places of public amusement.[27] And in 1896, in *Plessy v. Ferguson*, it upheld a Louisiana statute requiring

> that all railway companies carrying passengers in their coaches in this State, shall provide equal but separate accommodations for the white, and colored races, by providing two or more passenger coaches for each passenger train, or by dividing the passenger coaches by a partition so as to secure separate accommodations.[28]

Although this "separate but equal" provision was considered in *Plessy* as part of the Louisiana statute, it soon became a constitutional standard against which state laws requiring racial segregation would be tested.[29]

In reaching its decision, the *Plessy* majority dismissed arguments by the plaintiff and a dissenting Justice Harlan that Louisiana was attempting to use racial segregation as a means of subjugating blacks in violation of the Equal Protection Clause of the Fourteenth Amendment, responding:

> We consider the underlying fallacy of the plaintiff's argument to consist in the assumption that the enforced separation of the two races stamps the colored race with a badge of inferiority. If this be so, it is not by reason of anything found in the act, but solely because the colored race chooses to put that construction upon it.[30]

The Court distinguished between political and social equality, insisting that "[i]f one race be inferior to the other socially, the Constitution of the United States cannot put them upon the same plane."[31]

Plessy defended the state's decision to segregate the races in the exercise of its police power by urging that courts had long recognized state authority to segregate, notably in "the establishment of separate schools for white and colored children, which has been held to be a valid exercise of the legislative power even by courts of States where the political rights of the colored race have been longest and most earnestly enforced."[32] Thus, through a decision over railroad legislation the Supreme Court endorsed the state practice of segregating educational facilities by race.

Plessy's legacy was far-reaching and devastating. United States Circuit Court Judge Nathaniel R. Jones calls it a "tragedy,"

> for it stripped black Americans of the protection that the Constitution and laws had set out to afford them. The divestment of rights was done under a ruse that provided a bogus equality in segregation, suggesting that ex-slaves would somehow become ennobled in their second-class, segregated status. Using the law in such a fashion, in reality, unleashed forces of ignorance, evil, and hate against a group of people long repressed by a system of slavery. It denied to them the tools essential for advancement. In the wake of this situation came waves of violence—physical, economic, and political—waves that washed persistently over virtually all of the nation's institutions, exuding heavy mist containing suffocating gases of racism.[33]

Fortunately, it also helped inspire a new champion for black civil rights: In 1909, the NAACP was formed to fight the system of racial subordination, and *Plessy's* doctrine of "separate but equal" was a natural target.[34]

The NAACP's Prospective Strategy

In the broad efforts of the NAACP and the LDF to attack school segregation can be discerned a prospective strategy, though one that was constantly adjusted in light of resources, the changing legal and political terrain, and the inclinations of the various men who headed the political and legal efforts by these organizations.[35] In other words, there was no singular plan that was consistently followed between the 1909 founding of the NAACP and the final victory in *Brown v. Board of Education* forty-five years later. Perhaps this is why Tushnet contends that

> It seems likely that the [NAACP] staff had in mind little more than the general approach of attacking segregation wherever they could: any positive outcome was seen as a victory, whether or not strategic analysis suggested that a particu-

> lar result would have a domino effect or make any other contribution to the accomplishment of the long-term goal.[36]

But Tushnet's notion of "strategy" is too limited here. When viewed not simply as a *legal* strategy (that is, a legal means to win decisions that create precedents supportive of a final Supreme Court victory), but as a *rhetorical* strategy (that is, a means to create the *conditions* for effective persuasion in a series of cases leading to an ultimate precedent-reversing Supreme Court case), we must judge the efforts of the NAACP differently.

As a rhetorical strategy, the desegregation effort had to be broad, complex, and adapted to the long-term challenge of overturning *Plessy*. Yet, in its first effort to outline a long-term strategy, the NAACP was narrowly legalistic in its approach. Using money from a grant by the Garland Fund, the organization commissioned a study by New York attorney Nathan Margold to identify a route for attacking disenfranchisement, segregation in housing, segregation on public carriers, and segregation in education.[37] With respect to the latter, Margold rejected the funding agency's recommendation that seven lawsuits be filed, one in each of seven Deep South states, "to force *equal* if separate accommodations for Negroes and whites."[38] Unfortunately, he reported, finding a remedy would be difficult since no state laws *mandated* a discriminatory division of school funds, even though the *results* of such divisions showed clear discrimination along racial lines.[39] Lawsuits would have to be brought against each official making a discriminatory division of funds (with two or three levels of division in each state), and they would have to address the previous year only, requiring repeated annual lawsuits to convince state officials to end their discriminatory practices.[40] Margold determined that the fund managers' approach would be unproductive and inefficient, warning:

> It would be a great mistake to fritter away our limited funds on sporadic attempts to force the making of equal divisions of school funds in the few instances where such attempts might be expected to succeed. At the most, we could do no more than to eliminate a very minor part of the discrimination during the year our suits are commenced. We should not be establishing any new principles, nor bringing any sort of pressure to bear which can reasonably be expected to retain the slightest force beyond that exerted by the specific judgment or order that we might obtain. And we should be leaving wholly untouched the very essence of the existing evils.[41]

As an alternative, Margold recommended an approach that would build on one of the few promising civil rights precedents available: *Yick Wo v. Hopkins*.[42] *Yick Wo* involved Chinese launderers in San Francisco who were denied permits to operate in the city. Although no law explicitly discriminated against them—as was the case with most laws regarding the funding of black and white schools—a unanimous Supreme Court in 1886 found that the awarding of operating permits was "administered by public authority with an evil eye and an unequal hand, so as practically to make unjust and illegal discriminations between persons in similar circumstances," thereby violating the equal protection clause of the Fourteenth Amendment.[43]

Margold proposed applying this precedent to the unequal distribution of educational funding in states with segregated education, urging "that segregation coupled with discrimination resulting from administrative action permitted but not required by state statute, is just as such a denial of equal protection of the law as is segregation coupled with discrimination required by express statutory enactment."[44] Margold's approach did not contemplate attacking educational segregation itself, which appeared to him to be constitutionally permissible.[45] But, it was strategic in showing how establishing a particular precedent in constitutional law might give the NAACP a club to wield in an attack on the unequal distribution of funds to segregated schools. Margold did not give directions about where to instigate such suits, how long it would take, who the ideal litigants would be, which courts would be most receptive to them (though he did note courts that might resist), and so forth. His vision was limited to extensions of existing law, and the establishment and use of a precedent to address the problem of educational inequality.

Margold would not have an opportunity to implement his plan for challenging racial inequity in education, though he did win a short-lived victory in a Texas disenfranchisement case.[46] Indeed, Margold's plan would be followed in spirit only,[47] and would give way to a more sweeping and rhetorically savvy approach developed by many hands over many years, but chiefly directed by a former law school dean, Charles Hamilton Houston, and his most notable student, Thurgood Marshall. That plan would attack educational inequity and segregation at the graduate school level, which, as I will show, was a particularly vulnerable spot to challenge the "separate but equal" doctrine. The NAACP's attack on Jim Crow did not follow a "preordained plan" (as Tushnet might require of "strategic" litigation), but remained "sensitive to pressures of the movement, to the opportunities provided and those foreclosed by shifting local circumstances."[48] Given the countermoves made by the states to resist equalization and desegregation, such rhetorical adaptability was necessary. Nonetheless, the NAACP's approach was systematic and strategic in preparing the stage for success in a series of rhetorical situations that led up to the *Brown* decision, by carefully developing speakers, audiences, messages, and occasions. The following sections summarize some of the most critical elements of this prospective work in reaching a final victory in the landmark desegregation decision.

Developing Speakers

As I noted earlier, the primary "speakers" in litigation campaigns are the litigants whose names appear on the case titles and the lawyers who defend their interests and the long-term interests of the litigation campaign. I begin by considering the NAACP's development of the latter.

Since its beginnings in 1909 until the late 1920s, leadership of the NAACP was dominated by white men, such as its first national president, Moorfield Storey. This pattern extended to its Legal Committee, which was dominated by white lawyers.[49] Under Walter White's leadership, this changed, as a larger conception of the NAACP's legal efforts began to form. The NAACP leaders replaced the white Margold as chief litigator with the black Charles Hamilton Houston, believing that African American lawyers "would be responsive to black concerns, because there would be no need to educate the lawyers on the issues blacks might be sensitive to."[50] Not only would recruiting black lawyers appeal to the clients they would represent and the larger black community from which those clients might be drawn (encouraging lawsuits, memberships, and contributions), it also appealed to the growing cadre of talented black lawyers seeking recognition for their work, attracting new blood to the cause.[51] There also was something in this nondiscursive, yet symbolic change for white audiences: First, as White noted in urging the hiring of Houston, "a colored lawyer with the dignity, ability, and tact of Mr. Houston would encounter far less hostility than a white lawyer."[52] Moreover, intelligent, articulate, and adroit black lawyers would demonstrate to white judges, white juries, and the larger white American public, through rhetorical enactment of these qualities, that their prejudices were unfounded.[53]

Although Houston's appointment as special counsel to the NAACP was made in May 1934, his contributions to the long-term effort to develop the black legal "speakers" who White sought for the cause began before the stock market crash of 1929. In July of that fateful year, Mordecai Johnson, president of Howard University, recruited Houston to take over Howard's "fifth-rate law school" and turn it into a premier institution for educating black lawyers.[54] Not only did Houston's efforts raise the bar at Howard and ensure that its black graduates would be well qualified to practice law (and to enact rhetorically those qualities that challenged racial prejudice), but he also ensured they would be better prepared than any other law school graduates to practice civil rights law. Howard Law School offered the first course in civil rights law in the country, and instilled in its students the idea that law was a tool for social change.[55] Thus, not only did Houston's efforts yield well-qualified *black* lawyers, they also yielded *civil rights* lawyers. This would prove critical in laying the groundwork for developing successful messages—legal arguments challenging inequity and segregation in education. They also would aid the effort to attract the other necessary "speakers"—black litigants.

As I noted, the NAACP decided to launch a series of attacks on educational segregation and inequity at the graduate school level.[56] For such attacks, it needed black litigants who had been denied equal treatment in seeking a graduate school education. The work of identifying litigants to challenge segregation at the graduate school level was much more complicated than ensuring there were lawyers to represent them. The NAACP needed a pool of potential litigants from which it could select the most promising candidates on whose behalf it could file lawsuits. The NAACP staff used a variety of methods to reach potential litigants: They used a newspaper clipping service to identify stories recounting potential civil rights violations, and followed up by writing to the victims named in the reports to offer NAACP help.[57] They encouraged local NAACP chapters to identify and refer potential litigants.[58] They gave speeches, published articles in their newsletter *The Crisis*, and visited communities to educate African Americans on how to bring a lawsuit and to offer the organization's assistance if they did so.[59] Such efforts to get out the word had the secondary advantage of encouraging new memberships and raising the money necessary to carry on such lawsuits.

But the NAACP did not put its resources behind every request that came its way. The staff screened potential litigants to ensure the NAACP's investment in particular cases would support (or at least not harm) its long-term efforts to turn back Jim Crow. William Hastie, a close associate of Houston's, described the ideal graduate school litigant as a person "of outstanding scholarship, personable, and unmistakably a Negro."[60] Specifically, the ideal candidate needed to have a strong academic record, be a resident of the state where the school to which he or she was applying was located, and be committed to riding out the difficulties entailed by the legal challenge. Houston wanted black candidates with a stronger record than "qualified" white candidates.[61] Such "speakers" would give the NAACP a solid basis for claiming that race was the sole factor for rejecting their applications to white graduate schools.

Because of such requirements, the NAACP rejected a weak pharmacy school applicant. Houston passed on a medical student applicant with a low score on the medical aptitude test. The legal staff refused to support nonresident applicants, even though white nonresident applicants were readily accepted, because they presented a weaker case. It also ignored pleas from graduates of unaccredited schools who failed to get into white graduate schools.[62]

The NAACP did not simply strike weak candidates, but carefully selected those who would best support its goals. One case in particular illustrates the care with which the NAACP selected its litigant-speakers. In the 1950 victory in *McLaurin v. Oklahoma State Regents for Higher Education* (discussed below), the NAACP chose from among six applicants to Oklahoma graduate schools, settling on the least threatening applicant.[63] George W. McLaurin was sixty-eight years old when he applied for doctoral study in education at the University of Oklahoma. Not only was McLaurin qualified for admission and committed to the lawsuit, additionally, as Thurgood Marshall noted, "we didn't think he was going to marry or intermarry [a white female Oklahoma student]."[64] Thus did the NAACP adapt to deep-rooted segregationist concerns over miscegenation.

If such pickiness thinned the ranks of potential litigants, so did the difficulties facing those who did meet the NAACP's high standards when they applied to graduate schools, were rejected, and sought relief. As Tushnet notes, "applicants to graduate schools would have their life plans disrupted by delays of litigation and would occasionally have difficulty in finding work during the indefinite interval between suing and attending school."[65] Because "the material incentives for becoming a plaintiff were extremely small," Tushnet adds, "clients had to be in the fight as a matter of principle."[66] Unsurprisingly, some exasperated litigants dropped their lawsuits and went to school elsewhere, or simply disappeared.[67]

Because the NAACP asked a great deal of its litigants, it made the strategic choice to bide its time, waiting for the right client, rather than risk failure and the chance of creating a bad precedent. Indeed, as I will further demonstrate, kairos, or effective rhetorical timing, was a central virtue of the NAACP's long-term strategy. The NAACP sought to create situations in which the right person would be able to say the right thing to the right audience on the right occasion. Very frequently, that required patience, particularly when it came to getting the right audience.

Developing Audiences

The ability of the NAACP to shape its ultimate legal audiences—the judges presiding over its cases—was constrained by the limits of its political power, its foresight, and the venues afforded by the litigants' citizenship and the issues presented. Thus, speaker, occasion, and message were intimately connected to audience.

In the short run, the NAACP could choose its audience, to some extent, through jurisdiction shopping. Audience considerations could feed into decisions about whether to litigate an Alabama case or a Maryland case, or whether to appeal to a federal court or a state court. Choosing states in which to bring actions did offer some advantages. Although the attitudes of white judges and the populations from which they were drawn might be expected to be hostile in segregating states, in border states like Maryland and Missouri, Kluger notes, "[t]hey were relatively less hostile to black aspirations" than in Deep South states like Alabama and South Carolina.[68]

Concerning the choice between federal and state courts, there may have been too little strategic advantage in choosing one or the other. Tushnet insists that "[f]ederal judges and, at least, state appellate judges were similar sorts of people, drawn from the same segments of the white bar and white society. Thus, there could be no systematic advantage, but only random variation, in choosing one forum over the other."[69] In most cases, initial graduate school appeals had to be made in state courts anyway since they were the most appropriate place to file a mandamus—the typical approach used to compel school officials to admit an applicant.[70]

In the long run, the NAACP could attempt to influence the appointment of judges they would face, particularly those on the U.S. Supreme Court. This strategy required political power, which they largely lacked, and a kind of foresight which had proven elusive.[71] The highest profile example of such efforts during this early period involved the nomination of Judge John J. Parker to the U.S. Supreme Court by President Hoover in 1930.[72] Parker, who was from North Carolina, had run for governor in 1920. During that campaign, Parker announced his public support for a state constitutional amendment to add a "grandfather clause" to North Carolina's voting laws—a potent means for disenfranchising blacks. He also made a statement proclaiming: "The participation of the Negro in politics is a source of evil and danger to both races and is not desired by the wise men in either race or by the Republican Party of North Carolina."[73] In response to Parker's nomination, Walter White addressed the Senate Judiciary Committee, lobbied senators, and urged Northern blacks to do the same. The NAACP's efforts, when combined with those of labor, which had its own concerns about Parker, led to a 39 to 41 defeat of the nominee.[74] Unfortunately, Parker proved on the Fourth Circuit bench to be a more consistent ally of the NAACP than his replacement, Owen Roberts.[75]

The most effective strategy used by the NAACP in shaping the judicial audiences it would face was a passive one—simply biding its time. When the NAACP began formulating its long-term approach to challenging educational segregation in the early to mid-1930s, the audience sitting on the U.S. Supreme Court was unlikely to be responsive to its concerns. Only the appointments of more progressive justices by Franklin Roosevelt and Truman would turn the tide in favor of the civil rights claims for which the NAACP sought support. The changes in the Court are nicely framed by the 1935 decision in *Grovey v. Townsend*[76] and the 1944 reversal of *Grovey* in *Smith v. Allwright*,[77] with a successful challenge to educational segregation marking the transition between them in 1938.

Grovey involved the third attempt by the Texas legislature to ensure that the Democratic Party could hold an all-white primary. Twice before, the Court had struck down Texas's attempt to exclude blacks from the primaries.[78] The third time, Texas avoided the charge that it was engaging in state action in barring blacks from voting by removing laws concerning the primary and leaving it to the state Democratic convention to exclude blacks. In a unanimous opinion authored by Justice Roberts, the Court found that this approach to black disenfranchisement was constitutional because the Democratic Party was a private association that could lawfully engage in the "private action" of racial discrimination. The eight other members of the unanimous majority were Chief Justice Hughes and Associate Justices Van Devanter, McReynolds, Brandeis, Sutherland, Butler, Stone, Cardozo, and Roberts.

Nine years later, when the issue was again raised, the composition of the Court was completely different. Only Stone and Roberts remained from the *Grovey* Court. The other seven were new, more liberal-minded appointees of Franklin Roosevelt's administration, including Associate Justices Black, Reed, Frankfurter, Douglas, Murphy, Jackson, and Rutledge. FDR's fight against the conservative bloc that threatened to scuttle his New Deal was won by five retirements, two deaths, and two conversions.[79] The open-mindedness of these new jurists with respect to federal intervention in economic matters was accompanied by an open-mindedness about federal intervention in matters involving civil rights.[80]

Stone, now Chief Justice, reversed his earlier position and voted with the seven new members to overrule *Grovey*. Writing for the majority in *Smith v. Allwright*,[81] Justice Reed urged that the primary system was an integral part of the state's election system, making the exclusion of blacks a forbidden form of state action. He relied on the Fifteenth Amendment's protection of black voting rights to find the Texas primary unconstitutional. Only Justice Roberts, who had written the majority opinion in *Grovey*, dissented, worrying about the Court's reputation in reversing itself so quickly.

Between *Grovey*'s 1935 9 to 0 decision and *Smith*'s 1944 8 to 1 reversal, the NAACP was able to find a judicial audience receptive enough to civil rights appeals to hand it a 6 to 2 victory in challenging educational segregation in 1938. Three vacancies and two FDR replacements helped give the NAACP its first educational segregation victory in the graduate school admissions case of *Missouri ex rel. Gaines v. Canada*.[82]

Two years after *Smith*, the last of the Hoover appointees would be gone, and the Court would be run completely by a moderate-to-liberal group of Roosevelt and Truman appointees.[83] Although not all appointees could be assumed to be champions of black civil rights, they were considerably more promising than the *Grovey* Court.[84] And it would be President Eisenhower, ironically and to his chagrin, who would appoint a Republican governor who would meld together these New Deal appointees to render a unanimous decision overturning *Plessy* on educational segregation.[85]

Analyzing one's audience is basic to any rhetorical strategy. Yet, Margold's narrowly legalistic strategy simply identified constitutional arguments that could be derived from existing precedents, without considering whether the particular Supreme Court he might face in the 1930s would likely be receptive to those arguments. The NAACP was much more sensitive to these audience constraints.[86] They could foresee that President Roosevelt would have an opportunity to change the Court, and that he would appoint more progressive judges than those on the high Court in the early 1930s.[87] But whether they consciously chose to let time and a succession of Democratic administrations change the Court, or simply went slowly for lack of money, time, or good litigants, the rhetorical consequence was a continual improvement in their audience's receptivity to black civil rights claims.[88] And, as that audience became more receptive, claims for black civil rights in education could become bolder.

Developing Messages

The NAACP's development of messages involved the gathering or creation of evidence and arguments supportive of its litigation efforts. On the most basic level, this involved the collection of facts, statistics, scholarly studies, and examples describing, illustrating, and substantiating educational inequalities and the effects of educational segregation. The NAACP kept track of stories on incidents of potential civil rights violations and larger national trends, often publishing them in *The Crisis*.[89] They also relied on the work of scholars, such as Gunnar Myrdal, to summarize and publicize information concerning the plight of African Americans under Jim Crow. They developed relationships with legal scholars, educators, and social scientists who would conduct studies and serve as expert witnesses at trial, providing a factual basis for claims of unequal treatment and the harms of segregation.[90]

Another important data collection function of their prospective strategy was keeping track of legal developments in civil rights law. Even in the earliest days of the NAACP's existence, Arthur Spingarn, chair of the Legal Committee, started monitoring pending litigation and legislative initiatives that might need challenging.[91] And, in addition to keeping tabs on NAACP cases, he and his successors had to monitor civil rights cases undertaken by non-NAACP attorneys.[92] These tasks were related both to setting the stage for future actions and to avoiding constraints on future actions. Poor precedents set by those working outside of NAACP supervision could hamper its long-term efforts; therefore, the NAACP often insinuated itself into ongoing litigation efforts to avoid such problems.[93]

An early example of this effort at controlling others' cases came in 1914 in *McCabe v. Atchison, Topeka & Santa Fe Railway Company.*[94] Oklahoma required segregated railroad passenger cars, as Louisiana had, but allowed railroads to leave off hauling sleeping and dining cars for blacks if retaining such cars was economically unfeasible because of insufficient black demand. Spingarn learned that a group of black lawyers planned to challenge the Oklahoma law, but they ignored his request that they delay filing suit until the NAACP could look at the case. When lower courts rejected the challenge, the attorneys approached the NAACP for help. The Legal Committee took on the case and approached NAACP President Moorfield Storey about writing the brief and arguing the case. Storey balked because no one had yet been denied accommodations under the statute. Without Storey, the NAACP pulled out of the case. The original counsel on the case proceeded without the NAACP and won a notable victory.[95] The U.S. Supreme Court found the state's position "without merit" because "it makes the constitutional right depend upon the number of persons who may be discriminated against, whereas the essence of the constitutional right is that it is a personal one" since "it is the individual who is entitled to equal protection of the laws."[96]

McCabe would prove critical to the graduate school cases because, typically, states claimed that they had not provided law and other graduate schools for blacks because none had applied. If a single applicant or a handful of applicants could be denied equal protection for financial reasons, such as the enormous expense of providing a black law school for a small number of students, then the NAACP's efforts would be stymied. Obviously, a lack of oversight by the NAACP did not always hurt the long-term development of its message. It would be twenty-two years before the NAACP would capitalize on *McCabe* and win its first graduate school case.

Charles Houston may have drawn a lesson from *McCabe*: It was easier to attack the inequality of segregation when the state refused to provide *any* services at all to African Americans. In such instances, arguments of what counted as "equal" treatment by the state gave way to more fundamental questions about the state's ultimate duty to its citizens of color. Since opportunities for graduate education were rare to nonexistent in the segregating states, Houston could challenge such educational discrimination on similar grounds to those in the *McCabe* case.

If this approach made discriminatory practices stark, it also was adapted to several audiences. The NAACP's primary audience—judges—typically had experience in graduate schools (specifically, in law schools) and might have a better understanding of the characteristics of a good graduate education program. It was adapted to the litigant-speakers whom the NAACP needed in order to bring its challenges since graduate school applicants were generally better educated, more understanding of the long-term litigation goals, and less vulnerable to counter-pressures, such as threats against elementary school children who would be on the front lines in later cases. There was even something in this approach for the hostile white audience in the segregating states: There was less of a threat of miscegenation, since most graduate students were male, and those few females in graduate school were more mature and, presumably, less "susceptible" to the advances of black male graduate students than high school or undergraduate students. There was a stick for the segregating states as well: Successful challenges would force them to choose between providing expensive new graduate programs for blacks or taking the less expensive approach of desegregating graduate education. Finally, inroads into creating graduate education opportunities for African Americans would contribute to the development of W. E. B. Dubois's "talented tenth," a cadre of well-educated blacks to advance the race, including, of course, lawyers to carry on the legal battles ahead.

Theoretically, precedents requiring greater state efforts for equalizing educational opportunities for blacks at the graduate school level could be applied to undergraduate, high school, and elementary school education as well. This was the sort of stage that this message-constructing strategy could set for success in the future. And, although Houston and his successor Thurgood Marshall could not foresee exactly how these cases would unfold, they had a basic approach that was promising.

After a few false starts in the 1930s where litigants, local attorneys, and local communities were inadequate or uncooperative, Houston and Marshall won the NAACP's first graduate school victory.[97] The litigant, Donald Murray, was a member of a prominent Baltimore family and had graduated from Amherst College. He applied to the University of Maryland's Law School in his home city and, although he met the academic standards for admission, he was turned down solely because of his race. His appeal to the state university board of regents failed, and the NAACP sought a mandamus from a lower Maryland court to compel them to admit Murray. The lower court found the state's actions in violation of the Equal Protection Clause of the Fourteenth Amendment and ordered his admission to the all-white law school. When the state appealed this order, the state's highest court backed the lower court.[98]

The state had tried to avoid admitting Murray by meeting its equal protection obligations in another way: It proposed tuition scholarships for African Americans to attend out-of-state graduate schools. The appeals court found this offer inadequate for four reasons: First, the money had yet to be appropriated. Second, even if it had, the $10,000 Maryland set aside might not have been adequate to provide scholarships to all the qualified black applicants who sought them.[99] Third, although the $200 per student allowance might be enough to pay for the tuition, for instance, at Howard Law School, it would not be sufficient—nor was it intended—to defray the costs for Murray to commute or move to another city and pay living expenses away from his home. Finally, since out-of-state law schools did not specialize in Maryland law, or offer experience with the state courts, he would be handicapped in his legal education when he returned to practice in Baltimore.[100] Clearly, this court of law school graduates understood well the disadvantages Maryland's alternative brought.

A careful choice of litigants and an advantageous set of circumstances made this victory possible. Had Murray been marginally qualified, had Maryland guaranteed scholarships and offered money for living expenses, had Murray not intended to practice law in Maryland, had the appeal involved a type of graduate education about which the justices were less educated, or had the case been brought in a Deep South state where the judges were less hospitable to reasoned claims, the results might have been different. Furthermore, had *McCabe v. Atchison* not preceded this case, the judges might not have so handily rejected the state's pleas that the numbers of blacks affected by an adverse decision would be small. Quoting *McCabe*, the Maryland court noted: "the essence of the constitutional right is a personal one," and concluded that "the number [of applicants] seems excluded as a factor in the problem."[101]

Thus, *Pearson v. Murray* built on a precedent set before (with little help from the NAACP), and set its own useful, highly citable precedent. The most important feature of this precedent was its potential to cut off the state route to avoiding equalization and desegregation by offering out-of-state scholarships. It also demonstrated that a reasonable judicial approach to resolving inequality in graduate education was requiring the admission of black students to white universities.

Pearson provided critical ammunition to the NAACP two years later when the U.S. Supreme Court heard a graduate school case from Missouri. That case also involved a law school application by a qualified student, Lloyd L. Gaines.[102] Missouri did not make the same mistakes as Maryland had in its case. It had a first-rate university for African Americans—Lincoln. And it stood ready to build a law school there for Gaines or any other applicant. To avoid opening such a school unnecessarily, Missouri waited for a qualified applicant before it began the process of building such a school. In the interim, the state offered a well-supported scholarship program (not merely a *chance* at a scholarship), which covered additional out-of-state tuition costs. Their only shortcoming was a failure to offer living expenses while their black citizens lived away from home.[103]

The case provided a logical next step in building a case against segregated graduate education: It could nationalize the state precedent in *Pearson*. On the other hand, if they lost and Missouri built a new law school at Lincoln, the NAACP could come back and question the equality of a newly minted school against the more established University of Missouri Law School.[104]

Tushnet criticizes Chief Justice Hughes's majority opinion in this case for a lack of "logical rigor," primarily because the Court appeared to assume that a legal education in Kansas or Illinois would be "equal" to that of a Missouri education, even though Missouri state law would not be offered and living expenses might be higher.[105] But, Hughes's discussion of equality simply reiterated claims by the state, finding them "beside the point":

> The basic consideration is not as to what sort of opportunities other States provide, or whether they are as good as those in Missouri, but as to what opportunities *Missouri itself* furnishes to white students and denies to negroes solely upon the ground of color. The admissibility of laws separating the races in the enjoyment of privileges afforded by the State rests wholly upon the quality of the privileges which the laws give to the separated groups *within the State*. . . .
>
> . . . Manifestly, the obligation of the state to give the protection of equal laws can be performed only where its laws operate, that is, *within the state*. It is there that the equality of legal right must be maintained.[106]

This was a novel finding to be sure. No precedents were cited to support a requirement that a state meet its constitutional obligations within its borders. However, the point that a state's constitutional obligations could not hinge upon another state's actions, such as offering programs a state itself will not offer, has a logical appeal.

The decision drew upon *Pearson*, citing it three times.[107] But *Gaines* did more than nationalize *Pearson*'s holding that the state's failure to provide an equal educational experience through its problematic out-of-state tuition plan amounted to a violation of the Fourteenth Amendment. It rejected outright any sort of out-of-state method for providing equal educational opportunities to blacks.[108] Thus, it cut off state routes for meeting equal protection obligations inexpensively. After *Gaines*, states would need to build graduate schools for blacks equal to those it offered for whites. And because of *McCabe*, the states could not deny equal rights on economic grounds. If only one African American wanted to study law, journalism, education, or any other subject provided for whites, the state would have to set up a separate and equal school, or else desegregate. To remain segregated, states had to put their money where their racist mouths were.

At this point, the NAACP had a foreseeable direction for case development. First, it needed to establish that a state's obligation to meet the needs of its black graduate school applicants could not be delayed interminably. *Gaines* did not resolve that issue. Obviously, if a state intended to maintain segregation, yet had no equal graduate school for blacks, it would have to build one. How long they would be allowed to take in providing an equal if segregated education without running afoul of the Fourteenth Amendment was not clear. Ideally, the NAACP would find that no period of delay was allowable. Second, assuming that segregated graduate institutions would be thrown up overnight, the NAACP would have good grounds for challenging their equality with long-established, well-respected programs for white graduate education. The NAACP would want to show that inequality still existed—a possibility that could undermine the second state strategy for avoiding graduate school integration.[109] With this challenge, the focus would move from clarifying state obligations to assessing state compliance with those obligations. Finally, this focus on equality could allow more rigorous scrutiny and conceptual development of the notion of "equal education." Here, the NAACP would want to take the broadest possible view of equality, not simply looking at physical facilities or curricular opportunities. Victories in these three areas would set the stage for a final, well-supported message challenging the validity of segregated education itself.

The message suffered when the NAACP made its first attempt to extend *Gaines*. Returning to Missouri, the NAACP's newly separate LDF, headed by Thurgood Marshall, brought an appeal from Lucile Bluford, managing editor of the *Kansas City Call*, a black newspaper. She wished to attend graduate school in journalism at the University of Missouri. Instead of asking for a graduate school to be provided at Lincoln University, she applied directly to the University of Missouri and was refused admission solely because of her race. She sued in both federal district court and in state court. At the federal level, she was defeated by a court that relied upon the state's interpretation of *Gaines*, which found that "the Gaines case did not deprive the State of a reasonable opportunity to provide facilities, demanded for the first time, before it abrogated its established policy of segregation."[110] The federal court's opinion revealed a weakness in the *Gaines* victory: The *Gaines* court had warned Missouri that "we cannot regard the discrimination as excused by what is called its temporary character."[111] The federal court in *Bluford* read that declaration "in the light of the fact that the State Supreme Court had not construed the obligation of Lincoln University to furnish the facilities as mandatory . . . , 'but on the contrary took the view . . . that the curators were entitled under the state law to refuse such an application and in its stead to provide for petitioner's tuition in an adjacent State.'"[112]

The key distinction from *Gaines*, the *Bluford* Court insisted, was that the legislature had reformed its equal educational requirements since *Gaines*, mandating that Lincoln University authorities provide graduate programs for black students when such were requested. Previously, this requirement had been at the officials' discretion.[113] Citing the constitutional right of states to segregate their education of whites and blacks, the District Court sought to balance that right against the claims of the black applicants, noting that the state could not simply maintain at Lincoln University versions of every program of study at the University of Missouri when no black students had requested them. Instead, the university needed to be given a reasonable time to develop programs *after* black graduate students requested them.[114] They directed Bluford to apply for a program to be developed for her at Lincoln before claiming her constitutional rights had been violated.[115] It appears that the LDF tried to move too quickly.

The state case, which reached the Supreme Court of Missouri, cited and approved of the District Court's findings, noting particularly the statutory change since *Gaines* that took away Lincoln University's discretion in deciding whether to offer graduate programs to qualified black applicants. It also weighed the state's goal of maintaining segregation against the Fourteenth Amendment, noting: "It is the duty of this court to maintain Missouri's policy of segregation so long as it does not come in conflict with the Federal Constitution."[116] And, from their perspective, asking black applicants to wait a "reasonable time" while a program was developed was not a constitutional violation. The Court did not define how much time was "reasonable." In 1942, citing dropping enrollments because of the war, Missouri ended the equalization challenge by closing its white journalism school.[117]

One year after the Missouri decision, a Tennessee court relied on *Bluford* in insisting that "reasonable advance notice" be given to university officials to allow them to develop graduate programs requested by African Americans.[118] Like Missouri, the Tennessee legislature made certain to include language that made the provision of equal graduate programs for black students mandatory, though it acted only after the commencement of this lawsuit.[119] The idea that such a delay of equal protection was constitutionally permissible was endorsed by a federal court in 1947. Relying on the *Gaines* ruling in finding that South Carolina was required to provide equal educational opportunities within the state, the Eastern District Court of South Carolina found that the state's plan to open a law school equal to the white University of South Carolina Law School two months later was reasonable.[120]

It would be another year before the LDF would get a case before the U.S. Supreme Court to challenge this period of "reasonable" delay. Lois Ada Sipuel was denied admission to Oklahoma's only law school solely because of her race. The state supreme court emphatically noted that the criminal code of Oklahoma prohibited integrated education, highlighting a point that other state cases merely referenced in passing: Compelling school officials to admit her (through a mandamus) would entail a violation of criminal laws.[121] The court assured Sipuel that she had advantages not afforded to white Oklahomans, for she could either take out-of-state tuition (not available to whites) or request that a law school be built for her. The court insisted "that while petitioner may exercise her preference between these two educational plans, she must indicate that preference by demand or in some manner that may be depended upon," and concluded "that such requirement for notice or demand on her part is no undue burden upon her."[122]

In 1948 the U.S. Supreme Court heard Sipuel's appeal and issued a *per curiam* (unsigned, "by the court") opinion reversing Oklahoma's highest court four days later.[123] Marshall used the opportunity to challenge *Plessy* directly, arguing in his brief that

> Segregation in public education helps to preserve a caste system which is based upon race and color. It is designed and intended to perpetuate the slave tradition. . . . Equality, even if the term be limited to a comparison of physical facilities, is and can never be achieved . . . the terms "separate" and "equal" can not be used conjunctively in a situation of this kind.[124]

The Court was not ready to go as far as Marshall requested. But, it did set the stage for future challenges by correcting lower courts' misreading of *Gaines* on the issue of state delays in providing equal educational opportunities for black graduate students like Sipuel: "The State must provide [a legal education] for [Sipuel] in conformity with the equal protection clause of the Fourteenth Amendment and provide it as soon as it does for applicants of any other group."[125]

Five days after the ruling, rather than order the admission of Sipuel to the white law school, the state court ordered that an "equal" law school be opened for Sipuel in twelve days (when the white law school's term would start). Marshall read this as defiance of the U.S. Supreme Court's order (since it was manifestly impossible), but the Court rejected the plea, deferring to Oklahoma's courts as bearing primary responsibility for ensuring compliance with the mandates they were obliged to hand down.[126] Justice Murphy thought the appeal had merit. And Justice Rutledge wrote a dissent that would foreshadow the next NAACP challenges, insisting:

> Obviously no separate law school could be established elsewhere overnight capable of giving petitioner a legal education equal to that afforded by the state's long-established and well-known state university law school. Nor could the necessary time be taken to create such facilities, while continuing to deny them to petitioner, without incurring the delay which would continue the discrimination our mandate required to end at once.[127]

Kluger focuses on the Supreme Court's failure to immediately deem Oklahoma's remedy patently inadequate and calls the decision in *Sipuel* "a setback."[128] But as part of a message-building strategy, it was valuable. If states had to provide immediate access to equal educational opportunities for black graduate students, then they could not simply sit around and wait for blacks to apply to graduate school, then drag their feet in complying. Indeed, in theory, they would not even have time to bring an unequal black graduate school up to speed with an established white graduate school by appealing to a "reasonable time" standard. And there would be plenty of opportunities to scrutinize the equality of newly minted black graduate schools and to further examine what "equality" requires in educational opportunities.

Sipuel would be critical to ensuring the development of an advantageous factual record for another graduate school case that followed on its heels. George W. McLaurin's application for doctoral study in education at the University of Oklahoma created a difficult problem for that state: how to immediately create a segregated doctoral program in education equal to that offered to white students. Marshall brought the case to a special three-judge federal district court, which relied on *Sipuel* in holding "the plaintiff is entitled to secure a post-graduate course of study in education leading to a doctor's degree in this State in a State institution, and that he is entitled to secure it as soon as it is afforded to any other applicant."[129]

Obviously, at this point, the LDF had developed a more receptive audience of jurists, a growing pool of litigants represented by increasingly experienced lawyers, and an evolving set of favorable precedents that were painting the segregating states into a corner. Although the strategic moves of the innovative and recalcitrant segregating states could not be predicted with certainty, it was becoming ever clearer that they would latch onto almost any tactic to avoid desegregating. And the more outrageous their efforts, the more they revealed the ugliness of their cause. Thus, the LDF could push the states to help build the rhetorical stage that would be used to overturn segregationist policies. And so it came that the Oklahoma's reaction to this sixty-eight-year-old doctoral school applicant would do for desegregation what Birmingham Police Chief "Bull"

Connor's fire hoses and attack dogs did for the political side of the black civil rights movement.

Oklahoma reluctantly admitted McLaurin while its Governor worked to develop a separate doctoral program in education for him.[130] But, shortsighted by their own racism, the state legislature amended the laws that made it a crime for blacks to attend white schools, but provided that such instruction "shall be given at such colleges or institutions of higher education upon a segregated basis."[131] By "segregated basis" the statute meant "classroom instruction given in separate classrooms, or at separate times."[132]

To comply with this statute, university officials put McLaurin alone in an anteroom adjoining the classroom where the white students sat, provided him a designated table in the library as the sole place he could sit, and made him eat in the cafeteria at a different time from the other students.[133] Marshall appealed to the District court, where McLaurin told the judges that it was "quite strange and humiliating to be placed out in that position."[134] The District court relied on *Plessy* in urging that it had no power "to obliterate social or racial distinctions which the State has traditionally recognized as a basis for classification for purposes of education and other public ministrations."[135] When Marshall appealed the case directly to the U.S. Supreme Court, Oklahoma adjusted McLaurin's situation, moving him into the white classroom, but surrounding his designated desk with a railing marked "Reserved for Colored," then later assigning him to a seat in a row designated for black students.[136]

Meanwhile, another case was working its way toward the Supreme Court where the two would be heard back-to-back. Heman Sweatt applied to the University of Texas School of Law at a time when white lawyers in Texas outnumbered blacks 7701 to 23.[137] Sweatt's application came a year before Sipuel's, but took longer to work its way up the judicial ladder. Without the *Sipuel* precedent requiring immediate relief, a trial judge gave the state six months to start a law school or else admit Sweatt. The state rented a few rooms in Houston, attached its new black law school to Prairie View University (which was more like a vocational school), and hired two African American lawyers to teach there. The trial court was satisfied that the school was equal to the University of Texas School of Law, and the NAACP appealed.[138]

Before the appeal reached the Texas Court of Civil Appeals, the state legislature appropriated $3 million for the new Texas State University for Negroes, with $100,000 earmarked for a law school. The black law school was moved to Austin, four University of Texas law professors were hired to teach there also, and students had access to the State Law Library. Because of these changes, the appellate court remanded the case for retrial on the new facts. The trial court found equality between the two schools, and the state appellate court affirmed.[139]

The U.S. Supreme Court heard arguments in the *McLaurin* case on April 3, 1950, finishing the next day when it heard arguments in *Sweatt*. Both decisions were handed down on June 5, 1950. Both cases raised the question of what equality in educational opportunity meant.

Marshall used these cases to launch a frontal assault on *Plessy*. He called on Yale Law School professor Thomas I. Emerson, who put together an amicus brief for *Sweatt* for a "Committee of Law Teachers against Segregation in Legal Education." The Committee's 187 members urged that "[a]s soon as laws make a right or responsibility dependent solely on race, they violate the 14th Amendment," and suggested that racial distinctions are always unreasonable, and therefore unconstitutional, classifications.[140] Marshall developed a trial record with testimony from a social scientist on the harms of educational segregation and a legal expert on the need for "a well-rounded, representative group of students in the classroom to participate in the . . . discussion which centers around previous decisions of the courts."[141]

This last testimony supported Marshall's successful effort to focus the Court on intangibles in its consideration of the equality question. Chief Justice Vinson, who authored the majority opinions in both cases, focused the *Sweatt* opinion on a comparison of the white and black Texas law schools, concluding:

> In terms of the number of faculty, variety of courses and opportunity for specialization, size of the student body, scope of the library, availability of law review and similar activities, the University of Texas Law School is superior. What is more important, the University of Texas Law School possesses to a far greater degree those qualities which are incapable of objective measurement but which make for greatness in a law school. Such qualities, to name but a few, include reputation of the faculty, experience of the administration, position and influence of the alumni, standing in the community, traditions and prestige. It is difficult to believe that one who had a free choice between these law schools would consider the question close.[142]

Additionally, Vinson made one the earliest arguments in favor of racial diversity as a virtue, noting that the black law school "excludes from its student body members of the racial groups which number 85% of the population of the State and include most of the lawyers, witnesses, jurors, judges and other officials with whom petitioner will inevitably be dealing when he becomes a member of the Texas Bar."[143] With this inequality established, Vinson turned to the constitutional questions.

Citing *Sipuel*, Vinson noted that the state was required to give Sweatt equal educational opportunities as soon as it did for whites. Citing *Gaines*, Vinson noted that it was the individual who was entitled to equal protection of the laws within the state's borders. Consequently, he noted, Sweatt "may claim his full constitutional right: legal education equivalent to that offered by the State to students of other races." Since "[s]uch education is not available to him in a separate law school as offered by the state," the only alternative was to admit him to the University of Texas Law School.[144] Vinson did not find it necessary to disturb *Plessy* since the case could be decided on the narrower issue of "equality."[145]

McLaurin also turned on intangible considerations of equality. The "internal segregation" of McLaurin from his fellow students "[set] McLaurin apart from the other students." That made him "handicapped in his pursuit of effective graduate instruction" because it "impair[ed] and inhibit[ed] his ability to study, to engage in discussions and exchange views with other students, and, in general, to learn his profession." As a teacher, McLaurin's ability to teach and lead his students could be affected. In response to state claims that social norms would set McLaurin apart from whites in any case, the Court responded that "[t]here is a vast difference—a Constitutional difference—between restrictions imposed by the state which prohibit the intellectual commingling of students, and the refusal of individuals to commingle where the state presents no such bar." Citing the just-decided *Sweatt* decision, the Court concluded that Oklahoma's actions deprived McLaurin "of his personal and present right to equal protection of the laws."[146]

Although the Court was not persuaded to revisit *Plessy*, its conclusions provided strong precedents for a final assault on "separate but equal." A year after the *Sweatt* and *McLaurin* decisions, one legal commentator noted: "The current issue to be judicially determined is whether a state can meet the equality in fact test and still insist upon segregation in the upper levels of education."[147] Indeed, if intangible factors were worthy of judicial notice, and Vinson's racial diversity argument was relevant, then assaults on undergraduate institutions, high schools, and elementary schools were possible.[148] The final step was clear: an argument that "separate" was inherently "unequal." That would lead to the demise of *Plessy*.

The message developed through this series of graduate school cases gave the LDF potent arguments for challenging segregation in *Brown*. But, obviously, this was a work of many hands, not only those of the NAACP, LDF, and its allies, but also of the increasingly progressive jurists, and, ironically, the states where segregationist tactics established a record illuminating the ultimate (if unstated) rationale for educational segregation—the subjugation of a minority by the majority.

If the LDF could not strategically plan how these graduate cases would unfold, they nonetheless could have faith that whittling away at segregating states' excuses would eventually reveal the racism at the core of their position. Changes in the contexts would cast a bright light on this racism.

Developing the Occasion

The chief consideration of the NAACP and the LDF in developing the occasion was timing. Kairos, or effective timing, would require the litigation strategists to find the right litigants, represented by the right lawyers, making the right arguments, before the right court. Underlying the question of "rightness" in timing is the larger legal, social, and cultural context which formed the backdrop for developing successful challenges to Jim Crow. I already have noted the challenges of developing a cadre of lawyers and a pool of litigants, waiting on a conservative court to be infused with new blood, and developing cases to progressively eat away at the underpinnings of *Plessy*. In addition to these specific developments, there were larger social, economic, political, and cultural changes that would help ripen the occasion for stronger and stronger challenges.

The Depression put financial pressures on segregating states that made it difficult to maintain separate graduate institutions. Since economic problems continued in the South longer than elsewhere, the 1938 *Gaines* decision's rejection of the cheaper out-of-state scholarship solution was particularly challenging for those seeking to maintain graduate school segregation. More important, FDR's New Deal led to a showdown with the Supreme Court that eventually encouraged an early changing of the guard and inspired the appointment of justices more open-minded about the use of federal power.

World War II brought to the public eye the horrors of racism, and challenged Jim Crow thinking. In the Cold War that followed, the embarrassment of Southern racism threatened the moral and political leadership of the United States in the world community. Such concerns inspired President Truman to create a Committee on Civil Rights, to desegregate the armed forces, and to put the Attorney General's office on the side of the LDF in some of its appeals.[149]

African Americans began emerging from centuries of obscurity to secure a place for themselves in American popular culture, challenging skepticism about their race's potential that had persisted since the slave days. White Americans began listening to Duke Ellington, Ella Fitzgerald, and Louis Armstrong; cheering for Jesse Owens, Joe Louis, and Jackie Robinson; and reading about the achievements of author and civil rights leader W. E. B. Dubois, labor leader A. Phillip Randolph, and Nobel Peace Prize winner Ralph Bunche. Despite the best efforts of the segregationists, they could not stop the emergence and recognition of African American successes and the inevitable—if slow and subtle—changes they wrought on the American consciousness.

In the narrower field of law, the work of the NAACP and LDF in challenging restrictive covenants, all-white juries, all-white primary elections, and so forth, influenced legal thinking about racial matters. The U.S. Supreme Court, in particular, was the site of dozens of final appeals in these and educational segregation cases, revealing the recalcitrant racism of the segregating states and, thereby, shaping the justices' experiences with racists and those who fought them. Additionally, developments in all of these areas had to give the justices and the larger legal community a sense of progress, of trajectory, and of a "directive principle" at work moving the law to support greater and greater freedom for African Americans.[150]

Philosophical changes in the way the legal community thought about law also had an impact, as I have suggested. In the 1920s and 1930s, law professors at Yale and Columbia began the new thinking about law that has been called the legal realism movement. Karl Llewellyn, one of the leading figures in the movement, summarized some of their beliefs in a 1931 *Harvard Law Review* article about these "new fermenters"; the first three are worth noting for our purposes:

> (1) The conception of law in flux, of moving law, and of judicial creation of law.
> (2) The conception of law as a means to social ends and not as an end in itself; so that any part needs constantly to be examined for its purpose, and for its effect, and to be judged in the light of both and of their relation to each other.
> (3) The conception of society in flux, and in flux typically faster than the law, so that the probability is always given that any portion of law needs reexamination to determine how far it fits the society it purports to serve.[151]

This view of the law was custom-made for challenging traditional ways of thinking about educational segregation, for pushing judges to think about the social consequences of their decisions, and for making judges less reluctant to overturn precedents like *Plessy*. The widespread influence of the legal realists during the period of the graduate school cases made the legal community more open to using the law to create social justice.

The trick for the NAACP and LDF legal strategists was to demonstrate kairos in recognizing when all the elements were right for a particular challenge: when good litigants and able lawyers were available; when the judicial audience was receptive; when the message had been sufficiently developed; and when the occasion, with all of its cultural complexities, was ripe. That was no small task. However, their success demonstrates their mastery of kairos. Four years after *Sweatt* and *McLaurin*, the rhetorical structure they had built (and waited for) was in place for a final reversal of "separate but equal."

Overturning *Plessy*

In *Brown v. Board of Education*, Chief Justice Warren determined that "[s]eparate educational facilities are inherently unequal," and that state racial segregation of public school students was a violation of the Equal Protection clause of the Fourteenth Amendment.[152] He reached that conclusion by relying on the graduate school cases. He cited *Gaines*, *Sipuel*, *Sweatt*, and *McLaurin* on inequalities in graduate school education and admitted that "[i]n none of these cases was it necessary to reexamine the [separate but equal] doctrine to grant relief to the Negro plaintiff" (491-492). However, he did note that *Sweatt* "expressly reserved decision on whether *Plessy v. Ferguson* should be held inapplicable to public education" (492). That caveat meant that this next-to-last in the line of cases (or at least this next-to-the-end of the line case) could not be taken as endorsing the doctrine of "separate but equal."

More important, the Court relied on *Sweatt* and *McLaurin*'s consideration of intangible factors in finding inequality. Warren noted that the central question in *Brown* was: "Does segregation of children in public schools solely on the basis of race, even though the physical facilities and other 'tangible' factors may be equal, deprive the children of the minority group of equal educational opportunities?" Here, the Chief Justice could turn to the two 1950 graduate school cases to find legal support for the proposition that intangible factors were sufficient to find inequality. He began with *Sweatt*, noting that the Court's ruling that the black law school was not equal to the white law school because of "those qualities which are incapable of objective measurement but which make for greatness in a law school" (quoting *Sweatt* at 493). In *McLaurin*, he continued, the Court "again resorted to intangible considerations: '. . . [McLaurin's] ability to study, to engage in discussions and exchange views with other students, and, in general, to learn his profession'" (quoting *McLaurin* at 493-494).

Having established the legal precedent for considering intangibles in assessing the equality of segregated schools, Warren drew upon psychological studies (some of it supported by the LDF[153]) showing that black children in segregated schools suffer "a feeling of inferiority as to their status in the community that may affect their hearts and minds in a way unlikely ever to be undone" (494). The *Plessy* ruling, he averred, suffered from a lack of such psychological knowledge, and must fall in light of new information (494-495).

Conclusion

Obviously, the graduate school cases prepared the ground for this argument. The justices hearing the *Brown* case were sufficiently liberal to support a unanimous verdict. The litigant-speakers were supportive, and the lawyers were well seasoned in arguing civil rights law before the U.S. Supreme Court. The occasion turned out to be ripe. The NAACP had to work diligently for nearly a half-century, but their efforts, particularly in the graduate school cases, set the rhetorical stage for success. And, rhetorically, we should judge their prospective efforts as strategic and a model of kairos.

As for the theory of prospective argument, I hope I have demonstrated that this theory provides a useful perspective from which to assess long-term litigation campaigns, particularly by reducing their complexity to basic and significant rhetorical considerations involving the development of speakers, audiences, messages, and occasions over time. Litigation campaigns, social movements, political campaigns, and other long-term rhetorical efforts often have been under-theorized, and their study reduced to interesting but rather unsystematic *his-*

tories of events, persons, ideas, and organizations.[154] A theory of prospective argument promises to structure such studies and ground them in strategic rhetorical concerns. That is not to say that serious interpretive issues, such as questions of intent, would not challenge analysts who apply this perspective. Nevertheless, it holds out the possibility of accounting for those rhetorical actions that look beyond the individual battles of limited rhetorical situations to longer-term rhetorical wars.

Notes

The author thanks the University of Alabama in Huntsville's Humanities Center for a grant that supported initial research on this essay. That grant afforded the valuable talents of Laura Orand as my research assistant. The author thanks John R. Lyne and Lelon Oliver for their valuable comments on drafts of this essay.

1. 163 US 537. I will be using the terms "black" and "African American" interchangeably in this essay. I do so out of respect for the African diaspora (which is not represented in the term "African American") and for stylistic reasons.

2. *Brown v. Board of Education of Topeka et al.*, 347 U.S. 483 (1954).

3. J. Clarke Rountree, III, "Prospective Argument: Constraining and Licensing Future Arguments," in *Argument and Critical Practices*, ed. Joseph W. Wenzel, Proceedings of the Fifth SCA/AFA Conference on Argumentation (Annandale, VA: Speech Communication Association, 1987), 207-213 (hereinafter, "Prospective Argument I").

4. I developed the concept of prospective argument in a series of essays beginning in 1987. Rountree, "Prospective Argument I"; "Reversing *Roe v. Wade* Through the Courts: The Rhetorical Strategy of *Americans United for Life*," paper presented to the National Convention of the Speech Communication Association, San Francisco, November 1989 (hereinafter "Reversing *Roe*"); "Prospective Argument, Part II: Laying the Ground for Future Argument," *Argument in Controversy*, ed. Donn W. Parson, Proceedings of the Seventh SCA/AFA Conference on Argumentation (Annandale, VA: Speech Communication Association, 1991), 58-63 (hereinafter "Prospective Argument II"); "'I Shot an Arrow in the Air . . .': The Rhetorical Trajectories of Knowledge Production" (with Robert Strikwerda), paper presented to the National Convention of the Speech Communication Association, San Antonio, November 1995); "Building up to War: Bush's 'Administrative Rhetoric' in the Persian Gulf Conflict," *The Speech Communication Annual* 10 (Spring 1996), 5-19.

5. Communication scholars began studying social movements after Leland M. Griffin's seminal essay, "The Rhetoric of Historical Movements," *Quarterly*

Journal of Speech 38 (1952): 184-188. Those studies peaked in the 1960s and 1970s when contemporary protests became the object of social movement criticism. In 1980, *Central States Speech Journal* featured a special issue on social criticism (vol. 31, 225-315). Rather than serving as an impetus for continuing social movement studies, it appeared as more of an epilogue for an area of study whose time had passed. For example, David Zarefsky, writing in that issue, argued "that extant theory of 'the rhetoric of social movements' fails to establish satisfactorily that there is such a thing." Despite this, he acknowledged that some social movement studies are useful for their historical insights. David Zarefsky, "A Skeptical View of Movement Studies," *Central States Speech Journal* 31 (Winter 1980): 252. The present essay does not attempt to revive movement studies, but it does seek to provide a more robust theoretical framework for analyzing long-term rhetorical processes, which include those found in social movements.

6. Rountree, "Prospective Argument I."

7. Rountree, "Prospective Argument II."

8. This most recent sponsored research was touted by Atkins' public relations group in "Atkins Research Update," *PR Newswire* 1.2 (7 November 2002) (downloaded from Infotrac).

9. Rountree, "Reversing *Roe*."

10. Rountree, "Building up to War."

11. Qtg. President Bush in Rountree, "Building Up to War," 6.

12. Qtd. in Rountree, "Building up to War," 15.

13. Kluger opens his book with a vivid account of the harassment one black litigant suffered from the white establishment.

14. These typically are carried out by advocacy groups. For example, I mentioned the campaign by Americans United for Life to overturn *Roe v. Wade*. The American Civil Liberties Union has been involved in a number of litigation campaigns, most recently challenging the Communications Decency Act and the Bush Administration's Patriot Act, as the watchdogs of civil liberties. Corporate groups often challenge environmental laws on an ongoing basis.

15. For the abortion campaign, they might represent "all parents who want to be notified before their minor daughters have abortions"; for the segregation cases, they might represent "all African American graduate students denied admission to a state graduate program because of their race."

16. Mark V. Tushnet, *NAACP's Legal Strategy, against Segregated Education* (Chapel Hill: University of North Carolina Press, 1987), 30.

17. For example, Americans United for Life used its political connections and its public advocacy to try and keep liberal judges off the bench and foster the appointment or election of conservative judges who were likely to overturn *Roe v. Wade*. For issues like abortion that require the U.S. Supreme Court to reverse an earlier decision, this effort could be very long indeed.

18. In its efforts to overturn *Roe v. Wade*, Americans United for Life sought to foster two types of research that would give it ammunition for argument: first, historical research to challenge the claim that abortion was freely available at the time the Fourteenth Amendment was written. Under an "original intent" argument, saying that abortion was not freely available at the time the Fourteenth Amendment was written might be used to suggest that the authors of that amendment never envisioned including such a right within the scope of that constitutional provision. Second, they encouraged medical research that showed that childbirth was becoming safer than abortion. That would be helpful because one of the arguments made by Blackmun in his majority opinion in *Roe* was that having a first-trimester abortion was safer than carrying a child to term; therefore, the pregnant woman ought to have the freedom to choose the safer route during the first trimester, without state interference. Showing that childbirth is becoming as safe or safer than abortion undermines the foundation of that position.

19. In trying to change abortion law, the strategy of Americans United for Life was to win rulings that increasingly limit abortion as an option by denying federal funding for abortion, upholding state laws that increase the regulation of abortion and, thereby, the costs of abortion; requiring the notification of parents by minors seeking abortions; requiring doctors to discuss fetal development and alternatives to abortion prior to giving abortions; and so forth. Their success in severely limiting the number of abortions performed will give them an easier time convincing the U.S. Supreme Court to take away this increasingly unobtainable right. Rountree, "Reversing *Roe*."

Thoroughgoing long-term litigation campaigns may even try to shape legislation that is the object of lawsuits, setting up the legal issues to challenge particular aspects of law they wish to overthrow. For example, antiabortion advocates would benefit from a Supreme Court finding that there are some state purposes for outlawing particular kinds of abortions, giving them a "foot in the door" for adding other state purposes to do so. For example, a state statute that forbade abortion solely for the purpose of sex selection (i.e., ensuring that one gets a boy or a girl) probably would survive judicial scrutiny since there are good social reasons for a state to want to ensure that its population remains roughly half male and half female. For a discussion of the causes and consequences of sex-selection abortion, see Gail Weiss, "Sex-Selective Abortion: A Relational Approach," *Hypatia* 12 (Winter 1995): 202-217.

The NAACP lacked the political clout to exert a great deal of influence over legislation in the period under study. And since they were trying to expand an existing right in the face of legislative restrictions (instead of limit an existing right in the face of constitutional restrictions, as Americans United for Life sought to do), encouraging legislation was not an obvious option.

20. Ripeness is encompassed by Article III's requirement that a "case or controversy" exist as a prerequisite to adjudication of constitutional issues. Courts typically avoid anything appearing as "advisory opinions." They also avoid intervening in a case before a clearly defined record has been created. They typically do not want to intervene in the normal course of conflict resolution (through the lower courts or other means) before those processes have been given a chance to work. See, for example, Gerald Gunther, *Constitutional Law*, 11th ed. (Mineola, NY: Foundation Press, 1985), 1580-1589.

21. Processes by which law is incrementally changed are discussed in a variety of places. Two classic sources are Benjamin N. Cardozo, *The Nature of the Judicial Process* (New Haven, Connecticut: Yale University Press, 1921) and Edward H. Levi, *An Introduction to Legal Reasoning* (Chicago: University of Chicago Press, 1949). My analysis of the incremental development of corporate criminal law provides a particular case study ("Judicial Invention in Cases Contributing to the Development of Corporate Criminal Liability: A Multi-Dimensional Dramatistic Analysis," Ph.D. diss., University of Iowa, 1988), as does Henry J. Steiner's study of tort accident law in *Moral Argument and Social Vision in the Courts* (Madison: University of Wisconsin Press, 1987).

22. For example, Americans United for Life fought efforts to support euthanasia to ensure that the sanctity of life in all forms was respected as it sought to argue on behalf of unborn fetuses. Rountree, "Reversing *Roe*."

23. On the relationship between reputation and inconsistency, see Rountree, "Prospective Argument I."

24. See Michael J. Klarman, "The Plessy Era," *Supreme Court Review* 1998 (1998), 303-414 (downloaded from Lexis-Nexis); Richard Kluger, *Simple Justice: The History of* Brown v. Board of Education *and Black America's Struggle for Equality* (New York: Alfred A. Knopf, 1976).

25. *Strauder v. West Virginia*, 100 U.S. 303 (1880) was such an exception. It found a violation of equal protection in a West Virginia statute explicitly limiting jury service to "all white male persons." *Yick Wo v. Hopkins*, 118 U.S. 356 (1886), discussed below, is another early exception.

26. *Slaughterhouse Cases*, 83 U.S. (16 Wall.) 36 (1873).

27. *Civil Rights Cases*, 109 U.S. 3 (1883).

28. Louisiana Acts, 1890, No. 111, p. 152, Quoted in *Plessy v. Ferguson*, 163 U.S. 537, 540 (1896).

29. By 1914 in another railroad segregation case, the Supreme Court could take it as a matter of settled law that "if facilities [such as sleeping cars] are provided [for anyone], substantial equality of treatment of persons traveling under like conditions cannot be refused" (*McCabe v. Atchison, Topeka & Santa Fe Railway Company*, 235 U.S. 151, 161). Even outside of specific statutory language such as found in the Louisiana railroad segregation statute, the use of the "separate but equal" standard was not unprecedented, perhaps reflecting a wide-

spread interpretation of "equal" in "equal protection" as requiring equality if segregation were to be enforced. In the U.S. District Court case of *United States v. Buntin* (10 F. 730 [S.D. Ohio, 1882]), fourteen years before *Plessy*, a federal judge found that an Ohio law requiring separate but equal educational facilities was constitutional. And he enforced the "equality" requirement in his charge to the jury, insisting that if

> you shall find that said colored school was so remote from the [black student's] residence that he could not attend it without going an unreasonable and oppressive distance; that he was thus placed at a material disadvantage with his white neighbors; that the school did not offer substantially the same facilities and educational advantages that were offered in the school established for the white children, and from which he had been excluded,—then and in that event he was entitled to admission in said last-named school, and his exclusion therefrom was a denial and a deprivation of his constitutional right. (*United States v. Buntin*, 10 F. 730, 735)

30. 163 U.S. at 551.

31. 163 U.S. at 552.

32. 163 U.S. at 544.

33. "The Harlan Dissent: The Road Not Taken—An American Tragedy," *Georgia State University Law Review* 12 (1996): 952.

34. Tushnet, *NAACP's Legal Strategy*, xi.

35. Tushnet argues this point and illustrates it throughout his book (*NAACP's Legal Strategy*).

36. Tushnet, *NAACP's Legal Strategy*, 52.

37. Nathan Margold, "Preliminary Report to the Joint Committee Supervising the Expenditure of the 1930 Appropriation by the American Fund for Public Service to the N.A.A.C.P.," Records of the NAACP, Group I (1909-1939), Series C., Box 200, Library of Congress.

38. Margold, 3.

39. Ibid., 30. At that time, South Carolina, for example, spent ten times more on each white student than each black student. Ibid., 3.

40. Ibid., 39-41.

41. Ibid., 93.

42. *Yick Wo v. Hopkins*, 118 U.S. 356 (1886).

43. 118 U.S. at 373-374.

44. Margold, 93.

45. Ibid., 15-25.

46. Margold won the U.S. Supreme Court case of *Nixon v. Condon* in 1932 (286 U.S. 73). Texas had tried to keep African Americans from voting by granting party executive committees the power to determine primary voting qualifications, and the Democratic executive committee promptly limited the primary to

whites. Justice Cardozo, writing his first opinion for a majority of the high court, found that the Democratic executive committee's actions amounted to unconstitutional state action since the committee's authority was vested in a state statute. Margold's victory was soon undone when Texas repealed all its primary election statutes and allowed a state Democratic convention (not merely the executive committee) to limit voting in its primaries to whites. The Court subsequently upheld this mode of discrimination as "private," and not a form of "state action" (*Grovey v. Townsend*, 295 U.S. 45 [1935]). That ruling was eventually reversed in *Smith v. Allwright*, 321 U.S. 649 (1944).

47. Kluger claims that Charles H. Houston, who directed the LDF's legal efforts from 1934 to 1938, put Margold's report in the drawer—"the top drawer"—but that "Margold's ideas were always on his mind" as he developed his own approach (136).

48. Tushnet, *NAACP's Legal Strategy*, 43.

49. Ibid., 29, 32; Kluger, 98. Two white attorneys, Moorfield Storey and Louis Marshall, argued all the NAACP's five Supreme Court cases between 1913 and 1927. Ibid., 16.

50. Tushnet, *NAACP's Legal Strategy*, 29-30.

51. Ibid.

52. Quoted in ibid., 29.

53. Tushnet makes a similar claim at ibid., 30.

54. Justice Louis Brandeis used the "fifth-rate" description in comments to Johnson. Kluger, 125.

55. Ibid., 126-131; Tushnet, *NAACP's Legal Strategy*, 29-31.

56. It was this series of graduate school attacks that lent the greatest legal support to the NAACP's arguments in *Brown v. Board of Education*. However, the NAACP also expended a great deal of effort in primary and secondary school equalization suits, in black teacher salary equalization suits, in suits challenging segregation on public transportation and in public spaces, and in defending the rights of black criminal defendants. The greatest successes in whittling away at *Plessy*'s "separate but equal" standard as applied to education, however, was in this series of graduate school cases, as the NAACP legal staff quickly recognized and sought to capitalize upon.

57. Susan D. Carle, "Race, Class, and Legal Ethics in the Early NAACP (1910-1920)," *Law and History Review* (Spring 2002), www.historycooperative.org/journals/lhr/20.1/carle.html (downloaded 20 June 2003).

58. Tushnet, *NAACP's Legal Strategy*, 154.

59. Ibid., 148. The effectiveness of this approach is reflected in the tour of Virginia undertaken by NAACP special counsel Spottswood W. Robinson, III and Virginia NAACP Executive Secretary W. Lester Banks, which spurred equalization suits in seventy-five school districts. Kluger, 472-473.

60. Quoted in Tushnet, *NAACP's Legal Strategy*, 37.

61. Ibid., 37.

62. Ibid., 37, 54, 82; Mark V. Tushnet, *Making Civil Rights Law: Thurgood Marshall and the Supreme Court, 1936-1961* (New York: Oxford University Press, 1994), 123.

63. *McLaurin v. Oklahoma State Regents for Higher Education*, 339 U.S. 637 (1950).

64. Quoted in Kluger, 266.

65. Tushnet, *NAACP's Legal Strategy*, 148. Such challenges led one local NAACP leader to provide financial support for a litigant, leading to the filing of ethics charges against the group. Tushnet, *Making Civil Rights Law*, 273.

66. Tushnet, *NAACP's Legal Strategy*, 148-149.

67. Kluger, 202; Tushnet, *NAACP's Legal Strategy*, 87. Lloyd L. Gaines, of the landmark graduate school case of *Missouri ex rel. Gaines v. Canada* (305 U.S. 337 [1938]; discussed below), disappeared after his suit was won but before Missouri could spend the $200,000 it pledged to create a black law school to educate him. Tushnet, *NAACP's Legal Strategy*, 73-74. Tushnet also recounts several troublesome cases where clients were lost at ibid., 86-87.

68. Kluger, 197. Alabama's hostility was amply illustrated in its handling of the cases involving the state government's attempt to shut down the Alabama NAACP. See "'A Mortal Blow from Which They Shall Never Recover': The Attack on the NAACP, 1955-61" in Tushnet, *Making Civil Rights Law*, 283-300.

69. Tushnet, *NAACP's Legal Strategy*, 51. The record bears out Tushnet's assumption. The NAACP won victories in both federal district court (e.g., *McLaurin v. Oklahoma*) and state court (e.g., *Pearson v. Murray*, 169 Md. 478 [1936]), and lost many cases in both.

70. As Tushnet notes,

> as a distinct remedy, mandamus was essentially available only in state court because the remedy was designed to require state officials to do their duty. Because those duties had to be defined primarily by state law, federal courts would be reluctant to use mandamus to direct officials to take actions that state law did not authorize them to take. (*NAACP's Legal Strategy*, 50)

71. Consider President Eisenhower's surprise and disappointment over Earl Warren, for example.

72. Later fights involved opposing the nominations of Clement Haynsworth, Harrold Carswell, Robert Bork, and Clarence Thomas. "National Association for the Advancement of Colored People," *Oxford Companion to the Supreme Court of the United States*, ed. Kermit L. Hall (New York: Oxford University Press, 1992), 571.

73. Quoted in Kluger, 142. Kluger discusses the Parker nomination and defeat at 141-144.

74. Ibid., 144. See also, Kenneth W. Goings, *The Defeat of John J. Parker* (Bloomington: Indiana University Press, 1990).

75. Parker ruled in the NAACP's favor in appeals involving teacher salary equalization and a disenfranchisement case (Kluger, 216, 300). He required equalization, but refused, as a mere Circuit judge, to overrule *Plessy* when asked and desegregate public schools in South Carolina (Kluger 344-366). Justice Roberts, on the other hand, wrote the Court's unanimous opinion upholding the constitutionality of the all-white Texas primary in *Grovey v. Townsend* (295 U.S. 45 [1935]) and dissented nine years later when it was overturned in *Smith v. Allwright* (321 U.S. 694 [1944]). He did, however, join the majority in the first graduate school victory in *Missouri ex rel. Gaines v. Canada.*

76. *Grovey v. Townsend*, 295 U.S. 45 (1935).

77. *Smith v. Allwright*, 321 U.S. 649 (1944).

78. In the first case, *Nixon v. Herndon* (273 U.S. 536 [1927]), a Texas law banning blacks from participating in the Democratic Party primary was ruled a violation of the Equal Protection Clause of the Fourteenth Amendment. Texas then gave the executive committee of the Democratic Party the power to determine primary voter qualifications, leading that committee to ban blacks. In *Nixon v. Condon* (286 U.S. 73 [1932]), the Margold victory noted earlier, the Court held that this delegation of authority to the executive committee still constituted prohibited "state action" under the Fourteenth Amendment.

79. Hughes, Van Devanter, McReynolds, Brandeis, and Sutherland all retired. Justice James Byrnes also served for one year, taking Stone's place after Hughes retired and Stone was elevated to Chief Justice, but resigned when Roosevelt tapped him to serve as director of economic stabilization. Byrnes was replaced by Rutledge in 1942. Butler and Cardozo died in office. As I will explain, Stone reversed himself on the white primary issue. Most critical for FDR's economic revitalization efforts were the departures of Van Devanter, McReynolds, Sutherland, and Butler, the "four horsemen" who consistently ruled against his New Deal legislation. Hughes and Roberts, who sometimes joined this conservative bloc, shifted allegiances and began supporting New Deal legislation.

80. The perspective that may tie these two progressive views together—one on government intervention in commerce and one on civil rights—is that of the increasingly influential legal realists, who believed that, ultimately, rules did not constrain decisions and decisions ought to be guided by a consideration of social consequences. Tushnet argues that Legal Realism exerted an influence on the justices' thinking about law during this period. *NAACP Legal Strategy*, 117-118.

81. *Smith v. Allwright*, 321 U.S. 649 (1944).

82. *Missouri ex rel. Gaines v. Canada*, 305 U.S. 337 (1938). Cardozo died in the summer of 1938 and had yet to be replaced by Frankfurter when the decision was handed down. As his about-face in *Allwright* indicated, Stone was open to persuasion on civil rights questions. Chief Justice Hughes, who wrote the majority opinion in *Gaines*, obviously was not an enemy of civil rights (despite his *Grovey* vote). He sided with the majority in *Powell v. Alabama* (287 U.S. 45 [1932]), an appeal from the Scottsboro Boys case, determining that the defendants' due process rights had been violated. Justice Roberts is difficult to classify on racial issues. Although he authored the *Grovey* decision, he also offered a passionate dissent against the Court's ruling in *Korematsu v. United States* (323 U.S. 214 [1944]) for refusing to find unconstitutional the internment of Japanese-Americans during World War II. (See my analysis of this dissent in Clarke Rountree, "Instantiating 'The Law' and Its Dissents in *Korematsu v. United States*: A Dramatistic Analysis of Judicial Discourse," *Quarterly Journal of Speech* 87 [February 2001]: 1-24). Justice Brandeis, best known for his defense of First Amendment rights, also championed the incorporation of the Bill of Rights into the Fourteenth Amendment, as a limit on state power. See *Gilbert v. Minnesota*, 254 U.S. 325 (Brandeis dissenting at 334-343). McReynolds, whose anti-Semitism interfered with his relationships with his judicial brethren, was an unbending dissenter in *Gaines*. See "McReynolds, James Clark" in *Oxford Companion to the Supreme Court*, 542-543. Butler, also dissenting, had a more mixed record on civil rights, supporting prior restraint on speech but opposing wiretaps. See "Butler, Pierce" in *Oxford Companion to the Supreme Court*, 110-111.

83. Justice Roberts was the last Hoover appointee to leave the Court. Truman added four to the Court: Chief Justice Vinson and Associate Justices Burton, Clark, and Minton.

84. Among the encouraging new appointments were Justices Clark and Minton. As Truman's Attorney General, Justice Clark had pushed the President's civil rights agenda. Justice Minton lost reelection to the Senate in 1940 after he denounced the Klan in his home state of Indiana. More troubling was the work of Chief Justice Vinson in the Roosevelt and Truman administrations, where he tended to support state and federal governments over individual rights. Justice Burton, appointed by Truman, was a Republican who appeared to be moderately conservative. Noting Truman's positive work on civil rights issues, Kluger contends of the Truman appointees: "It was not unthinkable that the politically attuned Justices that he had selected felt they owed him their allegiance on racial questions" (250-255, 271). Kluger provides a good overview of the justices at 210-212, 241-246, and 269-271. See also, *The Oxford Companion to the Supreme Court* under particular justices' names.

85. Eisenhower is widely credited with claiming that the appointment of Chief Justice Warren to the Court was his biggest mistake. See, for example,

Bernard Schwartz, "REMARK: Chief Justice Earl Warren: Super Chief in Action," 33 *Tulsa Law Journal* (Winter 1997): 477 (downloaded from Lexis-Nexis). Kluger gives a great deal of credit to Chief Justice Warren for creating consensus among the justices and ensuring a unanimous decision in *Brown.* Kluger, chapter 25.

86. As late as the early 1950s, after having made significant inroads into attacking segregated schools, LDF chief legal strategist Thurgood Marshall was worried about asking the Court to reverse *Plessy*. Kluger, 291-292.

87. Obviously, the progressivism FDR most desperately needed required his judges to think differently about the role of the federal government and its authority in combatting economic and social problems. That might not necessarily translate into a greater concern for individual civil rights. However, any shift of power to the federal government over the states (who were the main culprits in sustaining Jim Crow) could prove useful. Furthermore, such progressive judges were likely to view law more as an instrument for social change than as a straightjacket of unbending rules. FDR's progressives would need to be willing to overlook recently decided precedents that had undermined the New Deal and reverse course. As I noted earlier, the spreading influence of the legal realists in the 1930s and 1940s undoubtedly shaped the thinking of many lawyers and judges, contributing to a progressivism which could not but help FDR's cause and that of the NAACP.

88. Intent is central to prospective strategy to the extent that looking beyond the "given case" toward a long-term future carries the idea that avoiding constraints or building stages conducive to later success are ends sought and met by prospective strategies. It is very easy, through post hoc analysis, to read intention from a successful series of choices. Indeed, Tushnet's well-written historical analysis of NAACP legal strategy from 1925-1950 tries to establish what NAACP legal strategists were thinking and seeking at each point, and that such thinking was not as long-term as Kluger and others have suggested. However, as I attempt to show here, given the broad needs of this campaign, we need to consider the specific rhetorical outcomes of more general strategies, such as developing litigant-speakers, judicial audiences, messages, and occasions. Here, general "garden tending" of this sort, and developments based on hunches rather than fully articulated strategies, served important rhetorical functions. The problem of intent has led my collaborator John Lyne and me to consider "rhetorical consequentialism" as a better term than "prospective argument" for framing discussions of such long-term strategies, focusing less on intent and more on the rhetorical consequences of both intentional and unintentional actions by rhetors and by others around them who contribute to the development of rhetorical situations.

89. Kluger, 98-100, 193.

90. The most notable result of this is in footnote 11 of *Brown v. Board of Education*, 347 U.S. 483, 494 (1954). See Kluger on the relationship between the LDF and the social scientists they recruited to testify for them. David Droge's essay in this volume provides a detailed account of their relationship.

91. Carle. I mentioned previously that an ideal prospective strategy in litigation efforts would try to shape the laws passed to create useful challenges. Obviously, the NAACP did not have the political clout to shape legislation in segregating states. Only much later would their cause gain enough political momentum to pass national legislation, such as the Civil Rights Act of 1964, to challenge segregationist laws and practices.

92. Ibid.

93. See Kluger generally for various accounts of the NAACP's relationships with other lawyers and their lawsuits.

94. 235 U.S. 151.

95. Carle.

96. 235 U.S. at 161-162.

97. Tushnet, NAACP Legal Strategy 52-56.

98. *Pearson v. Murray*, 169 Md. 478 (1936). See also, Tushnet, *NAACP Legal Strategy*, 56.

99. The appeals court noted that 380 applications had been requested and 113 returned. At $200 per scholarship, the $10,000 might prove inadequate. *Pearson v. Murray*, 169 Md. 478, 485-486.

100. 169 Md. at 486.

101. 169 Md. at 487.

102. *Missouri ex rel. Gaines v. Canada*, 308 U.S. 337 (1938).

103. Kluger, 202.

104. Tushnet, *NAACP Legal Strategy*, 71.

105. Ibid., 71-72.

106. 308 U.S. at 349-350.

107. The most important reference to *Pearson* came in discussing the constitutional question, when the Court noted: "It is manifest that this discrimination, if not relieved by the provisions we shall presently discuss, would constitute a denial of equal protection. That was the conclusion of the Court of Appeals of Maryland in circumstances substantially similar in that aspect." *Gaines*, 308 U.S. at 345, citing *Pearson.*

108. *Pearson* left to the side the question of whether better out-of-state provisions might overcome the constitutional inadequacies of Maryland's approach. *Pearson*, 169 Md. at 488.

109. The first was the out-of-state tuition strategy.

110. *Bluford v. Canada*, 32 F. Supp. 707, 710 (1940) (downloaded from Lexis-Nexis).

111. *Gaines*, 308 U.S. at 352.

112. 32 F. Supp. at 710.

113. 32 F. Supp. at 709.

114. 32 F. Supp. at 710-711. The Court also was concerned because Bluford's suit asked for damages from the individual curators who refused to admit her.

115. 32 F. Supp. at, 711.

116. *State ex rel. Bluford v. Canada*, 348 Mo. 298, 309 (1941).

117. Tushnet, NAACP Legal Strategy, 85.

118. *State ex rel. Michael et al. v. Witham et al.*, 179 Tenn. 250, 256 (1942) (downloaded from Lexis-Nexis).

119. The new provision became effective on February 12, 1941, while the cases were pending. *Michael*, 179 Tenn. at 253.

120. *Wrighten v. University of South Carolina*, 72 F. Supp. 948 (E.D.S.C. 1947).

121. *Sipuel v. Board of Regents of Oklahoma et al.*, 199 Okla. 36, 42 (1947) (downloaded from Lexis-Nexis).

122. 199 Okla. at 45.

123. *Sipuel v. University of Oklahoma*, 332 U.S. 631 (1948) (per curiam).

124. Quoted in Kluger, 259.

125. *Sipuel*, 332 U.S. at 633.

126. *Fisher v. Hurst, Chief Justice, et al.*, 333 U.S. 147 (1948) (downloaded from Lexis-Nexis).

127. 333 U.S. at 152.

128. Kluger, 260.

129 *McLaurin v. Oklahoma State Regents for Higher Education et al.*, 87 F. Supp. 526, 528 (W.D. Okla. 1948) (downloaded from Lexis-Nexis).

130. *McLaurin*, 87 F. Supp. at 528.

131. *McLaurin v. Oklahoma State Regents for Higher Education*, 339 U.S. 637, 640 (1950) (downloaded from Lexis-Nexis), quoting 1950 Okla. Stat. Ann. tit. 70, §§ 455, 456, 457.

132. *McLaurin*, 339 U.S. at 640 (1950), quoting 1950 Okla. Stat. Ann. tit. 70, §§ 455.

133. This is recounted in *McLaurin*, 339 U.S. at 640, and also in Kluger, 268.

134. Quoted in Kluger, 268.

135. *McLaurin*, 87 F. Supp. at 530.

136. *McLaurin*, 339 U.S. at 640.

137. Kluger, 260.

138. Ibid., 261.

139. Tushnet gives a good description of the complicated procedural history of this case at *NAACP Legal Strategy*, 126.

140. Quoted in Kluger, 275-276.

141. The experts were University of Chicago Professor and Chair of Anthropology Robert Redfield and University of Pennsylvania Law School Dean Earl Harrison. Ibid., 264.

142. *Sweatt v. Painter*, 339 U.S. 629, 633-634 (1950).

143. *Sweatt*, 339 U.S. at 634.

144. *Sweatt*, 339 U.S. at 635.

145. *Sweatt*, 339 U.S. at 635-636.

146. *McLaurin*, 339 U.S. at 641-642.

147. R. C. Taylor, "The Demise of Race Distinctions in Graduate Education," *Duke Bar Journal* 1 (June 1951), 141.

148. Tushnet notes that "the Court's decisions in *Sweatt* and *McLaurin* were widely regarded as having direct implications for elementary and secondary education" (*NAACP Legal Strategy*, 136).

149. The first was a restrictive covenant case (Ibid., 117). The government filed amicus briefs in both *Sweatt* and *McLaurin* on the LDF's side.

150. Cardozo describes this "directive principle" in *The Nature of the Judicial Process*.

151. Karl N. Llewellyn, "Some Realism about Realism" in *Jurisprudence: Realism in Theory and Practice* (Chicago: University of Chicago Press, 1962), 53, 55 (reprinted from *Harvard Law Review* 44 [1931]: 1222-1264).

152. *Brown v. Board of Education*, 347 U.S. 483, 495 (1954). Further references to this case are in the text.

153. See Kluger for an extensive discussion of the recruitment of social scientists, as well as Droge in this volume.

154. See Zarefsky, for example.

4

From Natural to Cultural Inferiority: The Symbolic Reconstruction of White Supremacy in *Brown v. Board of Education*

David Droge

Vexing and emotionally disturbing, racial injustice has profoundly affected U.S. culture. As historian Ben Keppel has argued, the nation's struggle "either to avoid or to come to terms [with racism] is the single most important theme in American history." At the beginning of the twentieth century, W. E. B. Dubois prophesied: "the problem of the twentieth century is the problem of the color-line." The end of that century was marked by Daryl Michael Scott's claim that this problem has been constructed using "damage imagery in the process of making and justifying social policy." Unable to confront the evil of racism, mainstream U.S. culture has continually viewed African Americans as objects of "amused contempt and pity."[1]

The *Brown v. Board of Education* case (hereinafter *Brown I*), decided half-way through the century of the color line, stands in popular memory as a land-mark in the struggle to end racial injustice.[2] This decision was heralded for a number of years for its reliance on social science evidence. Psychologist Otto Klineberg, in his 1986 Presidential Address to the Society for the Psychological Study of Social Issues (SPSSI), described the Court's use of social science as "the greatest compliment ever paid to psychology by the powers-that-be in our own or any other country."[3] In *Brown I*, the Court cited a finding by a lower court that segregated schools harm black children; Chief Justice Earl Warren, writing for a unanimous Court, claimed that this finding was "amply supported by modern authority."[4] This phrase was accompanied by the "most disputed footnote in American constitutional law,"[5] *Footnote 11*, which cited seven social science publications.

The passing of time has not been kind to the Court's use of social science evidence. Recently, as John Jackson has concluded,

> [t]he idea that the social scientists' testimony in *Brown* was unfounded has become the dominant understanding of the case. Within four decades, what was once conceived as psychology's greatest achievement in social engineering has been proclaimed a miserable failure.[6]

This contemporary criticism by psychologists and historians has been acknowledged by at least one sitting Justice. In a 1995 concurring opinion in *Missouri v. Jenkins*, Clarence Thomas stated that "the studies cited in *Brown I* have received harsh criticism."[7] Denunciation of the scientific evidence has led some legal analysts to dismiss the social science evidence as "wholly irrelevant to the Court's desegregation verdict"[8] and to claim instead that the Court simply recognized that school segregation was a violation of the Fourteenth Amendment.

This chapter focuses on the growing criticism of the Supreme Court's use of social science evidence to justify the ruling that segregated public education is inherently unequal. The critique of the Court's use of social science in *Brown*, I will contend, fails to account adequately for the rhetorical situation faced by the attorneys for the NAACP's Legal Defense and Education Fund (hereinafter LDF), who argued the desegregation cases, and also faced by the Warren Court. Studying the Court's use of social science evidence through the lens of rhetorical history will lead to a deeper understanding of this event as a moment in the struggle for racial justice. In particular, examining the historical context of *Brown I* through "messages that reflect and construct that context" will help illuminate the mixed legacy of this decision in the battle to overcome the pervasive and persistent ideology of white supremacy in the United States.[9]

My main claim is that the rhetorical actors in this decision constructed their appeals during an era in which white supremacy was being challenged for the first time. The rhetorical force of this ideology led these actors to replace the image of African Americans as biologically inferior with one of black cultural pathology. This characterization, which reflected the consensus of progressive social scientists at that time, resulted in a selective use of the social science evidence by the Court in both of the school desegregation decisions. Chief Justice Warren's decisions to invoke the scientific evidence in *Brown I* and ignore that evidence in *Brown II* (the follow-on case which determined a remedy for educational desegregation) set the stage for Southern resistance to desegregation. The Court's reasoning in the *Brown* decisions also unintentionally established a set of unrealistic expectations regarding the outcomes of integration.

This analysis begins with a brief summary of the major criticisms of *Brown I*. The rhetorical dimensions of the Supreme Court are examined next as a framework for the present study. The struggle to overcome the belief in the "natural" inferiority of African Americans, which had justified legal segregation, is reviewed to provide a context for the Court's turn to social science research as justification for rendering segregation illegal. As I will show, this challenge to white supremacy by progressive social scientists led to a troublesome image of African Americans as psychologically "damaged" people.

This background material is used to examine the development of two key texts: a summary of social science evidence appended by the LDF attorneys to their brief in the desegregation cases, and the Warren Court's unanimous opinion in *Brown I.*

"Flimsy" Evidence

Denunciation of the Court's use of psychological evidence has been a recurrent theme in the critical analysis of this important but controversial decision. The critique centers on three claims. The first assertion is that social science evidence used by the Court was unnecessary since it was based on a self-evident truth. Anthony Lewis, writing in the *New York Times* shortly after the decision, remarked: "It took no reference to social scientists to know that state-enforced segregation was a calculated device to exalt one group and debase another." Ernest Cahn, in one of the first articles criticizing the *Brown* decision, maintained in 1955 that "[f]or at least twenty years, hardly any cultivated person has questioned that segregation is cruel to Negro school children. The cruelty is obvious and evident." Lino Graglia, writing in one of the works cited by Justice Thomas in his *Missouri v. Jenkins* opinion, claimed that "[n]o principle is more generally accepted, appealing on its face, or basic to American ideals than that a human being or, at least, an American citizen in America should not be disadvantaged by government because of his race or ancestry."[10]

Even if the social scientific findings were obvious, some commentators thought that citing them helped the Court counter Southern resistance to desegregation and convinced reluctant justices to join the opinion. Historian Daryl Michael Scott, for example, has argued that the *Brown I* opinion was a "masterful work of judicial diplomacy and public relations." Scott maintains that highlighting the "intangible harm" of segregation allowed the more conservative members of the Court to join in a unanimous decision. Because the justices recognized that the desegregation decisions were likely to meet resistance, they sought unanimous opinions in all these decisions in the early 1950s. By focusing on this intangible damage, they could affirm that segregation was illegal without claiming that the 1896 Court ruling in *Plessy v. Ferguson*, which established the "separate but equal" doctrine, was a mistaken reading of the Fourteenth Amendment. Sanjay Mody argues that the social science evidence helped the Court preempt a "crisis of institutional legitimacy" due to anticipated strong resistance from Southern states.[11]

The other two criticisms of the use of social science in *Brown I* call for a more comprehensive examination. The second claim is that the Court wrote new law in the 1954 decision and thus usurped the role of the legislative branch. In June 1954, the *Saturday Evening Post* editorial staff wrote that "decisions which imply the duty of the federal government to prevent inferiority complexes certainly suggest a tendency to move in on the legislative function." Graglia maintained that "so important a social change should not be made by unelected, lifelong appointees."[12] This line of reasoning is consistent with the theory of *judicial restraint* which guided several members of the 1954 Court, particularly the influential Felix Frankfurter. Adherents of judicial restraint argue that if the judiciary makes new law through court decisions, then the will of the majority, as expressed through their elected representatives, is thwarted. They maintain that only in rare cases, when a violation of the Constitution can be demonstrated unequivocally, should the judiciary overturn a law. Since judicial restraint is seen as promoting majority rule in a democratic society by preventing government by a judicial oligarchy, the role of judicial restraint is examined in detail in this chapter.

The third criticism centers on the social science practices and the motivations of the social scientists who testified in the desegregation cases. This line of analysis is based on two claims. First, the social science evidence in the desegregation cases was methodologically flawed. No empirical evidence of the damaging effects of segregation existed at that time. In 1951, a psychologist at NYU's Graduate School of Arts and Sciences studied "the experimental evidence on the effects of school segregation" and consulted "with a number of her colleagues." Elsa Robinson wrote to Robert Carter, one of the LDF attorneys, that "there is as yet no scientifically verified material of an empirical nature which bears directly on the case."[13]

The evidence used by the LDF attorneys, these critics claim, was "bad social science" and "methodologically unsound."[14] In particular, a set of projective tests conducted by Kenneth and Mamie Clark in the late 1930s and replicated in the desegregation cases was strongly denounced. In this "dolls test," black children were shown a series of light- and dark-colored dolls and asked questions about their preferences; they were then asked to identify "the doll that looks like you." In the original study, a substantial proportion of black children identified the dark-skinned doll as the "bad" one and picked the light-skinned doll as "the one that looks like me." The Clarks had argued that these findings indicated that young black children were learning that they were marked by their color with a badge of inferiority, and that some had succumbed to "self-hatred."[15]

Critics of this research claimed that the results of the dolls tests did not single out legal segregation as the cause of this inferiority. Indeed, the original data demonstrated that "a smaller percentage of black children picked the white doll in segregated than in unsegregated schools." Further, Kenneth Clark, the lead social scientist working with the NAACP whose name had appeared first in the list of references in the infamous *Footnote 11*, seems to have found evidence of psychological damage regardless of whether the black child became upset or remained calm when describing the brown doll as "bad."[16]

In addition to the conclusion that the social science evidence was "feeble" and "flimsy," these critics offer a second, and more serious, denunciation. As John W. Davis, the famous attorney who argued for the Southern states before the Supreme Court in *Brown I* asserted: "Much of that which is handed around under the name of social science is an effort on the part of the scientist to rationalize his own preconceptions. They find usually, in my limited observation, what they go out to find." The current consensus seems to reflect Davis' conclusion—that the "social science in *Brown* was merely a political argument dressed in scientific garb."[17]

Each of these criticisms of the use of social science in *Brown I* seems to imply that the actors who overcame legal segregation chose expediency over accuracy. The Court focused on social science rather than common sense for "public relations" purposes; instead of using the slower but more appropriate legislative branch to overturn segregation, the Court overstepped its boundaries and made new laws; finally, the social scientists involved in *Brown I* distorted the research evidence for political ends. The critique thus represents a recurring theme in the history of rhetoric—that social actors who make rhetorical choices profane the search for truth and justice in order to gain adherence to their policy proposals.

This critique, which has gained currency in recent years, represents a rhetorically and historically impoverished perspective on the school desegregation decisions. The critique fails to consider the inherently persuasive nature of the judicial branch, particularly the rhetorical exigences which shaped the *Social Science Statement* appended to the *Brown I* opinion (and described later) and the opinion itself. The perspective also ignores the struggle over the scientific backing for white supremacy which framed the arguments of the rhetorical actors.

"The Least Dangerous Branch"

As Alexander Hamilton noted in *The Federalist No. 78*, the judicial branch has "no influence over either the sword or the purse." Absent monetary or military power, claims Steven Goldberg,

> judicial opinions . . . are successful or unsuccessful depending on the extent to which they effectively draw on commonly held values to persuade the interested segments of the population. Judges . . . engage in rhetoric . . . in the older sense of persuasive communication designed to win support for views on questions of values.[18]

From this perspective, controversial decisions like *Brown* underscore an ongoing rhetorical problem for the judiciary, particularly the Supreme Court.

Every decision, in order to gain the adherence of other branches which control the purse or the sword, must be perceived as a legitimate exercise of judicial authority, even though some people may disagree with the decision. Thus, the credibility of the Court is a potential issue in every ruling.

Until the late nineteenth century, the predominant judicial solution to the legitimacy issue was to view legal decision making as an exercise in syllogistic reasoning. A judge would search the records of past cases to discover the "proper rules and precedents involved," then apply those rules to the particular case under review. "Once he had done that, the judge could decide the case with certainty and uniformity."[19]

Beginning in 1870, however, Oliver Wendell Holmes, Jr., who was to become one of the most influential Supreme Court justices, challenged this tradition of "mechanical jurisprudence." Holmes provided an alternative view of judicial decision making which was to affect profoundly the arguments of both the LDF attorneys and the Warren Court.

"It is the merit of the common law," Holmes wrote, "that it decides the case first and determines the principle afterward." Judges made decisions in specific cases; even though they thought they were using deductive logic, they were thinking "the way everybody else does—by the seat of their pants. First they decide, then they deduce."[20] Since practical exigencies, "necessitated by the needs and conflicts of human society," were more important than logical propositions, Holmes rejected the notion that "the law is discovered, and not made."[21]

In Holmes' view, law was not a body of universal statements; it was "the product of social struggle." This view of the law had two consequences. First, the study of law in the future was to be the province of "the man of statistics and the master of economics." Second, the appropriate institution for settling matters of social and political struggle was the legislature, not the judiciary. Holmes was both "the father of legal realism" and the founder of the doctrine of judicial restraint.[22]

Legal realism came to define the work of a loose coalition of law professors who taught primarily at Columbia and Yale during the 1930s. William O. Douglas, Hugo Black, and Felix Frankfurter, who were sitting Supreme Court justices at the time of the school desegregation decisions, were influenced by legal realism. Legal realists believed "human knowledge could never be certain"; they thought of the law as a "constantly changing phenomenon"; they denounced "abstract verbal formulas or absolutes" as impediments to "clear legal thinking"; they called for "careful empirical studies of the way the law actually operated in society"; they examined the "practical impact of legal rules"; finally, they "suggested that judicial logic was in part rationalization."[23]

Roscoe Pound, dean of the Harvard Law School, developed a variant on legal realism that has come to be known as "sociological jurisprudence." Pound claimed that the "overemphasis on logical uniformity and theoretical reasoning" that characterized mechanical jurisprudence often frustrated the cause of justice.

"Only by studying the social impact of legal principles and rules could men know whether the law in fact brought about the administration of real justice." He envisioned close cooperation with social scientists "in order to obtain insights into legal behavior."[24] Therefore, by the time the desegregation cases reached the Supreme Court, mechanical jurisprudence had been challenged overtly by the realist view that judicial decisions could be used to change social policy, especially if those decisions took advantage of social scientific knowledge.

Pound's ideas also became a cornerstone of the legal philosophy of the attorneys who prosecuted the desegregation cases, many of whom attended Howard University Law School in the early 1930s.

Social Engineers or "Parasites"

No individual had a greater impact on the legal fight to end segregation than Charles Hamilton Houston, who became dean of the Howard University Law School in 1929. Houston brought a philosophy of law as social activism that he used to motivate his students.[25]

Houston incorporated sociological jurisprudence into legal education at Howard. Pound was a frequent guest lecturer at the law school. Houston "brought the realist emphasis on the use of social science to an entire generation of African-American attorneys" who would challenge legal segregation. Thurgood Marshall, the lead attorney in the desegregation cases, recalled that "Houston made public statements that the black lawyers he trained at Howard would become social engineers rather than lawyers—that was our purpose in life." Otherwise, lawyers were "parasites." Houston defined the mission of Howard lawyers as overturning the "separate but equal" doctrine the Court had laid down in the 1896 *Plessy v. Ferguson* case; this doctrine had been used for nearly fifty years to justify legal segregation in transportation, restaurants, lodging, restrooms, and, most important, education. Houston saw education as the key to breaking the back of segregation. If blacks and whites went to integrated schools, he argued, "then smart black children, like smart white children, could be captains of industry."[26]

Because Houston and Marshall saw themselves as social engineers, they approached the law as a vehicle for racial justice. The NAACP's legal strategy afforded a prominent role for extralegal information, particularly economic and sociological evidence. Eventually, the Supreme Court itself would open the door for the introduction of the evidence of the harms of segregation as relevant evidence in reconsidering *Plessy.*

The Court's use of sociological jurisprudence in *Brown* was not, however, an innovation. The *Plessy* court had also relied on the available social scientific knowledge in 1896 to rule that the provision of segregated facilities was consistent with the Fourteenth Amendment.

To understand the court's use of social scientific evidence to respond to *Plessy*, it is necessary to examine the view of African Americans that came to dominate mainstream culture at the time of the desegregation decisions. The years immediately following World War II witnessed the culmination of a dramatic shift in the scientific consensus regarding blacks. Rather than being seen as a biologically inferior group who could not benefit from quality education, their social situation came to be viewed as analogous to immigrants awaiting cultural assimilation through improved education. The attorneys and social scientists who battled segregation in the *Brown* case believed that equality for African Americans could be achieved simply by removing legal barriers to their educational, residential, and economic opportunities.

"Hewers of Wood and Drawers of Water"

To strike down segregation in *Brown*, the Court needed to counter the justification offered to support the "separate but equal" doctrine in *Plessy*. To justify segregation as consistent with the Fourteenth Amendment, the *Plessy* Court had relied on "conservative sociological jurisprudence."[27] Chief Justice Henry Brown, writing for an eight to one majority, based his ruling in *Plessy* on two popular sociological beliefs—social Darwinism and white supremacy. "If one race be inferior to the other socially," wrote Brown, "the constitution of the United States cannot put them on the same plane." Government could not overcome natural inequality. "If the two races are to meet upon terms of social equality, it must be the result of natural affinities, a mutual appreciation of each other's merits, and a voluntary consent of individuals."[28] The state was powerless against the forces of nature, which had made blacks inferior.

Plaintiff Homer Plessy, the Court majority determined, committed the "fallacy" of assuming that "enforced separation of the two races stamps the colored race with a badge of inferiority. If this be so," Justice Brown concluded, "it is not by reason of anything found in [the state statute], but solely because the colored race chooses to put that construction on it."[29] Those who believed that segregation caused inferiority, the *Plessy* Court implied, should look to nature instead.

Justice Brown's ruling was consistent with the state of scientific knowledge in 1896. The contemporary view of white supremacy, of course, is that the term entitles a set of opinions that is inaccurate, irrational, and frequently symptomatic of a pathological personality. However, as historian George Fredrickson has demonstrated, between the 1830s and the 1930s, white supremacy was a virtually unchallenged belief system. The central propositions of this ideology were that African Americans are by nature both different from and inferior to

European Americans; that these differences are either permanent or subject only to gradual change; that cross-breeding between the races is dangerous; that prejudice is a natural and inevitable response to the inferior race's aspirations for equality; and that the destiny of African Americans is either continued subordination or extinction. Blacks were condemned by nature to be "a nation of mere hewers of wood and drawers of water."[30]

The pervasive discrimination and prejudice encountered by African Americans within this system has been widely recounted. This legacy of justifications for slavery, which emerged only after abolitionist agitation grew in the 1830s, affected the thinking and research of anthropologists, biologists, sociologists, and psychologists throughout this era.[31] The northern migration of African Americans during and after World War I, and the widespread use of the Army's administration of standardized intelligence tests during that conflict to heighten public fears of an inundation of waves of mentally defective immigrants, both solidified segregation and led to the passage of restrictive immigration laws in the 1920s.

Remarkably, by the end of that decade, social scientists had begun to abandon the belief that intelligence was solely determined by biology and to recognize the role of different environments in determining individuals' life outcomes. Influenced by the work of a generation of anthropologists who had trained with Franz Boas at Columbia University and of sociologists who had studied with Robert Park at the University of Chicago, these researchers began to embrace the belief that social conditions, rather than innate biological differences, determined the life outcomes of different social groups.[32]

Both groups of researchers rejected the biological inferiority thesis. Boas' students, however, studied the cultural practices of African Americans descriptively. Grounded in Boas' cautious empirical approach and sensitive to the ways groups with different histories developed different cultural practices, they investigated continuities between African culture and "Negro" cultural practices. Park's students, some of whom became prominent African American social scientists teaching at Howard University in the early 1930s, were grounded in a "social evolution" perspective. They saw most African American cultural practices as indicative of a backward, "folk" culture, which had developed as a response to prejudice, discrimination, and segregation. Once afforded equal opportunity to participate in mainstream culture, "Negroes" would quickly abandon their uncivilized practices and join the modern American culture.[33]

The emerging public view of African Americans in the 1950s was influenced strongly by a massive study which established a "liberal orthodoxy" regarding race relations; this orthodoxy dominated progressive thought and social policy until the mid-1960s. This study reflected the *social evolution* perspective of the Park-trained sociologists rather than the *cultural relativism* perspective of the Boas-educated anthropologists.

Swedish economist Gunnar Myrdal had been commissioned by the Carnegie Commission of New York to supervise a comprehensive study of race relations. The results of this study, published in 1944 as *An American Dilemma*, reflected the view of blacks as culturally deficient, rather than biologically inferior. This influential volume provided the background set of assumptions used by the social scientists and attorneys to frame their arguments against segregation. By focusing on the deficiencies of African American culture, Myrdal clothed the myth of white superiority in different raiment.[34]

Myrdal's monumental study centered on "a problem in the heart of Americans." Mainstream Americans face "a moral dilemma"; the "American creed" of equality and freedom is in "ever-raging conflict" with specific beliefs and practices that discriminate against blacks.[35]

For Myrdal one consequence of this dilemma is that black Americans, denied equal access to American culture, have been restricted to a distorted imitation of that culture. As he says in his chapter on black "Institutions":

> In practically all its divergences, American Negro culture is not something independent of general American culture. It is a distorted development, or a pathological condition, of the general American culture. We assume it is to the advantage of American Negroes, as individuals and as a group to become assimilated into American culture, to acquire the traits held in esteem by the dominant white culture.[36]

Myrdal was disdainful of black social groups which "appear ludicrous" to many white Americans, and he dismissed efforts like Carter Woodson's Negro History movement as "propaganda." For Myrdal, and for the generation of academic researchers, civil rights leaders, and public officials influenced by *An American Dilemma*, African Americans were "only white men with black skins, nothing more, nothing less."[37] Any evident differences were the product of the damage caused by prejudice and discrimination.

In the years following the publication of *An American Dilemma*, this book was cited on numerous occasions by civil rights organizations filing *amicus curiae* ("friend of the court") legal briefs in lawsuits challenging segregation. As David Southern has concluded, by the time the Supreme Court ruled in the *Brown* cases, the clause "see Myrdal, *An American Dilemma*, passim" had become a common reference in a number of these briefs.[38] Because the book was so comprehensive and so widely celebrated, the view of black Americans in *An American Dilemma* became the dominant perspective among the rhetorical actors in the school desegregation decisions. African Americans were seen as "white men with black skins"; if barriers like segregation, which had been justified by an outmoded belief in the natural inferiority of Negroes, were removed, they would smoothly and easily be assimilated into the prevailing American culture, and the "Negro problem" would disappear. The pervasiveness of this cultural deficiency perspective is revealed by examining development of the arguments in two key texts in the school desegregation decision: the *Social Science Statement* appended to the LDF brief in the school desegregation cases, which was a product of the cooperation between attorneys and social scientists, and Justice Warren's opinion in *Brown I*.

"Intangible" Harms

From the beginning of their assault on school segregation, the LDF attorneys turned to empirical evidence to support their arguments. The legal strategy Charles Houston developed was prompted by a 1930 report authored by Nathan Margold, Houston's former Harvard law classmate. Margold's report proposed an attack on segregation from within the "separate but equal" doctrine established in *Plessy*. The NAACP should challenge segregation "as now provided and administered," demonstrating *empirically* that the disparity in expenditures for white and "colored" schools in the seventeen states with legally segregated education made the segregated schools unequal. Thus, states would have to decide between a program of costly school improvement or integration of black children into existing white schools.[39]

Houston decided to use the Margold strategy in an arena "where whites were most vulnerable and least likely to respond with anger." He focused the LDF efforts on graduate and professional education, where educational facilities for blacks were "neither separate nor equal but nonexistent." A successful case in this arena, he felt, would either "result in improved all-black facilities" or, if integration were required, "demonstrate that blacks and whites could attend school together to the mutual benefit of the students as well as the state treasury."[40] Thurgood Marshall, reflecting on this strategy years later, found it puzzling that "those racial supremacy boys" who were worried that integration would give "little kids of six or seven . . . funny ideas about sex or marriage," for some reason thought "youngsters in law school aren't supposed to feel that way." "We didn't get it," he admitted, "but we decided that if that was what the South believed, then the best thing for the moment was to go along."[41]

As they pursued the graduate education cases, the attorneys repeatedly advanced two scientific arguments against segregation. First, they relied on the research in the Boas tradition to claim that there was no scientific foundation for the belief that blacks were biologically inferior to whites. Second, they relied on the Park research tradition to argue "that segregation denied African-Americans the opportunity to embrace true American values."[42] African Americans were portrayed as a group desiring only to join mainstream American culture.

The strategy resulted in a major victory when, on the same day in June 1950, a unanimous Supreme Court ruled in two cases that separate law and graduate schools were unequal. In *Sweatt v. Painter* in particular, the Court identified "qualities which are incapable of objective measurement but which make for greatness in a law school" as the main inequality of segregated legal education. Since the focus of the case was on legal education, the Justices could rely on their own law school experiences, in addition to the social science evidence presented by the LDF attorneys, to conclude that a segregated law school could not provide equality in terms of "reputation of the faculty, experience of the administration, position and influence of the alumni," or "traditions and prestige."[43] Demonstrating the intangible harms of segregation in the public education of children, however, was a more formidable task.

An appellate case in California near the end of World War II had opened the door for the introduction of the psychological damage argument into the LDF strategy to defeat school segregation. *Westminster School District v. Mendez*, originated by five Mexican American parents, challenged the segregation of Mexican American children in the California school system. Robert Carter, who had recently joined the LDF, wrote an *amicus* ("friend of the court") brief for this case. In addition, the Commission on Law and Social Action (CLSA) of the American Jewish Congress submitted an *amicus* brief written by Alexander Pekelis, a Russian expatriate and legal realist. The arguments offered in these briefs laid the foundation for the public school desegregation cases.

In *Westminster*, Carter argued that segregated schools, even if the physical facilities were equal, failed to ameliorate "the most important inequalities of all"—the "feeling of second-class citizenship" implied by the power of the majority to discriminate. This second-class citizenship, he argued, "expressed itself in criminality and rebellion against constituted authority."[44] Carter proposed that segregation was damaging even if the "tangible' factors were equivalent. The argument appeared compelling to the other members of the LDF team, but Carter provided no research evidence to support the damage argument.

In the CLSA brief, Pekelis argued that the Court's claim in *Plessy* that segregation was not inherently harmful had been refuted by "the sociological and psychological findings of the past fifty years." In education, the consequences of segregation were especially pernicious. "By giving official sanction to group separation based on the assumption of inferiority," he said, "it helps to perpetuate racial prejudice and contributes to the degradation and humiliation of the minority child." Again, the argument was presented without evidence of this degradation and humiliation.[45]

The California appellate court ruled narrowly in favor of the plaintiffs on the grounds that segregation was not sanctioned by California law, thus avoiding the question of the constitutionality of *Plessy*. These *amicus* briefs, however, crystallized the arguments that NAACP attorneys would use in their fight to end public school segregation. Because they recognized that there was no existing empirical research on the psychological harms of school segregation itself, the LDF planned to assemble relevant data, but a scarcity of funds resulted in the abandonment of this effort in 1947.[46] Throughout the legal campaign against school desegregation, therefore, NAACP attorneys tried to use existing social science research findings as indirect support for their claim that segregated schools were unconstitutional.

The organizations that participated in the *Westminster* case began to marshal evidence supporting the psychological harms of segregation. The CLSA commissioned psychologist Isador Chein to conduct a survey of social scientists' opinions regarding the outcomes of legal segregation. Chein's survey, which he published along with statistician Max Duetscher in 1948, reported that 90 percent of the social scientists he surveyed believed that segregation damaged the segregated group psychologically, and a strong majority believed that this conclusion was supported either by their own research and experience or the experience and research of other social scientists. Although not direct scientific evidence of the harms of segregation, this survey aggregated the "expert witness" tradition in the court system. Expert witnesses were often called on to provide opinions rather than give reasons for their opinions. LDF attorneys called two dozen expert witnesses to offer their opinions in the desegregation cases; the survey was used to support the claim that these social scientists represented, if not a consensus, certainly a plurality of expert opinion on the harms of segregation.[47]

Carter also looked for direct empirical evidence of psychological harm. This search led him to the work of Kenneth and Mamie Clark, who were using projective techniques to study "the incorporation of racial custom by individual children." These studies explored the "genesis of racial attitudes," and, in the social engineering tradition the Clarks shared with Gunnar Myrdal, asked whether the social environment could be "altered in ways that would encourage children to become more tolerant, more democratic." Reflecting on this research project years later, Kenneth Clark stated that they were "surprised by our findings," especially "the degree to which the children suffered from self-rejection. . . . I don't think we had quite realized the *extent* of the cruelty of racism and how hard it hit."[48]

Kenneth Clark's "Gloomy Observations"

In 1950 Clark wrote a report on the problems of minority youth for the White House Mid-Century Conference on Youth. When Robert Carter began looking for expert social science witnesses, it was suggested that he contact Clark.[49] In the White House report, Clark had argued that minority children early on "learn the inferior status" assigned by society to their caste, and "they react with feelings of inferiority, aggressive and hostile impulses toward themselves and toward others," and suffer a "lowering of personal ambition" which "seems to be associated with a humiliating and inferior role assigned to minorities." Carter read the report and told Clark, "It's almost as if it were written for us." The scientific evidence of psychological damage apparently had been discovered. Clark was recruited by the LDF to both serve as an expert witness and organize the testimony of other social science experts.[50]

From his very first meeting with Carter, however, Kenneth Clark had told him that it was not possible to "isolate the effects of school segregation from the psychological damage . . . from the collective impact of prejudice." Heeding Clark's admonition, in his instructions to the expert social science witnesses, Carter wrote that research by Clark and Eugene Hartley "found little differences . . . among northern and southern Negro and white children." Hartley had concluded that "attitudes towards Negroes are now chiefly determined not by contact with Negroes, but by contact with prevalent attitudes toward Negroes." In the very first trial in South Carolina, Clark testified that "discrimination, prejudice, and segregation" have "detrimental effects on the personality development of the Negro child."[51]

The fact that both Northern and Southern children experienced a sense of inferiority, and the unorthodox nature of the projective tests themselves, led some LDF attorneys to resist including the social science evidence in the Supreme Court appeals. Thurgood Marshall, however, supported the use of the social science research. Marshall argued that in a "direct challenge to segregation . . . there was no reason not to use sociology, psychology, or anything else that might be helpful to the case."[52] The importance of the evidence, he claimed, was that it refuted the conservative sociological jurisprudence offered by the majority in the fifty-year-old *Plessy* case. The Clarks' research seemed to demonstrate that the harm of segregation was not simply a fiction in the minds of African Americans.

Segregation was demonstrably damaging because it was linked to prejudice and discrimination. At the heart of legal segregation was the belief that blacks are inherently inferior. After all, "it was actionable defamation in the South to call a white man a Negro," and " a small portion of Negro blood put one in the inferior race for segregation purposes." Legal segregation contributed to "feelings of inferiority in the African-American population" by providing "environmental support" for the idea that blacks were inferior. Carter and Marshall believed that "the state could not consciously inflict such damage because such action would constitute discrimination." In his oral argument before the Court Marshall stressed that "not a single lawyer for any of the states with segregated schools has refuted any of the sociological evidence of the damage done to black children." Thus, the continuation of legal segregation meant that the government would continue to sanction the damage caused by discrimination and prejudice. Perpetuating this damage, the LDF attorneys argued, was unconstitutional.[53]

Segregation as a "Symbol of Inferiority"

The LDF collaborated with the SPSSI to produce a *Social Science Statement*, which summarized the expert testimony in the five cases consolidated under *Brown v. Board of Education*.[54] The *Statement* was signed by thirty-two social scientists and presented by the attorneys as "a consensus of social scientists" relying on "the best available scientific evidence" (42). As psychologists Kenneth Clark, Stuart Cook, and Isador Chein created the *Statement*, they faced the rhetorical challenge of crafting a document that supported desegregation while remaining consistent with the limited research evidence available to challenge segregation directly.

Their solution was to incorporate segregation into the existing research on the effects of prejudice and discrimination. In the opening section of the report, titled "Definitions," they stressed that segregation marks a "restriction of opportunities for different types of associations" between groups which is supported by an "official body or agency" of the government. Stressing the inherent inequality of legal segregation, they characterized the "segregated" group as possessing "lesser social status" (44).

Segregation, these authors argued, cannot be separated from a "social milieu in which 'race' prejudice and discrimination exist." By linking segregation to these "social concomitants," the authors could draw on research which addressed the effects of racial prejudice and discrimination, including studies that examined prejudice directed at other groups (e.g., anti-Semitism). In an important disclaimer, the authors admitted that it is "difficult to disentangle the effects of segregation" from the effects of prejudice and discrimination; in addition, segregation helps create a "pattern of social disorganization" among blacks. Consistent with Myrdal's characterization of African American culture, they listed "high disease and mortality rates, crime and delinquency, poor housing, disrupted family life and generally substandard living conditions" (45) as indicators of this social pathology. In adopting Myrdal's perspective, the authors of the *Statement* affirmed adaptation to mainstream culture as the only rational goal for African Americans.

The first section of the *Statement*, which deals with the "consequences of segregation" (44), began with a summary of Kenneth Clark's White House Conference report. That report is titled "Effect of Prejudice and Discrimination on Personality Development." Segregation was introduced in Clark's report through his summary of the Deutscher and Chein survey. Addressed to social scientists and educators, the report emphasized the effects of prejudice on both the targets of discrimination and the perpetrators of prejudice, and concluded with an examination of educational efforts to reduce prejudice. To move this body of observational and experimental research into the domain of constitutional law required the invocation of the symbolic effects of segregation.

When the *Social Science Statement*'s authors turned to the question of the effects of segregation per se, they argued that segregation is "a significantly contributing factor to these effects" because it is perceived as " a symbol of inferiority" (50). Enforced segregation, they claimed, "results from the decision of the majority group without the consent of the segregated" and rests on "the assumption of the inferiority of the segregated" (51).

The *Statement* also cited Deutscher and Chein's survey to indicate that the conclusion they reached represented a consensus of social scientists. Consistent with the state of the available scientific evidence, the *Statement* embedded segregation in the context of prejudice and discrimination. In making this connection, however, the authors stressed the harms of segregation on black children; the "somewhat more obscure" (48) material on the effects of prejudice on children from the majority group disappeared. The absence of direct scientific evidence regarding the harms of segregation led the *Statement*'s authors to focus their attention on the role of the "American dilemma" in perpetuating the "social disorganization" of black children.[55]

The second argument in the *Statement* was that desegregation can be achieved with a minimum of disruption. To support this argument, the *Statement*'s authors claimed that concerns about the possible harms of including "an intellectually inferior group" in a "competitive" educational setting are based on a false assumption. "The available scientific evidence," they asserted, "indicates that much, perhaps all, of the observable differences among various racial . . . groups may be adequately explained in terms of environmental differences" (54). In this section, the authors also summarized a large number of historical reports and research studies which demonstrated that desegregation can be successful. Reflecting the interest among social scientists in overcoming prejudice and discrimination rather than merely providing data to support the harmful effects of discrimination, this body of evidence was simply summarized by the *Statement*'s authors with little interpretive text. In a dramatic contrast to the first section, this part of the *Statement* contained far less text (ten paragraphs rather than twenty) and many more references (fifty-one rather than twenty-two) than the first section. A more well-developed body of research supported the conclusion that integration was likely to be successful if a particular set of conditions were established. To be successful, desegregation must be introduced "simultaneously into all units of a social institution . . . e.g., all of the schools in a school system" (16). Second, desegregation efforts require "consistent and firm enforcement . . . by those in authority" (17). Desegregation also is more successful in a situation free from competition for limited resources, when opportunities of individuals to interact as individuals is provided, and when equality of status can be maintained. The authors affirmed that "public schools" are institutions in which these conditions can be achieved (59).

The social scientific arguments summarized by the LDF in the *Statement* claimed that segregation, discrimination, and prejudice were harmful to black children. Because segregation was sanctioned by the law, the attorneys and social scientists felt they did not need to claim that segregation itself was the "independent variable" that caused psychological damage. Law was unjust if it reinforced the harms of prejudice and discrimination; legal segregation was thus harmful to the personality development of African American children and therefore constitutionally unjustified. The authors also asserted that desegregation could be socially engineered by a strong and consistent policy, in spite of anticipated resistance. Central to both these arguments was the contention that the problems of educational achievement of African Americans were a result of environmental deprivation, rather than biological inferiority.

In his attempt to develop a unanimous opinion in these cases, Chief Justice Earl Warren made rhetorical choices that led directly to the three criticisms of social science that have become popular in contemporary readings. Attempting to appease anticipated Southern anger over desegregation, Warren omitted the challenge to white supremacy which formed the basis of the LDF claims regarding the psychological harms of segregation. To obtain the consent of Justices who advocated judicial restraint, Warren used the social science evidence selectively to avoid claiming that the *Plessy* decision was a mistaken verdict. Concerned over potential resistance to enforced integration, the Court ignored the strong body of social science evidence regarding successful integration and focused on political considerations in writing the implementation decree in *Brown II.* In making these choices, Warren substituted a view of blacks as culturally deprived rather than biologically inferior as a justification for ending school segregation, perpetuating white supremacy in a different mode. Warren also made the implicit claim that ending legal (*de jure*) segregation would solve "the Negro problem."[56]

Crafting Unanimity

> A unanimous opinion of the Court inspires a measure of respect and obedience that even a single dissent bespatters. A single opinion says that the nine men have in union apprehended the truth and now reveal it; more than one opinion suggests that truth may be glimpsed from many angles—or that there is none, only conflicting opinion among mere mortals, and that another season may bring a different outcome.—Richard Kluger[57]

Supreme Court deliberation occurs in an intimate rhetorical scene. Arguments are directed at nine individual justices who can represent diverging political opinions and judicial philosophies. At the same time, opinions must be crafted with an eye toward their rhetorical impact. Having neither "purse nor sword," the Court's decisions must be seen as legitimate to be effective. Unanimity provides powerful rhetorical support for any decision.

Oral argument in the consolidated desegregation cases began on December 9, 1952, and ended two days later. When the Justices met on the following Saturday, they comprised "the most severely fractured Supreme Court in history." Justice Frankfurter, fearing a bare majority opinion would emerge, worked "to prevent the Court from taking a premature vote." Frankfurter believed that any decision rendered at that time would have "produced . . . a number of clashing opinions that might have reduced the Court's standing and ignited racial warfare in the South." Frankfurter successfully persuaded his colleagues to hear additional arguments in 1953 on two issues: (1) Could the original intention regarding school segregation of the framers of the Fourteenth Amendment be ascertained? and (2) What program of implementation of desegregation was likely to be successful? Frankfurter's call for reargument, however, was little more than a delaying tactic.[58]

After the sudden death of Chief Justice Vinson, President Dwight Eisenhower appointed California Governor Earl Warren as the new Chief Justice. Warren had only recently joined the Court when the reargument occurred on December 7, 1953. On the next Saturday, the new Chief Justice convened a conference of all nine Justices. Warren began by proposing that the Court delay taking a vote and continue to deliberate about the case. Reflecting on this decision a year later, Chief Justice Warren said that "the fact that we did not polarize ourselves at the beginning gave us more of an opportunity to come out unanimously."[59]

According to the notes of those who attended the conference, Warren's next statement set the agenda for the Court's deliberation. "The more I've read and thought," he said, "the more I've come to conclude that the basis of segregation . . . rests upon a concept of the inherent inferiority of the colored race. . . . If we are to sustain segregation, we must do it upon that basis." If the argument before the Court had proven anything, "it proved that this basis was not justified."[60]

This statement by Warren, which ironically was never included in the *Brown I* decision, struck a responsive chord with the other justices. In the 1952 conference, Frankfurter had indicated he was ready to strike down segregation in Washington, D.C., but could not find grounds to overturn *Plessy* with regard to state laws. As a champion of judicial restraint, Frankfurter could not bring himself to say that the 1896 Court "had misread the Constitution." "What justifies us," he had asked, "in saying that what *was* equal in 1865 [when the Fourteenth Amendment was passed] is not equal *now*?" Frankfurter also had rejected the notion that scientific evidence of black inferiority was convincing. "To attribute such a view to science," he had written in a memorandum in 1953, "as is sometimes done, is to reject the very basis of science, namely the process of reaching verifiable conclusions." For Frankfurter, therefore, the relevant scientific evidence appeared in the *Social Science Statement* when the social scientists affirmed that differences between the races were "environmental."[61]

Justice Robert Jackson was the other strong adherent of judicial restraint. In the 1953 conference, he saw the problem as making "a judicial decision out of a political conclusion," and implied that he would support a "properly written decision striking down segregation." Even Stanley Reed, considered by most commentators to have been the Justice most likely to dissent in any decision to overturn *Plessy*, stated in the 1953 conference that he rejected "the argument that the Negro is an inferior race. Of course, there is no inferior race, although they may be handicapped by lack of opportunity."[62] The rejection of biological inferiority, although never directly addressed in the Court's opinion, seems to have been a fundamental assumption underlying the desegregation decision.

Warren, however, was concerned about the tone of the opinion. "We should abolish the practice of segregation," he said at the 1953 conference, "but in a tolerant way." He wanted to avoid making accusations against the South, but Warren felt that the Court could say that segregation was no longer justifiable "in this day and age."[63]

In his memorandum transmitting a draft of the *Brown I* decision to his colleagues, Warren indicated that he felt that the opinion should be "short, readable by the lay public, non-rhetorical, unemotional and, above all, non-accusatory."[64] To avoid an accusatory tone, Warren emphasized the damage argument and avoided confronting directly the claim that blacks were inferior, which would have accused the South of basing segregation on an irrational prejudice.

The final draft of the opinion in *Brown I* reflects a realist perspective by emphasizing changed circumstances as the reason for overturning *Plessy*. Warren's text avoided the necessity to declare that the *Plessy* court was wrong in offering the "separate but equal" doctrine. Thus, he could minimize the likelihood of separate concurring or dissenting opinions from the Justices who advocated judicial restraint. Warren chose non-accusatory language, avoiding a direct assault on the belief in black inferiority, in hopes he could minimize resistance to the decision. These rhetorical choices emerge in the central passages of the decision.

Warren's opinion began with a review of the judicial history of the desegregation cases; he then summarized the main claim of the plaintiffs: "that segregated schools are not 'equal' and cannot be made 'equal'"(488).[65] The opinion then addressed the question of the intent of the framers of the Fourteenth Amendment, finding the arguments "inconclusive" (489).

In the next paragraph, Warren invoked the legal realist perspective. One of the limitations of the quest for the framers' intent was that the "status of public education" at the time of the Amendment's adoption differed dramatically from public schooling in the early 1950s. "Even in the North, the condition of public education did not approximate those existing today" (490). The arguments advanced at the time of the adoption of the Fourteenth Amendment, according to Warren, need to be interpreted in light of changing historical circumstances.[66] The subsequent paragraph, which reviewed briefly the relevant cases, contains the following key sentence: "The doctrine of 'separate but equal' did not make its appearance in this Court until 1896 in the case of *Plessy v. Ferguson*" (491). The *Plessy* doctrine, Warren implied, was not a part of the Fourteenth Amendment debates; it was instead an interpretation of the Amendment offered thirty years later. The paragraph continued with a summary of the cases involving public education in which the *Plessy* doctrine was involved. The current cases were different because "the question of whether *Plessy v. Ferguson* should be held inapplicable to public education . . . is directly presented" (492).

Unlike the previous cases, some of the defendant school districts were moving to improve segregated educational facilities so they would be equal in "tangible" factors. Warren claimed that the court must therefore look to "the effect of segregation itself on public education" (492). In accordance with a realist perspective, he next noted that changes in the importance of public education warrant a reexamination of the "separate but equal" formula. "Education is perhaps the most important function of state and local governments" (493). Educational opportunity had become essential for success. And so the central question the Court must address, Warren said, is whether "segregation of children in public schools solely on the basis of race . . . deprive[s] children of the minority group of equal educational opportunities" (493).

"We believe that it does," he asserted. "To separate them from others of similar age and qualifications solely because of their race generates a feeling of inferiority as to their status in the community that may affect their hearts and minds in a way unlikely ever to be undone" (494). To support this claim, he cited the finding from the Kansas court:

> Segregation of white and colored children in public schools has a detrimental effect upon the colored children. . . . The policy of separating the races is usually interpreted as denoting the inferiority of the Negro group. . . . Segregation with the sanction of law, therefore, has a tendency to (retard) the educational and mental development of negro children and to deprive them of some of the benefits they would achieve in a racial(ly) integrated school system. (494)

The Kansas finding, he concluded, is "amply supported by modern authority," referring to the infamous *Footnote 11* (495). Because *Plessy* was based on "the state of psychological knowledge" in 1896, it was appropriate for the Court to consider the current state of psychological knowledge. Warren turned to extralegal information, specifically the Social Science Statement, as the source of "modern [scientific] authority."

Six of the seven sources cited in *Footnote 11* were also in the *Statement.* The seventh, a 1952 book called *Personality in the Making*, contains Kenneth Clark's White House report. All the sources come from the first section of the *Social Science Statement*, which addressed the damage claim. The last citation in the note, which by this time had become familiar, was "And see generally Myrdal, *An American Dilemma.*"

What was the role of the *Footnote*? Some legal historians have claimed that the controversy surrounding *Footnote 11* stems from "ignorance of the manner in which Supreme Court opinions are prepared." Citing evidence from conference notes and retrospective interviews, they echo Warren's dismissive reply in his interview with Richard Kluger: "After all, it was only a footnote." A rhetorical reading of this controversial reference, however, would view *Footnote 11* as a refutation of the Court's claim in Plessy that segregation was not inherently harmful.[67]

A year after the decision, Warren told psychologist Otto Klineberg that the Court "probably would have come to the same conclusion" but "felt that their case was strengthened by the clear support of the present generation of psychologists." Both Warren and his clerk Earl Pollock stated in later interviews that the purpose of *Footnote 11* was to refute the statement in *Plessy* that any perception of damage from segregation was "only in the mind of the Negro." Warren felt that the sources in the note were sufficient to refute this argument.[68] To counter *Plessy*, Warren focused on the social science evidence that stressed that the damage from segregation was real, rather than imagined. Since the question of damage to the majority had not been raised in the 1896 case, that question was not addressed in *Brown I.* Instead, Warren followed the scientific consensus reflected in *An American Dilemma* and made the harms that segregation inflicted on black children the major justification for overturning *Plessy*.

The question the Court avoided in the first case was how to implement the end of segregation. Anticipating Southern resistance, the Court called for additional arguments regarding implementation and, following these arguments, issued a subsequent ruling in 1955. In that unanimous decision, the Court required desegregation, which was to monitored by federal district courts, to proceed with "all deliberate speed." The Justices hoped that gradual, rather than immediate, implementation would lessen Southern resistance. In this decision, the Court ignored the second part of the *Social Science Statement*, which used a strong body of historical precedent and research evidence to suggest policies likely to lead to successful integration.

Read against the recommendations in the *Statement*, the Court's requirement seemed to be a formula for failure. Rather than requiring integration across the board in public schools, the Court allowed for gradual desegregation. Rather than mandating consistent action on the part of elected leaders, the "all deliberate speed" formula afforded opportunities for evasion and resistance by Southern elected officials. Where the Court could have been aided by a strong body of social science research, the justices chose to ignore this body of work and attempted to mollify anticipated political resistance.[69]

Brown's Legacy: Damaged Psyches and Cultural Deficiency

Brown I changed American society, but it was an equivocal victory for the civil rights of African Americans. Although states could no longer legally use race to separate public school pupils after *Brown I*, the decision could not integrate public schools. Desegregation required enforcement by governmental branches with money and military force, and those branches were reluctant to move quickly, if at all.[70] More important, the Court had unintentionally endorsed the transformation of white supremacy that social scientists had brought to the case. Chief Justice Warren had affirmed the social scientific claim that there were no inherent biological differences in talent between black and white Americans in the private conference; in his written opinion, however, he omitted this claim in order to craft a non-accusatory opinion and alluded to this premise only by quoting the Kansas court's finding. Instead, Warren relied on the indirect evidence of psychological damage from segregation *and its concomitants* to claim that new knowledge warranted a reexamination of the extralegal justification for the 1896 "separate but equal" doctrine. Later claims regarding the quality of the evidence are inappropriate attempts to criticize research which was never designed to directly test the effects of segregation. Criticisms of the motivations of the social scientists improperly disparage the use of social engineering for racial justice as "unscientific."

The inadequacies of the *Brown* decisions stem from two rhetorical choices made by the justices that have proven problematic. First, the attempt in *Brown II* to be non-accusatory and ameliorative, rather than to offer a decision that was consistent with the best available social science evidence, did little to prevent resistance to desegregation.

Second, the emphasis on evidence of the psychological damage of segregation on black children stressed the role of African Americans in public life *only* as objects of "contempt and pity." Rather than ruling that segregation violated the Fourteenth Amendment, the Court concluded that changing times required a different interpretation of that amendment. African Americans, in the Court's view, were simply another group that wanted to be in the mainstream, but segregation had prevented their full incorporation as "Americans." Remove the barrier, and they would assimilate as easily as other immigrant groups had.

In a review of *An American Dilemma* written at the time the book was released, but published twenty years later, novelist Ralph Ellison asked, "Are American Negroes simply the creation of white men, or have they at least helped to create themselves out of what they found around them?"[71] The social evolution perspective affirmed by the Court in *Brown*, following Myrdal, denied Ellison's implicit claim of the self-creation of African American culture. Instead, African Americans were viewed as culturally deprived, rather than naturally inferior; the Court's decision encouraged the hope that eliminating segregation would quickly and easily eliminate "the Negro problem."

Although the scientific community had rejected the idea of racial inferiority by 1954, this ideology persisted as a set of social myths that supporters of segregation relied on to justify their resistance to integration, as Burnette shows in chapter 5 of this volume. The Court was constrained from offering a different set of justifications for desegregation by both the legal and extralegal rhetorical constraints at the time of the *Brown* opinions. Thus, the Court's emphasis on the damage to black children from segregation reflected an accommodative version of white supremacy.[72] Blacks, the Court concluded, wanted only to assimilate; they were willing to turn their backs on their "pathological" culture once the barrier of segregation was removed. As damaged Americans, they had nothing unique to contribute to American society.

Chief Justice Warren's opinion helped perpetuate the liberal orthodoxy established in *An American Dilemma.* Contrary to the Court's hopes, attending integrated schools did not transform African Americans into "white men with dark skins." The national legacy of white supremacy, rather than the sectional legacy of segregation, continues to plague the struggle for equality even as we leave behind the century of the color line and move into the twenty-first century.

Notes

1. Ben Keppel, *The Work of Democracy: Ralph Bunche, Kenneth B. Clark, Lorraine Hansbury, and the Cultural Politics of Race* (Cambridge, MA: Harvard University Press, 1995), 1; W. E. B. Dubois, "Forethought" (from *The Souls of Black Folk*), in *W. E. B. Dubois: Writings* (New York: Viking Press, 1986), 359; Daryl Michael Scott, *Contempt and Pity: Social Policy and the Image of the Damaged Black Psyche, 1880-1996* (Chapel Hill: University of North Carolina Press, 1997), xviii; Dubois, 364.

2. One indicator of the power of Dr. Dubois' prophecy is the differing racial perceptions of that decision at the end of the century of the color-line. For example, *USA Today Weekend* magazine in 1999 conducted an electronic survey of the top news events of the twentieth century. The 35,000 volunteer respondents ranked the desegregation decision thirtieth in importance. Among African American respondents, however, this decision was ranked third, behind only the assassinations of President Kennedy and Dr. King.

3. Otto Klineberg, "SPSSI and Race Relations, in the 1950s and After," *Journal of Social Issues*, 42 (1986): 54.

4. *Brown v. Board of Education*, 347 U.S. 493, 494 (1954). A subsequent ruling in 1955, also called *Brown v. Board of Education* (349 U.S. 294), dealt with the implementation of school desegregation. This second decision is called *Brown II.*

5. Sanjay Mody, "Note: Brown Footnote Eleven in Historical Context," *Stanford Law Review* 53 (2002): 801.

6. John Jackson, Jr. *Social Scientists for Social Justice: Making the Case Against Segregation* (New York: New York University Press, 2001), 2.

7. *Missouri v. Jenkins*, 515 U.S. 70, note 2.

8. Mody, 794.

9. Kathleen J. Turner, "Rhetorical History as a Social Construction" in *Doing Rhetorical History: Concepts and Cases*, ed. Kathleen J. Turner (Tuscaloosa: University of Alabama Press, 1998), 2.

10. Anthony Lewis quoted in Keppel, 117; Edmond Cahn, "Jurisprudence" *New York University Law Review*, 30 (1955): 150; Lino Graglia, *Disaster by Decree: The Supreme Court Decisions on Race and the Schools* (New York: Cornell University Press, 1976), 30.

11. Cahn, 168, note 32; Scott, Chapter 7; Mody, 824. For a discussion of the "intangible harm" strategy, see Clarke Rountree, chapter 3 in this volume.

12. Keppel, 117; Graglia, 32.

13. Richard Kluger, *Simple Justice* (New York: Random House, 1975), 336.

14. Graglia, 289; Mark Yudoff, "School Segregation: Legal Realism, Reasoned Elaboration, and Social Science Research in the Supreme Court," *Law and Contemporary Problems*, 42 (1978): 70.

15. Kenneth B. and Mamie P. Clark, "Racial Identification and Preferences in Negro Children," in *Readings in Social Psychology*, ed. Theodore Newcomb and Eugene Hartley (New York: Henry Holt and Company), 602-611.

16. Scott, 122; Graglia, 28; Cahn, 163.

17. Kluger, 573; John Jackson, *Social Scientists for Social Justice*, 181.

18. Steven Goldberg, *Culture Clash: Law and Science in America.* (New York: New York University Press, 1994), 15-16.

19. Edward A. Purcell, Jr., *The Crisis of Democratic Theory: Scientific Naturalism and the Problem of Value* (Lexington: University of Kentucky Press, 1973), 74-75.

20. Louis Menand, *The Metaphysical Club* (New York: Farrar, Straus, and Giroux, 2001), 338; Purcell, 76; Menand, 342.

21. Purcell, 75; Morton Horowitz, *The Transformation of American Law 1870-1960: The Crisis of Legal Orthodoxy* (New York: Oxford University Press, 1992), 142, 140.

22. Horowitz, 130, 127, 142; John Johnson, *American Legal Culture, 1908-1940* (New Haven: Greenwood Press, 1981), 125.

23. Purcell, 85-86.

24. Johnson, 127.

25. Kluger, 125. Houston's role is also discussed in Rountree's chapter in this volume.

26. Juan Williams, *Thurgood Marshall: American Revolutionary* (New York: Random House, 1998), 59, 63.

27. Barton J. Bernstein, "Plessy v. Ferguson: Conservative Sociological Jurisprudence," *Journal of Negro History*, 48 (1963): 196-205.

28. *Plessy v. Ferguson*, 163 U.S. 537, at 552, 550, 551 (1896).

29. *Plessy v. Ferguson*, 551.

30. George Fredrickson, *The Black Image in the White Mind: The Debate on Afro-American Character and Destiny 1817-1914* (New York: Harper & Row, 1971), 321; Dubois, 365. The use of white supremacist arguments in the Southern resistance to *Brown* is described by Ann Burnette, chapter 5 of this volume.

31. See, for example, William Tucker, *The Science and Politics of Racial Research* (Urbana: University of Illinois Press, 1994); Stephen J. Gould, *The Mismeasure of Man* (New York: Norton, 1981); Carl N. Degler, *In Search of Human Nature* (New York: Oxford University Press, 1991); Hamilton Cravens, *The Triumph of Evolution* (Philadelphia: University of Pennsylvania Press, 1978).

32. See, for example, Degler, Part II and Cravens, Part 2 and 3.

33. Lee Baker, *From Savage to Negro: Anthropology and the Construction of Race 1896-1954* (Berkeley: University of California Press, 1998), chapter 8.

34. Gunnar Myrdal, *An American Dilemma* (1944; reprint, New York: Harper & Row, 1962). Analyses of the background and influence of Myrdal's work are provided by Walter W. Jackson, *Gunnar Myrdal and America's Conscience* (Chapel Hill: University of North Carolina Press, 1990) and David A. Southern, *Gunnar Myrdal and Black-White Relations* (Baton Rouge: Louisiana State University Press, 1987).

35. Myrdal, lxxi.

36. Myrdal, 928, 929.

37. Myrdal, 954,752; Kenneth Stampp, *The Peculiar Institution* (New York: Vintage Books, 1956), vii.

38. Southern, 145.

39. Kluger, 134-135. For more discussion of Margold's strategy, see chapter 3 in this volume.

40. Kluger, 137

41. In John Simon, *The Antagonists: Hugo Black, Felix Frankfurter, and Civil Liberties in Modern America* (New York: Simon and Schuster, 1989), 215.

42. Baker, 198.

43. *Sweatt v. Painter*, 339 U.S. 634.

44. John Jackson, Jr., "The Triumph of the Segregationists: A Historiographic Inquiry into Psychology and the *Brown* Litigation," *History of Psychology* 3 (2000): 84-86.

45. John Jackson, "The Triumph of the Segregationists," 89-90.

46. Ibid., 92.

47. Kluger, 492-493; John Jackson, "The Triumph of the Segregationists," 94-95.

48. Keppel, 105; Kenneth Clark interview in Kluger, 318.

49. Kluger, 318.

50. Keppel, 115; Kluger, 321.

51. Kluger, 353; John Jackson, *Social Scientists for Social Justice*, 127, 30; Kluger, 353.

52. Williams, *Thurgood Marshall*, 197.

53. Charles Lawrence, "'One More River to Cross': Recognizing the Real Injury of *Brown*: A Prerequisite to Shaping New Remedies," in *Shades of Brown: New Perspectives on School Desegregation*, ed. Derrick Bell (New York: Columbia University, 1980), 51; John Jackson, "The Triumph of the Segregationists," 132; Kluger, 358; John Jackson, *Social Scientists for Social Justice*, 251.

54. The *Statement* appears in Phillip B. Kurland and Gerhard Caspar, *Landmark Briefs and Arguments of the Supreme Court of the United States, Constitutional Law* (Arlington, VA: University Publications of America, 1975), 42-61. Subsequent references to this document will be made in the text.

55. In his White House report, Clark had stressed that the scientific evidence regarding even the effects of prejudice on personality development was sparse. Clark speculated that one of the reasons for this paucity of evidence was that "the effort of research workers has gone into finding ways of eliminating the obviously bad situation." Kenneth Clark, "The Effects of Prejudice and Discrimination," *Personality in the Making*, ed. Helen Witmer and Ruth Kotinsky (New York: Harper and Brothers, 1952), 136.

56. *Brown II* is analyzed by Ann Gill in chapter 6 of this volume.

57. Kluger, 708-709.

58. Johnson, 53; Kluger, 206; Simon, 97.

59. Bernard Schwartz, *Super Chief: Earl Warren and His Supreme Court—A Judicial Biography* (New York: New York University Press, 1983), 73.

60. Schwartz, 84-85.

61. Schwartz, 86; Kluger, 570; Williams, 272.

62. Schwartz, 76; Kluger, 680.

63. Schwartz, 87, 36.

64. Schwartz, 87.

65. Additional references to *Brown I* will be included in the text.

66. Legal realism is also described in chapter 3 of this volume.

67. Bernard Schwartz, *A History of the Supreme Court* (New York: Oxford University Press, 1993), 303.

68. Klineberg, 56; Kluger, 706.

69. Walter Jackson, 126, *Brown v. Board of Education*, 349 U.S. 294.

70. On the reluctance of the federal government to enforce segregation, see Ann Burnette's discussion of the events surrounding the 1957 Arkansas case, chapter 6 of this volume.

71. Ralph Ellison, "An American dilemma: A Review," in *The Death of White Sociology*, ed. Joyce Ladner (New York: Random House, 1973), 94.

72. George Fredricksen distinguished between accommodative white supremacy, which sees equality as a distant possibility when the "primitive" group develops civilization, and competitive white supremacy, which views interaction between racial groups as leading inevitably to the extinction of the non-white group. See *The Black Image in the White Mind*, 284.

5

The Rhetoric of Virginia's Massive Resistance Movement

Ann E. Burnette

In February 2003, the Virginia Legislature passed a resolution expressing "regret" for the closing of Prince Edward County public schools in the aftermath of the 1954 *Brown v. Board of Education* decision.[1] In response to the *Brown* ruling that *de jure* (or legally sanctioned) segregation in public schools was unconstitutional, Virginians who sought to continue segregation organized a "massive resistance" to the Supreme Court's decision. The massive resistance movement in Virginia resulted in the temporary closing of public schools in Warren County, Charlottesville, and Norfolk, and a five-year closure of Prince Edward County schools in defiance of the order to desegregate public schools. Nearly a half-century after this response to *Brown*, legislators and citizens still debate the import of the massive resistance movement.

The *Brown* decision was significant for many reasons—the Court cast public education in a new light by calling it "the very foundation of good citizenship," and the Court supported its arguments for the first time with social science findings.[2] One of the most fundamental effects of this ruling was the way in which it promised to change the system of racial segregation that formed the basis of many laws and customs in Southern society. Civil rights advocates hailed *Brown* as a watershed event that would lead to a more egalitarian society. Those who opposed *Brown* also perceived the decision as the dawn of a new era. The Supreme Court's decision against segregation challenged a worldview which had enforced segregated behavior for generations.

Many Southern segregationists channeled their discontent with *Brown* into a campaign that came to be known as "massive resistance." While the massive resistance movement had many proponents and took various forms, its essence was that Southern states could simply and legally resist the orders of the Supreme Court if they chose to override the decision. This position was based on the assumption that the Civil War had not settled the issue of states' rights; although the Union had thwarted the Confederacy's attempt to secede, the Union's military triumph had not necessarily resolved the legal and political questions raised by secession. Advocates of massive resistance revived and defended this assumption in their discourse. In theory, massive resistance meant that the states could refuse both the constraints and the support of the federal government altogether. In practice, massive resistance translated into legislative action that was designed to nullify the Court's ruling or at least hinder its implementation. In defending these actions, advocates of massive resistance argued that the South was thus taking its last stand.

Citizens and politicians throughout the South endorsed massive resistance and defended segregation. Louisiana, Alabama, Mississippi, North Carolina, and South Carolina passed legislation to avoid complying with the *Brown* ruling.[3] As state and federal agencies clashed over the issue of integration and Southern indignation over the *Brown* decision mounted, many of the South's national representatives took up the debate and introduced "The Southern Manifesto: Declaration of Constitutional Principles" into Congress. This resolution denounced the *Brown* decision as "a clear abuse of judicial power" which "threatened to destroy the system of public education in some of the States."[4]

In Virginia, a group of legislators and citizens were among the most aggressive in the South to attempt to maintain a system of segregated schools. Government response at first seemed moderate. In the months immediately following the 1954 *Brown* decision, Governor Thomas Stanley affirmed that the state would follow the Court's edict, and he promptly appointed a commission to study the question of desegregation. Yet private citizens and political figures more closely allied with the political machine of Virginia U.S. Senator Harry Byrd quickly drew up their battle plans. In 1954 concerned citizens formed the Defenders of State Sovereignty and Individual Liberties, which helped propel the resistance effort. By 1956, the state's General Assembly had passed an interposition resolution addressing the Supreme Court's rulings. In the fall of 1958, the new governor, J. Lindsay Almond, ordered the public schools of Warren County, Charlottesville, and Norfolk closed to avoid integrating black and white students. And in the fall of 1959, the resisters continued the effort by closing the schools of Prince Edward County, which remained closed for five years.

This study analyzes the arguments that emerged during Virginia's campaign to resist the *Brown* decision. Virginia serves as a significant case study for three reasons. First, the closing of public schools in Virginia was the logical result of the state's massive resistance effort as it was articulated. While other Southern leaders such as Orval Faubus, George Wallace, and Ross Barnett took measures to close their schools in response to the prospect of integration, their stands, though highly publicized, were short-lived and not sustained by subsequent actions of the state. The massive resistance movement in Virginia was the most extreme instance of resistance exercised by a state legislature. Second, Virginia legislators and commentators were instrumental in framing the goals and methods of the massive resistance movement. It was Byrd who coined the term "massive resistance," and James J. Kilpatrick, editor of the *Richmond News Leader*, who spelled out the theory and provided the historical and philosophical underpinnings of the movement. Politicians and journalists from other states frequently consulted and referred to Virginia as the leader of the massive resistance movement. Virginia politicians and critics were therefore conscious of their roles as leaders in the movement, and it was common for public debate in Virginia to dwell upon the provenance and viability of the ideals of massive resistance. Finally, the public discourse that culminated in the closing of Virginia schools represented a view of the legal, political, and social ramifications of desegregation that many Southerners shared.

As Virginia leaders made their case for massive resistance, two categories of arguments emerged. One was a series of constitutional arguments based on the principle of state sovereignty. The other category contained arguments against segregation based on race. In making the constitutional argument for massive resistance, advocates used legal arguments regarding states' rights and drew on history as a framework for interpreting their experience. Proponents of massive resistance also frequently used racial arguments to justify the movement. The resisters asserted that African Americans were less intelligent than whites, that African Americans had debased moral values which threatened white society, that the inferiority of African Americans was innate, and that there were compelling practical reasons for the continuation of a racially segregated society. The constitutional argument gave the resisters a means to characterize their resistance to *Brown* as a stand for principles other than racism in the conflict over segregation. Indeed, some advocates recognized and commented on this opportunity to elevate their rhetoric in response to *Brown*. Yet the movement's simultaneous reliance on racial arguments seemed to sully the elevated nature of a constitutional debate. The development of these arguments and the relationship of these arguments to each other provide insight into the sometimes conflicting and ultimately untenable rhetoric of this twentieth century "Lost Cause."

The Constitutional Argument

One of the major themes of the massive resistance movement was that the *Brown* decision, and the resistance of it, did not raise primarily a racial issue, but rather one of states' rights. The states' rights argument was an important component of the resisters' discourse throughout the massive resistance effort. It enabled resisters to make an historical appeal for opposing *Brown* and to transcend the racial dimension of the segregation debate. The leaders of the movement drew from two sources to mount their constitutional argument: legal definitions and interpretations of history.

Legally and intellectually, the argument of massive resistance turned on a particular interpretation of state sovereignty. One of the principal theorists of massive resistance was James J. Kilpatrick, editor of the *Richmond News Leader*. He devoted many of his editorials as well as his books to explaining his view of state sovereignty and, from the beginning, used historical examples to build and illustrate his definition of the idea.

When Kilpatrick introduced his interposition strategy in his December 1955 *News Leader* editorials, he printed passages from the 1798 Virginia and Kentucky Resolutions, an excerpt from a 1799 report by James Madison in response to criticism of the Virginia resolutions, and an address by John C. Calhoun on the right of interposition. Kilpatrick offered to his readers "certain historic documents that shed light upon the evils of today that were prophetically seen long ago."[5] Quoting the language of the second Kentucky Resolution, Kilpatrick asserted that states "faced with a 'deliberate, palpable and dangerous exercise'" of federal powers had "'the unquestionable right' of a sovereign State, in such an emergency, to judge of the infraction of the Constitution," and to declare nullification of such acts.[6] Kilpatrick presented his most thoroughly documented argument for states' rights in his book *The Sovereign States: Notes of a Citizen of Virginia*, which appeared in 1957. In it, he was able to expand upon the case for state sovereignty that he had been printing in the *News Leader* since he introduced the idea in his editorial page.

Kilpatrick's strategy in *The Sovereign States* was to establish a working definition of a state, determine the powers that followed from statehood, and demonstrate that nullification of federal actions is one of the powers that naturally springs from the definition of a state. To this end, he traced a selective history of thought, legislation, and court decisions that concerned the respective roles of state and federal government since the American Revolution. He discussed the Continental Congress and the ratification of the Constitution, the Virginia and Kentucky Resolutions, Calhoun's theory of nullification, and the Fourteenth Amendment in order to argue that the *Brown* decision was a violation of states' rights. He summarized his definition of state sovereignty as "The will to make, the power to unmake."[7]

The state sovereignty argument of the 1950s' massive resistance movement had its roots in the historical debate regarding the relative powers of state and federal government. In 1798, Thomas Jefferson, in protest against the Alien and Sedition Acts passed during the John Adams administration, prepared a set of resolutions that was approved by the Kentucky Legislature. These resolutions asserted that the Constitution did not require states to demonstrate "unlimited submission to their general government"; rather, the Union consisted of a compact among states that delegated certain powers to a "general" federal government but reserved for states "the residuary mass of right to their own self-government."[8] If the federal government should assume "undelegated" powers, its actions would be "unauthoritative, void, and of no force," and each state in the compact had the power to declare such acts unconstitutional.[9] Later in 1798, the Virginia Legislature adopted similar resolutions which James Madison had written after he consulted with Jefferson. These resolutions declared that, "in the case of a deliberate, palpable, and dangerous exercise" of federal powers, the states "have the right, and are in duty bound, to interpose."[10] In 1799 the Kentucky Legislature passed a second set of resolutions authored by Jefferson. These resolutions echoed the Virginia Resolutions by calling for the states' right to nullify unconstitutional federal acts.

The Alien and Sedition Acts expired in 1800 and Jefferson was elected president that year; neither Virginia nor Kentucky attempted to nullify the Alien and Sedition Acts. In 1803 the Supreme Court handed down *Marbury v. Madison*, which asserted the authority of the Supreme Court to declare acts of Congress unconstitutional. During and after his presidency, Jefferson continued to argue against what he saw as the danger of an unchecked federal judiciary. He also defended the state powers outlined in the Virginia and Kentucky Resolutions, but during that time, no state attempted to exercise those powers, leaving the prospect of state nullification untested.

John C. Calhoun revived the compact theory of states with his doctrine of nullification. Calhoun proposed this doctrine in response to the 1828 "tariff of abominations" and the 1832 tariff bill, both of which heavily taxed the staples of the South's agrarian economy. Calhoun borrowed the idea that a state can nullify federal actions from the Kentucky and Virginia Resolutions. Calhoun called for South Carolina to exercise its right of nullification; this test of the doctrine proved to be moot. The South Carolina legislature passed a nullification resolution in 1832, and Congress countered by passing President Jackson's "force bill" in 1833. South Carolina lifted its nullification resolutions on the 1828 and 1832 tariffs before federal action was taken, and then nullified the federal force bill. South Carolina could claim rhetorical victory in that their nullification of the force bill was the last word. Advocates of the doctrine of nullification could also claim that nullification was a viable, constitutional right since it had not been invalidated.

Even after the Civil War, some Southern defenders of states' rights argued that states had a constitutional right to nullify federal actions. They disputed that the war had settled the matter of state sovereignty. Instead they claimed that the war had only settled a military issue and that congressional and state representatives of former Confederate states had passed and ratified the Thirteenth, Fourteenth, and Fifteenth Amendments under duress. Many Southern leaders included this interpretation of states' rights as part of the "Lost Cause" for which the South had nobly, but unsuccessfully fought.[11] According to Southern apologists, the Lost Cause which compelled the Confederacy to go to war was not slavery, but the defense of constitutional ideals.

The idea of state sovereignty appeared early in the discourse of Virginia politicians and legislators who responded negatively to *Brown*. Many state leaders used the language of state sovereignty to define the Supreme Court's action as unconstitutional and therefore untenable. On the day the ruling was announced, Senator Harry F. Byrd proclaimed the decision "the most serious blow that has yet been struck against the rights of the states in a matter vitally affecting their authority and welfare."[12] J. Lindsay Almond, then Virginia's attorney general, announced on the day the ruling was handed down that it "is a drastic blow at the right of the state to maintain its own public school system without interference from the Federal government."[13] These early statements foreshadowed the legal and philosophical basis that opponents of desegregation would try to establish.

As the massive resistance movement continued, its advocates remained determined to cast the segregation crisis in terms of this constitutional issue. In his 1958 gubernatorial inauguration address, Almond warned that the Supreme Court's usurpation of state power would hurt not only Virginia, but all the United States.[14] At a 1958 Labor Day picnic, Byrd told his guests, "We Virginians seek only to preserve . . . the sovereignty of our Commonwealth."[15] The strongest citizens' group in the massive resistance movement, The Defenders of State Sovereignty and Individual Liberties, took their name and their purpose from the idea of states' rights. Members pledged that they believed "the segregation of the races is a right of the state government; [and] in the sovereignty of the several states."[16]

During the late 1950s, several judicial rulings chipped away at the legal basis for Virginia's interposition against *Brown*. Still, resisters insisted that the idea of states' interposition was still viable. For example, Defenders of State Sovereignty and Individual Liberties President Robert B. Crawford refused to acknowledge the validity of the 1959 state and federal rulings against Virginia's massive resistance laws:

> My organization is no more ready to accept a little bit of integration than we were four years ago, because as soon as we accept a little integration we come down off the high plane of states' rights and recognize the authority of the Supreme Court. We still believe there has been an illegal interference by the federal courts and that Virginia has the right to operate its schools the way it wants to operate them.[17]

Crawford's description of the conflict over education pitted the Virginia educational system against the federal judiciary. His description of the "high plane of states' rights" was a notion that other resisters explored in much greater depth.

The leading Richmond newspapers and the governor tried to differentiate the larger philosophy of states' rights from its particular application to massive resistance. On the eve of the Virginia Supreme Court of Appeals decision on the constitutionality of the state's massive resistance laws, the *Richmond Times-Dispatch* reported that the legality of the state's massive resistance laws would be decided, but massive resistance as a state policy would be unaffected.[18] On January 19, 1959, the court announced its 5 to 2 decision invalidating massive resistance laws. In response to the decision, the *Times-Dispatch* editorialized that "The first thing we must do is retain our perspective. . . . The simple fact . . . is that this tangible abuse of federal power has not lessened Virginia's will to resist."[19] The *Richmond News Leader* called for the same perspective, telling its readers that "in yesterday's opinions, we lose some ground," but that the cause of states' rights was still alive.[20]

Governor Almond responded at first by supporting the massive resistance program, saying, "I will not yield to that which I know to be wrong."[21] A week later, though, he gave up the cause in his January 28 speech to a joint session of the legislature. Even while he acknowledged defeat in this speech, he did not surrender the idea of state sovereignty. "The General Assembly had pledged that it would resist unwarranted federal encroachment within honor and within the framework of the law," said the governor. "I have repeated that pledge to the people. It is as solemn and sacred now as when it was made."[22] In the speech, Almond made a distinction between what was practicable in terms of keeping the schools segregated and what was not. While he was admitting that not only the massive resistance laws, but any extralegal strategies or protests, were doomed to failure, he attributed this turn of events to "the dark maze of judicial aberration and constitutional exploitation" in which Virginia was stuck.[23]

Kilpatrick kept the states' rights debate alive even in the early 1960s, by which time most Virginia schools had been peacefully desegregated and the massive resistance movement was commonly disavowed. In his 1962 book *The Southern Case for School Segregation*, he admitted that "the immediate battle over school segregation has passed Virginia by," but he still insisted that the states' rights principles behind massive resistance should be understood.[24] He offered his familiar defense of state sovereignty and argued that this issue was still vital, despite the defeat of the states' rights argument in the segregation debate.

Kilpatrick's insistence on clinging to this argument is a dramatic illustration of the importance which resisters attached to it. The argument was a difficult one for them to abandon, despite its ultimate failure. The laws that the General Assembly passed based on a staunch view of states' rights were in effect for a relatively short period of time before they were struck down by federal and state courts. The idea of states' rights was one of the driving forces of the movement not only because of its legal ramifications (however short-lived), but because of the rhetorical possibilities it afforded the resisters. The states' rights argument enabled supporters of the movement to evoke a historical tradition, to place the

Brown decision in a larger political context, and to direct the argument against *Brown* away from the obvious racial dimension of the ruling.

Virginians also invoked their forebears to bolster their argument for massive resistance. Senator A. Willis Robertson delivered an Independence Day speech titled "The Origin and Meaning of Virginia's Declaration of Rights" at Shadwell, Virginia, the birthplace of Thomas Jefferson. In the speech, Robertson discussed Virginia's Declaration of Rights, authored by George Mason. Robertson traced the most important influences on Mason, including the Bible and the writings of John Locke. He finished his speech by applying Mason's ideas to the *Brown* decision and concluded: "All this heritage is now threatened . . . by those who would abandon the ancient landmarks."[25]

By turning to history to support their position on massive resistance, the leaders of massive resistance found ready-made arguments for the idea of interposition. But these rhetors did not merely borrow legal arguments from history; they also recalled the dramas that these legal conflicts had engendered, and they cast figures such as Jefferson, Madison, and Calhoun as heroes in these conflicts. Invoking these historical figures was a way to encourage support for massive resistance and motivate supporters to action.

As the massive resistance movement met with judicial setbacks, its discourse echoed the rhetoric of another historic episode—the South's articulation of its role in the Civil War. In 1958, Byrd declared, "We face the greatest crisis since the War Between the States."[26] In 1959, after the Virginia Supreme Court ruled against the state's massive resistance laws, supporters of the movement were quick to evaluate this event in terms of the Civil War. Virginia Congressional Representative Howard Worth Smith characterized the aftermath of the ruling by stating, "My own State of Virginia is today in a state of disturbance that has never existed since the Civil War."[27] This allusion to the Civil War called forth both the constitutional justifications of the war and the postbellum Lost Cause rhetoric which maintained that the war itself had not settled these constitutional issues. After the rejection of the state's massive resistance program, the president of the Defenders of State Sovereignty and Individual Liberties, Robert B. Crawford, stated, "We've always defended our public schools, but we'll go along with closing all the public schools rather than have any integration anywhere in the state."[28]

Advocates of massive resistance used the legacy of Jefferson, Madison, and Calhoun to help interpret and articulate their situation. Faced with the prospect of desegregating their public schools, they framed their response to *Brown* in terms of the historical debate over states' rights. By recalling the positions of Jefferson, Madison, and Calhoun, they were able to assume the role of protectors of a noble and neglected ideal. The fact that Jefferson and Madison had espoused this ideal enabled the resisters to align themselves with Founding Fathers who were widely revered. Massive resistance discourse honored ideals and heroes of the sectional conflict as well as the Revolutionary era. In declaring that they were willing to take their last stand, resisters echoed the theme of the Lost Cause in the rhetoric following the Civil War. The myth of the Lost Cause offered a source of regional pride and identity.

Another advantage to this use of history was that it portrayed massive resistance as conservative rather than radical. By drawing on the ideas of Jefferson and Madison in particular, the resisters could represent themselves as consistent with the founders of the union. In this light, massive resistance was not a defiant challenge of the Supreme Court's authority, but an attempt to rectify the imbalance of federal power.

A successful argument for school segregation on the basis of constitutionality was highly valued because it provided a way for the state to defend a racial practice without having to argue for it on racial grounds. Virginia, as one of the Jim Crow states, was vulnerable to the charge of racism. While many massive resistance advocates also articulated racist beliefs, the states' rights argument gave resisters a way to contend they were not racist.

Kilpatrick fully appreciated this ramification of the states' rights argument. At the time he was preparing and publishing his interposition editorials, he wrote to North Carolina Governor Luther Hodges, "[T]he significant thing, it seems to me, is that this approach transcends the racial issue, and thus elevates us to a higher ground of fundamental principles."[29] These fundamental principles were embraced by Byrd, Stanley, Almond, the editors of the *Richmond Times-Dispatch*, the Defenders of State Sovereignty and Individual Liberties, and the state delegates who fought to keep Virginia public schools segregated.

The argument of states' rights gave the resisters practical and argumentative strategies to fight *Brown*. Practically, the idea of states' rights gave rise to a legislative program designed to forestall public school integration. Although this practical application of the states' rights argument won the resisters only a temporary victory that was taken away from them fairly easily, the resisters pursued it nevertheless as a cogent plan to combat desegregation. The argumentative possibilities that the states' rights theme gave the resisters were perhaps more valuable to them. Massive resistance leaders used the idea of states' rights to refocus and elevate the debate and to assume the force of morality even though the legislative strategy did not prevail.

The Racial Argument

While proponents of massive resistance developed elaborate constitutional arguments defending segregation, they also utilized racial arguments to convey their objection to desegregation. Often the same rhetors would invoke both arguments to the same audience, and both arguments circulated widely during the massive resistance movement. The racial argument featured development of four themes. Resisters argued that African Americans were significantly less intelligent than white Americans. Second, proponents of massive resistance asserted that African Americans did not exhibit the same standard of morality as white Americans, particularly with regard to sexual behavior. Third, spokespersons of the movement sought to establish that these deficiencies in intellectual ability and morality were due to innate qualities rather than social conditioning. And, finally, advocates of massive resistance reasoned that segregation was necessary and beneficial because of pragmatic considerations related to differences between the races.

Although the journalists and politicians advocating massive resistance resurrected interposition to support their contentions, it is notable that legal arguments frequently included claims about race to supplement the legal pleadings for continued segregation. The attorneys for the Commonwealth of Virginia incorporated racial themes into the rearguments they submitted to the Court in late 1954 and early 1955. In this legal context, the Commonwealth argued that desegregation was undesirable because African Americans were less intelligent than their white counterparts. The evidence submitted by Virginia counsel specified the problems that would arise from black and white students sharing educational programs and facilities. "Is it not relevant to consider the general level of educational capacity and attainment between the two races?" asked the brief.[30] The commonwealth provided supplemental information that detailed the differences between white and black school children. A memorandum detailed the obstacles that served as impediments to integration, including the "level of educational attainment" of black and white children, as reflected in compulsory reading test scores and IQ test scores.[31] The state argued that the highest scoring quarter of black students did not perform as well as the lowest scoring quarter of white students. Although the memorandum stated that the argument for continued segregation was "not taken out of racial dislike," its overriding concern was that white students would be harmed by attending school with black students, whose educational capacities were far lower.[32]

Other opinion leaders expressed the concern that disparate intellectual levels would interfere with the education of white students. Virginius Dabney, editor of the *Richmond Times-Dispatch*, reiterated many of the state's objections to integrated education. In a 1957 address to the National Association of Secondary School Principals in Washington, D.C., Dabney observed that even in states where the integration of public schools had been "proceeding smoothly for the most part," there was still a "2- to 3-year educational lag . . . in the performance of Negro students by comparison with white students of the same age."[33]

Kilpatrick, who tried to develop nullification into a rigorous and compelling constitutional justification for massive resistance, also argued explicitly that blacks were inferior to whites intellectually, socially, and culturally. Although he purported in *The Sovereign States* to frame the South's resistance to integration in a historical and legal context, he devoted a short section of the book to discussing the nature of the Southern white and that of the Negro. One of the distinctions he made between the white and black populations was their relative IQ scores.[34]

In his books, Kilpatrick developed the claim that blacks were intellectually inferior in order to argue that black culture was itself inferior. He sought to establish that African culture was impoverished as compared to other cultures of the world, and that Africans had not contributed significantly to the collective knowledge or progress of humanity. To support this position, he wrote that he could not find any achievements of note among African civilizations. "From the dawn of civilization to the middle of the twentieth century, the Negro race, as a race, has contributed no more than a few grains of sand to the enduring monuments of mankind."[35] Responding to claims that historians traditionally have not studied African cultures and therefore have not recorded their accomplishments, Kilpatrick asked, "Well, then, where is this contrary evidence? What library houses the works of a Nubian Thucydides? Who was the Senegalese Cicero?"[36]

Kilpatrick also rejected the contention that African cultures have been creative and productive, although not by white European standards. He reasoned that the concern of the American South was not the value of black accomplishments to African societies, but the contribution of blacks to the culture of the South, which had a majority of white citizens who were primarily of Western European descent. He dismissed the question of a possible white bias in the judgment of black achievements:

> The Ubangi's mud huts may be the most artistic mud huts ever set out in the sun to bake; by tribal esthetics of the African bush, the Ashanti may be vastly more cultured than the Yorubas, and the Balubi superior to the Mogwandi. Or vice versa. These critical judgments are interesting. They are irrelevant, too.[37]

For the purpose of the school integration issue, Kilpatrick concluded that Africans' so-called lack of cultural accomplishments was another argument for segregating the races in educational facilities. Objections could be raised to Kilpatrick's argument on the grounds that desegregation involved American blacks rather than members of an African community. Kilpatrick contended that the meager accomplishments of African culture strengthened the claim that people of African descent—even those in the United States—were racially inferior to whites.

In his second book, *The Southern Case for School Segregation*, Kilpatrick echoed the state's argument that desegregating schools was not viable because intelligence test scores varied so dramatically between black and white students. According to this argument, the education of white students would be hampered by the presence of black classmates. Moreover, black and white adolescents could not realistically aspire to the same vocations; their educations did not serve the same function and therefore required different types of programs. Desegregation would also have a negative impact on both black and white educators; black teachers would lose the status they enjoyed within the segregated school system, and white instructors would often refuse to teach in an integrated setting.[38]

Arguments that black adults and black children were not as intellectually gifted as the white population led to claims that focused on the viability of desegregation. Even if this lack of intellectual ability could be demonstrated, African Americans could be pitied rather than despised. To create an appropriate scapegoat, the discourse of massive resistance had to invest blacks with more threatening qualities. Many of the racial arguments for massive resistance attacked the moral standards of the black population and frequently invoked sexuality. Massive resistance supporters did not hesitate to espouse this aversion openly; their discourse indicates that they assumed this sentiment was widely appreciated.

This argument appeared in the commonwealth's reargument brief. The supplemental memorandum listed "standards of health" as an impediment to integration. In this category was information about the relative incidence of tuberculosis, syphilis, and gonorrhea among the populations of black and white Virginians. According to the statistics presented, tuberculosis was nearly twice as common among blacks, and the rates of syphilis and gonorrhea were disproportionately high for the black population. The memorandum did not state what sectors of the population were the source for the figures (e.g., whether the statistics included children or only adults), but it did conclude that "[n]o white parent will welcome Negro students into the white schools when to do so would increase his child's exposure to such contagious diseases."[39] In addition, the state cited figures, under the category "standards of morality," regarding the higher rate of black illegitimacy.[40] The statistics that black children were ten times as likely as white children to be illegitimate led the lawyers to conclude that the "background of parental morality indicated by these figures dismays Virginia's white parents."[41]

Segregationists repeatedly pointed to the figures on the incidence of venereal disease among blacks, the black illegitimacy rate, and sexually permissive attitudes which they attributed to blacks. Kilpatrick supplemented his development of the constitutional case for massive resistance in *The Sovereign States* by describing the incidence of venereal disease and promiscuity among African Americans, as well as the black homicide rate.[42] In *The Southern Case for School Segregation*, Kilpatrick characterized the prevailing sexual mores among blacks as an attitude "which views the sexual act as casually as a good-night kiss," and which found its ultimate expression in "interracial 'Sex Clubs.'"[43] In a 1958 speech to the American Carpet Institute, U.S. Representative Burr P. Harrison described the consequences of public school desegregation in the District of Columbia. He told his audience that black students had contributed "the vilest sex talk, dirty writing on walls, foul and unspeakable language to teachers, and vicious and obscene tongue battles in classroom, as well as during recess."[44] In addition, Harrison warned, observers "reported an enormous increase in venereal disease, which included 13 colored girls of 6 years of age."[45] Two days after the Virginia massive resistance laws were struck down in 1959, Almond warned of "the livid stench of sadism, sex immorality and juvenile pregnancy infesting the mixed schools of the District of Columbia and elsewhere" which now might find their way into Virginia schools.[46]

The supporters of massive resistance frequently invoked the fear that desegregation would lead to a black invasion of previously white sectors of society, both in the public and private spheres. James Ely noted that, "Whether phrased discreetly or openly, aversion to social mixture with Negroes was a major element behind massive resistance."[47] Almond delineated an apocalyptic vision at a campaign rally during his gubernatorial race. "When the sociological hallucinations of the Supreme Court, backed by the bayonets of the Army, descend on Virginia and when Southside schools are closed," he told his audience, "Negroes will come knocking at your door."[48] In submitting a recommendation to the state's commission on education, F. D. G. Ribble and Hardy C. Dillard, two University of Virginia law professors, observed that white Virginians feared "engulfment." "The fear is that in a critical sector of life—the education of our white children—we will be engulfed and that, as a consequence of engulfment, our standards and the tone and quality of our way of life will be lowered," they wrote.[49] Pointing to the example of integrated schools in the District of Columbia, the Newport News's *Daily Press* reported that black students were both more likely to drop out of school and less likely to find employment after dropping out of school. The editor argued that local police attributed "sickening waves of crime" in the District to "this pool of idle youth."[50]

The vehement reaction to desegregation in schools was due in part to the resisters' belief that integration in education would naturally lead to integration in other, more intimate arenas. Because schooling has social as well as intellectual aims, desegregated schools would mean that black and white children would be engaging in social activities together, and this could quite easily spill over into other aspects of their lives. Several months after the first *Brown* ruling, C. Vann Woodward noted:

> It goes much deeper into the lives of the people and affects more of them and for a longer time than any previous decision. . . . It bears much more directly on the sensitive area Southerners call "social equality" than does the mixing of races at the polls, on the trains, in sports and amusements.[51]

Woodward was describing a slippery slope argument where school desegregation would lead to miscegenation.

Many supporters of massive resistance made these slippery slope arguments. Cary P. Flythe of the *Emporia Independent Messenger* warned in an editorial that no one could "improve on God's plan to keep the races separate and identifiable."[52] The *Richmond Times-Dispatch*'s Virginius Dabney addressed this fear more openly. He acknowledged that "it may be possible to argue that integration would not increase the likelihood of racial amalgamation." But, he continued, "even if we accept this argument, which I do not, the desirability that every race strive to maintain its own integrity seems to me to be indisputable."[53] Nevertheless, massive resistance proponents responded not only to the possibility of integrated schools, but also to the even more dire potential of black and white Virginians forming other kinds of social relationships that were not based, as traditional social arrangements had been, on black subservience.

This fear helps to explain the preoccupation with sexuality in some of the massive resistance discourse. Resisters made references to the possibility of interracial sexual unions; many equated desegregation with miscegenation. U.S. Representative Watkins M. Abbitt warned his Congressional colleagues that "[o]ur people are not going to accept integration of the races in the public schools or the mongrelization of the races."[54] Governor Almond told his constituents that he would not yield to "those whose purpose and design is to blend and amalgamate the white and Negro race."[55]

When discussing the immorality of blacks, the advocates of these racial arguments needed to claim that it was the innate nature of blacks and not segregated society itself which produced such an appalling moral standard. The NAACP Legal Defense Fund had sought to prove that it was segregation that produced feelings and behavior that reflected a sense of inferiority among Southern blacks. Kenneth and Mamie Clark testified that their research findings demonstrated that segregation had a negative psychological effect upon black school children.[56] Spokespersons of the massive resistance movement had to provide counterarguments for such claims.

As discussed earlier, the rearguments submitted by the Commonwealth of Virginia contained data indicating that black and white students performed at vastly different academic levels. The supplemental memorandum that was submitted with the brief also cited the results of "the standard psychological examination of the American Council on Education, generally designated as IQ tests, given to all high school seniors."[57] The score of the top quarter of white students was 103.2 (the scale of the test was not described), and the score of the lowest quarter of white students was 71.2. The score for the top quarter of black students, however, was 63.9.[58] By including these statistics in conjunction with the figures on school performance, the Virginia counsel suggested that black students had lower educational results than white students because of innate abilities. Neither the brief nor the memorandum addressed the possibility that the difference in these psychological test scores might, in fact, be caused by a segregated school system.

The Virginia Methodist Advocate, a statewide publication, published an example of this counterargument. An editorial titled "Integration and Moral Standards" listed statistics indicating a high rate of illegitimate black births, relative to the white rate of illegitimacy. The editor provided this interpretation of these data:

> There will be those, no doubt, who will say, "Well, it's all the result of segregation." But is it? Why then did not the white percentage equal that of the Negroes? Or there will be those who claim that the low economic status of the Negroes is the reason. But the State is filled with multitudes of poor whites. Besides, the Negroes have had much larger incomes in recent years than formerly, better schools and more cultural advantages. Yet, their record is getting worse rather than better as regards this matter of illegitimacy.[59]

This argument implicitly claimed that the high rate of illegitimacy among blacks was due solely to their race; moreover, this measure of black immorality showed signs of getting worse despite improvements in their material situation.

Kilpatrick also tried to dispel the idea that societal forces such as segregation, economic need, and prejudice accounted for the differences in health and crime statistics for whites and blacks. In discussing illegitimacy, he rejected the argument that the higher rate among blacks was due to social and economic factors. He wrote that the disparity did not result from a trend for the white community to underreport illegitimate births, the fact that white women had greater access to abortions, the social conditions in which blacks lived, or the historical influence of slavery on the structure of the black family. Furthermore, he pointed out that black leaders such as Carl Rowan and Thomas Henderson had stated that illegitimacy was a serious problem within the black community.[60] In addition, Kilpatrick argued that the black illegitimacy rate had increased since the advent of civil rights legislation, thus indicating that the socioeconomic status of blacks was not a factor.

The discourse of massive resistance routinely represented African Americans as less intelligent and capable than whites, highly likely to transmit disease, and possessing sexual attitudes that were not only indecent, but irresponsible. Segregationists who convinced their audiences that this was the real and immutable character of blacks provided a more immediate and threatening source of motivation than constitutional principles for resistance to desegregation.

A final dimension of the racial argument was pragmatism based on an assumption of racial differences. Massive resisters argued for the practicality of segregation in two ways. First, they claimed that desegregation was too logistically difficult to enact. And, second, leaders of the movement invoked pragmatism when they explained how black and white Southerners had managed to live together in Southern society. In this sense, pragmatism was not just a social tool, but a Southern virtue.

One of the racial arguments included in the briefs for reargument was that Virginia counties varied in terms of their black population, and desegregation would be more difficult in areas with a high percentage of black citizens. "The question of ratio of population has particular significance in Virginia," the brief stated. "The percentage of Negro school children ranges from zero in Buchanan, Craig and Highland Counties to 77.3% in Charles City County."[61] Virginia's counsel anticipated that forced integration was a more threatening prospect in counties with many blacks since this population ratio would be reflected in the schools. The emergence of staunch segregation advocates, such as The Defenders of Individual Liberties and State Sovereignty from the "black belt" counties of Virginia, supported this assumption. The brief argued that the sentiment against desegregation in these counties threatened the school systems throughout Virginia. School systems that faced the possibility of integrating a majority black population with a minority white population would move to close the state's schools rather than mix the black and white children in the county. In asking for the Court to permit "gradual adjustment" to the desegregation ruling, the Virginia brief warned, "It would be most unfortunate if the decision of this Court on May 17, 1954, affected adversely the schools in Craig County where there are no Negro pupils as well as those in Charles City County."[62]

The memorandum also developed another claim that was made in the brief. Under a system of integration, it would be impossible to reassign the black teachers currently employed by the state because they would be responsible for white children. "Virginia is not prepared to place Negro teachers in charge of white pupils," the commonwealth flatly asserted. According to the state, this condition presented two dilemmas: It would not be fair to the state's black teachers, and it would force the state to hire more teachers.[63]

While this defense of segregation emphasized the separation of the races, black and white Southerners nevertheless had frequent contact. Because of their minority status and their relatively impoverished economic standing, a routine employment situation for African Americans in the South was to be employed by whites. White Southerners frequently hired black laborers or domestics. It was common for black domestic workers to become intimately associated with white families. In this way, the races had a great deal of contact with each other, with status clearly defined. Because of this association, many segregationists needed to make allowances for some positive qualities demonstrated by blacks. Kilpatrick, for instance, acknowledged that there existed "hosts of decent, respectable, law-abiding Negro teachers, bankers, students, artisans, and servants," and noted, "*The South knows this better than any other region.*"[64] But these positive qualities of the black community could only exist in a narrowly defined context—a context where blacks were subservient and deferential to whites. In both of his books, Kilpatrick described comfortable interactions between black and white Southerners which depended on the participants of both races knowing and respecting the social hierarchy that Kilpatrick defended. He also depicted negative consequences that resulted from either white or black Southerners violating that hierarchy.[65] Outside of this context, in society at large, white segregationists claimed that blacks did not meet the minimum standards of decent white society. Kilpatrick spoke for this viewpoint when he asserted that "instead of ambition . . . we have witnessed indolence; instead of skill, ineptitude; instead of talent, an inability to learn."[66]

Describing African Americans as inherently inferior and yet tolerable within certain societal constraints suggests a contradiction. This inconsistency was not unusual in white Southerners' attitudes toward blacks. Myrdal noted:

> The trait which the whites perhaps associate most with Negroes is a tendency to be aggressive. . . . The tendency is exaggerated in the minds of the whites, and whites are ambivalent in their beliefs since they also frequently speak of the Negroes as docile, subservient, and dull.[67]

White Southerners who agreed with Kilpatrick addressed this ambivalence by arguing that Southerners were merely realistic about social inequality. Kilpatrick wrote that "the first reality he [the white Southerner] faces squarely is the one reality most often shunned: the *inequality* of man."[68] Segregationists defined this inequality as a condition where southern blacks may show aptitude for some limited skills or interactions, but ultimately were inferior. "Down deep," observed Kilpatrick, the relationship between white and black Southerners was "that of master and servant, superior and inferior."[69] This presumed black inferiority made a dual society necessary.

The dual society in Virginia, as in other southern states, was codified by the Jim Crow laws mandating the separation of blacks and whites in most public facilities. Spokespersons for massive resistance defended the tradition of segregation and suggested that both races lived contentedly in segregated society; presumably, the issue of desegregation would never have arisen had the Supreme Court not ordered it. Senator A. Willis Robertson bemoaned the call for desegregation and expressed his fear that "bitter animosities have been engendered in areas where heretofore peace and harmony have characterized racial relations."[70]

A final component of the resisters' pragmatic arguments was their assertion that white Southerners demonstrated wisdom in their pragmatic acceptance of the differences between the races. Kilpatrick noted in an editorial that "in defending racial segregation, we are defending a practice that to much of the Nation seems indefensible."[71] But, he argued, white Virginians knew and appreciated "the gulf that divides the mores of two disparate races."[72] The willingness to accept this fact demonstrated two things: that the South had a distinct history of race relations, and that the South should pride itself on its honesty regarding this issue. The resisters contended that their honesty, as represented in their discourse, was something that distinguished them from Americans who were either less perceptive, less honest, or both. When discussing the import of the *Brown* decision, Kilpatrick noted that the desegregation order called for the South to "breach the immutable law by which the South's character has been preserved."[73] The immutable law was that "white and black cannot come together, as equals."[74] The massive resisters used this idea of an immutable racial law to contrast themselves with Northerners in general and champions of desegregation in particular. Resisters argued that the South was not morally wrong to enforce a racial hierarchy; on the contrary, white Southerners were morally superior to people who were hypocritical enough to refuse to admit the nature of the law. Through this argument, supporters of massive resistance tried to turn the tables on those who would criticize the South's defense of segregation. The resisters could characterize their Northern critics as self-contradictory, which eroded the strength of any of their arguments for integration.

In an editorial describing white flight from New York City integrated schools, the *Richmond Times-Dispatch* noted, "Great numbers of white Northerners are fleeing headlong from the very thing the North wishes to force upon us."[75] Kilpatrick traced the present-day hypocrisy of the North to the days of the slave trade. He recalled the relationship between Northern slave traders and the Southerners with whom they did business and noted that "when the assignation ended, the South had all the problems, and the North had all the answers."[76] Representative Harrison also commented on this theme by remarking that racial integration "becomes an embarrassing cause when its practical applications approach too closely the ivory towers of the 'liberals.'"[77] Resisters represented themselves as pragmatic and honest about their motives, while Northerners, liberals, or anyone else who called for racial equality but did not enact it were hypocritical. This was consistent with the characterization of Southerners as realistic about social inequality. Resisters could thus claim moral superiority in their defense of segregation.

Conclusion

Advocates of massive resistance used a variety of channels and contexts to articulate their vision of the movement. The arguments appeared in traditional public sites, such as political speeches, newspaper editorials, and published books. Adherents of the movement also used communication channels to which the public had less widespread access, such as legal briefs and private correspondence. The wealth and variety of these sources give the critic an opportunity to assess the development of the massive resistance arguments in different stages and with regard to different audiences.

The architects of Virginia's massive resistance grounded their constitutional and racial arguments in historical arguments very early in the movement and relied on these historical arguments throughout the movement. According to the proponents of massive resistance, the legal strategy of the movement was not just a matter of legal arguments, but a continuation of the philosophical debates on the nature of state sovereignty in the eighteenth and nineteenth centuries. Similarly, the racial arguments supporting massive resistance represented a defense of long-standing cultural values. This use of history provided two benefits for the movement. First, early spokespersons for the movement, such as James Kilpatrick, could use these historical precedents to construct complete arguments early in the movement. Second, the invocation of history enabled the resisters to portray themselves as conservative in the face of the Supreme Court's decision. The *Brown* decision thus became a radical action that bespoke an encroaching federal agency and threatened the tradition the resisters represented and sought to preserve. The resisters could frame the outcome of massive resistance laws—the closing of public schools—as conservative rather than radical.

The variety of audiences to which the resisters addressed themselves is also significant. While it might be natural to assume that rhetors addressed different arguments to specific audiences, such patterns are not clear. Advocates of massive resistance seemed equally likely to use the constitutional and the racial themes of the movement whether they were addressing local, statewide, or national audiences. The two themes also appeared in both political and legal arguments. The resisters' decisions to use both the constitutional and racial arguments to local, state, and national audiences suggest that the resisters believed that their arguments would resonate with audiences within and outside of the state. Their framing of the constitutional and racial arguments as historical traditions can be viewed as an attempt to make the last stand of massive resistance more palatable to audiences who might otherwise view the movement as reactionary and racist.

Finally, the relationship of the constitutional themes to the racial themes within the massive resistance rhetoric invites examination. Virginia leaders worked assiduously to reestablish the constitutional arguments of states' rights and their right of interposition, and to base their justification for massive resistance measures on this higher ground. Rhetors within the movement expressed their awareness of this aspect of the constitutional argument. In his introduction of the idea of state sovereignty in the *Richmond News Leader*, Kilpatrick wrote that "measured against its solemn implications, problems of local school segregation, serious as they are, seem almost petty."[78] Yet, the advocates of massive resistance did not let that argument stand alone; they often invoked racial arguments to explain their position and move their followers. U.S. Congressional Representative William Tuck put the issue bluntly: "When these clouds are dispelled and dissipated and we get down to the plain unvarnished truth, there is but one question, and that is whether or not we favor or oppose the mixing of races in the schools."[79]

The dual line of argument may have been a reflection of the resisters' understanding of some of their audience members. Racism was a powerful social element and was, in all likelihood, more compelling than abstract constitutional principles were to an audience of citizens. The use of racial arguments also suggests that the constitutional argument was vulnerable. Although resisters viewed states' rights as the rhetorical high road, several, including Kilpatrick and former University of Virginia president Colgate Darden, expressed private doubts about whether or not that line of argument would be tenable. In this light, the use of racial arguments appears to be a disingenuous contradiction of the interposition claims. If the states' rights argument were truly transcendent, the race argument would not be necessary. The use of the race argument combined with the resisters' disclaimers about the transcendence of the states' rights argument called the sincerity of the states' rights argument into question. In this context, the constitutional arguments appeared to be a more respected and palatable cover for the resisters' race arguments. And the resisters' reliance on such blatant racial arguments may have signaled a fear that this last stand was more wishful than legitimate.

Notes

1. Karla Scoon Reid, "Va. Expresses 'Regret' for Closures Aimed at Resisting Desegregation," *Education Week*, 19 February 2003, 17.
2. *Brown v. Board of Education of Topeka*, 346 U.S. 483 (1954). References to social science data are in *Footnote 11*.
3. Francis M. Wilhoit, *The Politics of Massive Resistance* (New York: George Braziller, 1973), 34-36, 44.
4. "Declaration of Constitutional Principles," in 84th Congress, 2nd sess. *Congressinal Record* (12 March 1956), vol. 102, pt. 4, 4460.
5. "The Transcendent Issue, II," *Richmond News Leader*, 21 November 1955, 10(A).
6. "Kentucky-Virginia Resolutions," *Richmond News Leader*, 21 November 1955, 10(A).
7. James J. Kilpatrick, *The Sovereign States: Notes of a Citizen of Virginia* (Chicago: Henry Regnery Company, 1957), 9.
8. "Kentucky Resolutions, November 16, 1789," in *Great Issues in American History: From the Revolution to the Civil War 1765-1865*, ed. Richard Hofstadter (New York: Vintage Books, 1958), 177.
9. "Kentucky Resolutions," 177.
10. "Virginia Resolutions, December 24, 1798," in *Great Issues in American History: From the Revolution to the Civil War 1765-1865*, ed. Richard Hofstadter (New York: Vintage Books, 1958), 183.
11. See Waldo W. Braden, "Introduction," in *Oratory in the New South*, ed. Waldo W. Braden (Baton Rouge: Louisiana State University Press, 1979).
12. William S. White, "Ruling to Figure in '54 Campaign, *New York Times*, 18 May 1954, 20(A).
13. James Latimer, "Stanley to Confer on State's Next Step," *Richmond Times-Dispatch*, 18 May 1954, 7(A).
14. J. Lindsay Almond, "Inaugural Address," 11 January 1958, in 85th Congress, 2nd sess. *Congressional Record*, 13 January 1958, vol. 104, pt. 1, 286.

15. Quoted in Ben Beagle and Ozzie Osborne, *J. Lindsay Almond: Virginia's Reluctant Rebel* (Roanoke, Va.: Full Court Press, Inc., 1984), 110.

16. Quoted in Robbins L. Gates, *The Making of Massive Resistance: Virginia's Politics of Public School Desegregation, 1954-1956* (Chapel Hill: The University of North Carolina Press, 1962), 161.

17. "Views Are Mixed Over Steps to Be Taken in School Crisis," *Richmond Times-Dispatch*, 20 January 1959, 5(A).

18. Latimer, "'Massive Resistance' Laws Face Fateful Tests Tomorrow," *Richmond Times-Dispatch*, 18 January 1959, 1(A).

19. "Now to Find a New Plan," *Richmond Times-Dispatch*, 20 January 1959, 12(A).

20. "The Vice Closes," *Richmond News Leader*, 20 January 1959, 10(A).

21. Quoted in Beagle and Osborne, 113.

22. Almond, "Virginia Won't Weaken," 20 January 1959, in 86th Congress, 1st sess. *Congressional Record*, 21 January 1959, vol. 105, appendix A365.

23. Ibid.

24. Kilpatrick, *The Southern Case for School Segregation* (New York: The Crowell-Collier Publishing Company, 1962), 8, 106.

25. A. Willis Robertson, "The Origin and Meaning of Virginia's Declaration of Rights," 4 July 1961, in 87th Congress, 1st sess. *Congressional Record*, 7 July 1962, vol. 107, pt. 9, 12010.

26. "Virginia: The Gravest Crisis," *Time*, 22 September 1958, 15.

27. Howard Worth Smith, "Our Federal Constitution and Our Supreme Court," in 86th Congress, 1st sess. *Congressional Record*, 27 January 1959, vol. 105, pt. 1, 1221.

28. "Views Are Mixed over Steps to Be Taken in School Crisis," *Richmond Times-Dispatch*, 20 January 1959, 5(A).

29. Kilpatrick to Luther Hodges, 21 December 1955, James J. Kilpatrick Papers (no. 6626-b), Manuscripts Department, University of Virginia Library, Charlottesville, VA.

30. *Davis v. County School Board of Prince Edward County*, 347 U.S. 483 (1954), Brief for Appellees on Further Reargument (15 November 1954), 15.

31. *Davis v. County School Board of Prince Edward County*, 347 U.S. 484 (1954), Supplemental Memorandum for Appellees on Further Reargument (8 April 1955), 4.

32. *Davis*, Supplemental Memorandum, 4-5.

33. Virginius Dabney, "Address to National Association of Secondary School Principals," 26 February 1957, in 85th Congress, 1st sess. *Congressional Record*, 8 March 1957, vol. 103, pt. 3, 3349.

34. See Kilpatrick, *The Sovereign States: Notes of a Citizen of Virginia* (Chicago: Henry Regnery Company, 1957), 279-282.

35. Kilpatrick, *The Southern Case for School Segregation*, 50.

36. Ibid.
37. Ibid., 52.
38. See ibid., 90-92.
39. See *Davis*, Supplemental Memorandum, 5.
40. Ibid.
41. See ibid.
42. Kilpatrick, *The Sovereign States*, 279-282.
43. Kilpatrick, *The Southern Case for School Segregation*, 63-64.
44. Burr P. Harrison, "Address to the American Carpet Institute," 23 October 1958, in 86th Congress, 1st sess. *Congressional Record*, 15 January 1959, vol. 105, pt. 1, 755.
45. Ibid.
46. Almond, "Virginia Won't Weaken," in 86th Congress, 1st sess. *Congressional Record*, 21 January 1959, vol. 105, appendix A365.
47. James W. Ely, Jr., The Crisis of Conservative Virginia: The Byrd Organization and the Politics of Massive Resistance (Knoxville: The University of Tennessee Press, 1976), 95.
48. Quoted in Ben Beagle and Ozzie Osborne, *J. Lindsay Almond: Virginia's Reluctant Rebel* (Roanoke, VA: Full Court Press, 1984), 91.
49. "Statement to Commission on Education," 6 March 1959, Leon Dure Papers (no. 9751), Manuscripts Department, University of Virginia Library, Charlottesville, VA.
50. "Where Integrated Schools Break Down," *Newport News Daily Press*, 16 February 1959, in 86th Congress, 1st sess. *Congressional Record*, 17 February 1959, vol. 105, appendix A1143.
51. C. Vann Woodward, *The Strange Career of Jim Crow*, 2nd ed. (New York: Oxford University Press, 1966), 149.
52. "Impressions and Expressions," *Emporia Independent Messenger*, 8 July 1954, in 83rd Congress, 2nd sess. *Congressional Record*, 15 July 1954, vol. 100, appendix A5101.
53. Dabney, "Address to National Association of Secondary School Principals," 26 February 1957, in 85th Congress, 1st sess. *Congressional Record*, 8 March 1957, vol. 103, pt. 3, 3350.
54. Watkins M. Abbitt, "Segregation of the Public Schools of Virginia," in 84th Congress, 2nd sess. *Congressional Record*, 18 January 1956, vol. 102, pt. 1, 851.
55. Almond, "Virginia Won't Weaken," A365.
56. Richard Kluger, *Simple Justice: The History of Brown v. Board of Education and Black America's Struggle for Equality* (New York: Vintage Books, 1977), 315-321, 544-545, 555-557.
57. *Davis*, Supplemental Memorandum, 4-5.
58. Ibid., 5.

59. "Integration and Moral Standards," *Virginia Methodist Advocate*, in 85th Congress, 2nd sess. *Congressional Record*, 18 July 1958, vol. 104, appendix A6456.

60. Kilpatrick, *The Southern Case for School Segregation*, 63.

61. *Davis*, Brief for Appellees, 14.

62. Ibid., 15.

63. See *Davis*, Brief for Appellees.

64. Kilpatrick, *The Sovereign States*, 281.

65. See, for instance, Kilpatrick, *The Sovereign States*, 255-258, and *The Southern Case for School Segregation*, 13-101.

66. Kilpatrick, *The Southern Case for School Segregation*, 35.

67. Gunnar Myrdal, *The American Dilemma: The Negro Problem and Modern Democracy* (New York: Harper & Row, 1944; reprint, New York: Harper & Row, 1962) 957.

68. Kilpatrick, *The Southern Case for School Segregation*, 36.

69. Ibid., 24.

70. Robertson, "Freedom of Association," in 84th Congress, 2nd sess. *Congressional Record*, 5 March 1956, vol. 102, pt. 3, 3964.

71. "Interposition, Now!" in *Interposition: Editorials and Editorial Page Presentations* (Richmond,VA: Richmond News Leader, 1959), 18.

72. Ibid.

73. Kilpatrick, *The Sovereign States*, 281.

74. Ibid.

75. "They Flee but Force It on Us," *Richmond Times-Dispatch*, 3 February 1957, in 85th Congress, 1st sess. *Congressional Record*, 4 February 1957, vol. 103, appendix A726.

76. Kilpatrick, *The Southern Case for School Segregation*, 35.

77. Harrison, "The Unsteady Liberals of Morningside Heights," in 85th Congress, 1st sess. *Congressional Record*, 26 June 1957, vol. 103, appendix A5143.

78. "The Right of Interposition," *Richmond News Leader*, 22 November 1955, 10(A).

79. William M. Tuck, "Address at Longwood College," 5 January 1956, in 84th Congress, 2nd sess. *Congressional Record*, 18 January 1956, vol. 102, pt. 1, 851.

6

The Supreme Court's Rhetoric of Legitimization

Ann M. Gill

A central rhetorical task facing the Supreme Court when it renders a decision upsetting the actions of a democratically elected legislative body is the need to assert its authority to do so. Any rhetorical text must establish its authority to speak, according to James Boyd White, who situates law as a branch of rhetoric.[1] The nature of such authority is both intellectual and institutional, as the perceived stature of the individual or institution that creates the text as well as the perceived rationality of the text combine to establish its legitimacy.[2] Following its 1954 decision in *Brown v. Board of Education*,[3] the Court faced a crisis of legitimization, to which it responded in very different ways in its next two school desegregation decisions.

The Supreme Court must establish its authority to declare acts of Congress or state legislatures unconstitutional because that power is not articulated in the Constitution. Learned Hand finds some judicial authority in the Preamble; he argues that courts derive their power "from the 'People of the United States' who 'ordain[ed] and establish[ed]' the Constitution."[4] However, the Supreme Court specifically gave itself the power to "say what the law is" in *Marbury v. Madison*, an 1803 case authorizing courts to determine whether legislative action runs afoul of the Constitution; this activity is "the very essence of judicial duty," according to Chief Justice John Marshall writing for a unanimous Court.[5] The legitimacy of the Court, along with its continued authority to "say what the law is," therefore, is implicit in all its decisions. When this authority is challenged, the Court must find ways to reestablish itself as the authoritative voice of constitutional interpretation as well as its final arbiter.

This is the circumstance the Supreme Court faced in the second half of the decision in *Brown v. Board of Education* and even more directly in *Cooper v.*

Aaron, a case arising out of the attempt to desegregate Central High School in Little Rock, Arkansas. In the former, the Court attempts to bridge the constitutional chasm between its decision in the first half of *Brown* and Southern resistance to desegregation by adopting rhetorical strategies of appeasement. The opinion features a narrative of desegregation that proposes a partnership between federal courts and school districts, which will make good faith efforts to transition from segregated to integrated public schools. However, when Southern resistance intensified rather than abated following that decision, the Court switched strategies. The story in *Cooper v. Aaron* vilifies the Arkansas governor and legislature for challenging *Brown*, articulates the duty of states to desegregate public education and revises the timetable for doing so, and, in the strongest available manner, reasserts its own authority.

Response to *Brown*

Brown v. Board of Education has been hailed as the most important case handed down by the U.S. Supreme Court in the twentieth century. Called the beginning of the "revolution in the American law of race relations"[6] and "a nuclear event in American constitutional law,"[7] the decision provoked immediate public response. Newspaper editorials either praised or reviled the decision. *The Daily News* in Jackson, Mississippi, for example, editorialized: "Human blood may stain Southern soil in many places because of this decision but the dark red stains of that blood will be on the marble steps of the United States Supreme Court building."[8] Some Southern leaders denounced the decision, including Mississippi Senator James Eastland, who charged that the Supreme Court "in the false name of law and justice has perpetuated a monstrous crime"[9] and announced "we do not intend to permit a crowd of parasitic politicians, who now sit on the Supreme Court bench, to destroy those great institutions and the great culture which are now in full flower in the Southern States—the culture of the Anglo-Saxon."[10] A number of other white Southern politicians also spoke of defiance or resistance to *Brown*, but most did not threaten violent action. Others, including Arkansas Governor Francis Cherry, announced their intention to "obey the law."[11] In the South, the decision became an issue in the elections that year.[12] Numan Bartley summarizes the year as one of various reactions in the South: "The Deep South sank deeper into hysterical reaction, while border states cemented their psychological identification with the nation, and the peripheral South, like an unstable planet, swayed between the magnetic attraction of North and South."[13]

There was little federal government support following the decision. President Eisenhower is reported to have condemned the decision in private as morally repugnant and politically confusing, although he publicly denied having said anything other than the Court was moving too fast. Indeed, Eisenhower made few public statements on the topic and certainly none praising the Court's decision. Evidence suggests that the president was comfortable with the world of separate educational facilities that existed throughout the South, and while reaction to *Brown* and desegregation escalated, he remained disengaged.[14] Eisenhower's inaction followed a pattern of federal government behavior toward the South established during the first half of the twentieth century. Although immediately following the Civil War the federal government had intervened both with troops and criminal prosecutions to protect black citizens from white violence, by the turn of the century, federal nonintervention in the South was the norm. Michal Belknap notes that disengagement during the pre-*Brown* period not only was federal policy, but also "constitutional dogma," a reference to the Court's 1896 decision in *Plessy v. Ferguson* that upheld the constitutionality of a state law requiring blacks and whites to travel in separate railway cars.[15]

Most telling regarding the states' response to *Brown* was that few schools had made any move toward desegregation when they opened in the fall of 1954.[16] Despite the lofty place the *Brown* decision now occupies in U.S. law, the decision proved a necessary but not sufficient condition for social change. Southern recalcitrance played a major role, but the Court itself may have helped stall desegregation by bifurcating the *Brown* decision. Despite ruling segregation in public education denied equal protection in 1954, the Court failed to identify the remedy for the plaintiffs; instead, it set the issue of remedy for reargument, which did not occur until the following Court term. Agreeing to bifurcate the decision was part of the negotiation for unanimity in the first *Brown* decision; it allowed Justice Frankfurter to support the decision that separate schools were inherently unequal while remaining very apprehensive about the problem of implementing that decision. Frankfurter also was central to postponing the rehearing on remedy, first because of the death of Justice Jackson and then until after the election in fall of 1954, so the Court's decision on implementation would not become an issue in the campaign.[17]

When the Court took up the remaining issue in a decision now known as *Brown II*, it was faced with deciding how desegregation of public education was to proceed, what the timetable would be, and how progress would be monitored. The Court considered *amicus curiae* or "friend of the court" briefs from Southern states and the federal government on these issues. The federal government took the position that the Court should be flexible with regard to a timetable and seemed to reflect the same "hands-off-the-South attitude" that President Eisenhower exhibited.[18] When the Court delivered its decision on May 31, 1955, it did not back away from the constitutional principle it established the prior term, but it also did not deliver the expected clarity regarding deadlines for desegregation. It held that federal district courts were to supervise desegregation in education, and it was to happen "with all deliberate speed," taking into account the public interest and particular issues of a school system.[19] The decision did nothing to quell the anger engendered by *Brown I*; some commentators argue its ambiguous language encouraged Southern defiance and the violence that marked the ensuing years of the Civil Rights Movement.[20]

For the remainder of 1955, most resistance to the decisions in *Brown* took place in courtrooms and in campaigns for public opinion and political support. When black parents went to court to demand desegregation, white officials opposed them. The *Richmond News Leader* editorialized that automatic acceptance of the Court's authority followed the decision in *Brown I* because Southerners "too long accustomed to submissiveness" acknowledged the Court as "supreme." The editorial argued for the "*right of interposition*," a notion that states have the right to place their sovereign powers between citizens of the state and the federal government.[21] One week later, in another editorial, the paper called on the Virginia legislature to "challenge this deliberate, palpable and dangerous encroachment of the Federal Government upon the amendatory rights of the States" by asserting that states "are not bound in honor, or in duty, or in law to abide by unconstitutional decrees."[22] Some private political organizations were created to oppose desegregation, including the various Citizens' Councils of the Deep South, organizations that were overtly racist. Soon, there was discussion of interposition in every Southern state, and it was on the agenda of the Councils to nullify the Court's decision in *Brown.*[23]

Many of the writings about this period focus on the white community in the South and the growing resistance to desegregation. The black community generally became more focused on the goal of desegregation. As Daisy Bates writes in her account of the crisis at Little Rock's Central High School, to the black community, *Brown I* "meant that the time for delay, evasion, or procrastination was past."[24] Expecting but not receiving an immediate desegregation order as part of the Court's decision, black citizens grew impatient. A series of murders then galvanized the community to action, particularly the kidnapping, brutal beating, and murder of Emmett Till, a teenager from Chicago who was visiting relatives in the Mississippi Delta. Till, in response to a dare from local youth, apparently either whistled at or said something like "bye, baby" to a white woman working in a store. The Northern youngster, who was not familiar with the racial etiquette demanded by white Southerners, was later abducted from his uncle's home by the white woman's husband and brother-in-law, according to eyewitness testimony. A grand jury refused to indict the two men for kidnapping, and an all-white jury acquitted both of murder charges. The press gave wide coverage to this travesty of justice, and when Emmett's mother held an open casket funeral in Chicago so the world could see her son's battered body, the case became a cause célèbre.[25]

White resistance to *Brown* became a revolutionary force in March of 1956.[26] Ninety-six Southern members of Congress signed "The Southern Manifesto," a document that excoriated the decision and pledged to "right this wrong." The strident language of the "Manifesto" proclaimed the Court had "exercise[d] their naked judicial power and substituted their personal political and social ideas for the established law of the land." Citing states' rights to control public education, the "Manifesto" labeled the Court's decisions in *Brown* and other civil rights cases as "encroachments" on those rights and "a clear abuse of judicial power." The "Manifesto" praised the 1896 decision *Brown* eviscerated, *Plessy v. Ferguson*, as displaying "elemental humanity and commonsense" in ruling that "separate but equal" public transportation facilities did not violate the Fourteenth Amendment.[27] The "Manifesto" argued that *Plessy's* interpretation had become "a part of the life of the people"; it "confirmed their habits, customs, traditions, and way of life." [28] Legislatures in Alabama, Georgia, Mississippi, South Carolina, and Virginia enacted forty-two pieces of prosegregation legislation in the first few months of 1956, adopting a strategy of "massive resistance" to *Brown* and desegregation.[29] Demagogues characterized the issue as not only states' rights versus federal rights, but also as a question of survival of the so-called Southern way of life.

The Court waded directly into this maelstrom of Southern defiance in 1958 when it heard *Cooper v. Aaron*. This was the only major opinion involving desegregation that the Court issued between 1955 and 1963.[30] One commentator argues that, during these years and on the issue of school desegregation, the Supreme Court "spoke mainly when it absolutely had to: at the point of crisis when obstruction was so apparent, delay so prolonged, or violation of constitutional principle so manifest that quiet was no longer feasible."[31] Such were the circumstances surrounding the *Cooper v. Aaron* case, which grew out of the attempt to desegregate Central High School in Little Rock, Arkansas. When Arkansas Governor Orval Faubus ordered the Arkansas National Guard to prevent nine black students from entering Central High, the Court's authority was challenged as it never had been before.

No one expected a crisis in Little Rock. The city seemed an unlikely site for this challenge to the Court's authority to declare segregated schools in violation of the Equal Protection Clause of the Fourteenth Amendment. Little Rock was not located in the Deep South, and the business community was considered progressive.[32] A number of interracial civic groups were in existence, and one of the city's newspapers supported integration in its editorials. Black citizens voted freely in party primaries and general elections, and the city bus system and other public sites were integrated.[33]

The Little Rock Independent School District worked for over a year on its plan for desegregation in compliance with the *Brown* decisions, nonetheless taking full advantage of the Court's invitation in *Brown II* to procrastinate. When first articulated, the plan called for the Little Rock high schools to be integrated first, then other levels of the school system. Superintendent of Schools Virgil Blossom, in the first draft of the plan, specified that two new buildings, one intended to be an all-black junior high school and the other an all-white high school, would be integrated high schools in the first phase. However, when the Little Rock School District published the final version of the plan, some changes had occurred. It provided token first steps at integration to be taken at Central High School, which served a working-class white population, starting in the fall of 1957.[34] This change in plan put the responsibility for integration on white working-class families and created not only racial, but class tensions.[35] The plan did not please the black community either; Daisy Bates argues that many black parents were convinced the superintendent "was more interested in appeasing the segregationists . . . than in complying with the Supreme Court's decision."[36] However, the superintendent and school board at least were moving forward with a desegregation plan as *Brown II* required.

Counter forces to this progress toward desegregation existed at the state level. In 1956, by a fairly close margin, the voters of the state had approved an amendment to the Arkansas state constitution that required the Arkansas General Assembly to oppose "in every Constitutional manner the Un-Constitutional desegregation decisions" in *Brown*.[37] Although this amendment provided some kindling, the real fuel for the Little Rock crisis came from a small group of Arkansas citizens involved in the Council movement, calling themselves the Capital Citizens' Council. The group launched a propaganda effort against integration, aimed at forcing the governor's hand. Members of the Council may have been responsible for rumors about impending violence and certainly were responsible for disruptions at school board meetings, which they then used in calling for the Arkansas governor to intervene in order to avoid violence and to preserve the system of segregated schools in Little Rock.[38] Governor Faubus started his political career appearing to be a progressive, but he soon bent with the political winds.[39] Determining that endorsement of desegregation would be political suicide, he announced support for the philosophy of interposition. The governor apparently gauged those political winds accurately, as he was reelected in a landslide in 1956.[40]

Black parents, meanwhile, became disenchanted with the desegregation plan as it devolved into the registration of a few token black students at Central High, and they took legal action. When the new high school, which was to have been integrated under the superintendent's original desegregation plan, opened, some black parents took children there in an attempt to register, but were turned away. The NAACP filed suit on their behalf in federal court in February of 1956. However, the federal district judge upheld the Little Rock desegregation plan, as nothing in *Brown II* made its policy of gradualism unconstitutional. The court found that the superintendent and school board "acted in the utmost good faith . . . to faithfully and effectively inaugurate a school system in accordance with the law as declared by the Supreme Court," and it refused to substitute its own judgment for that of the board's about an appropriate plan for desegregation. The court also maintained jurisdiction over the plan.[41]

The Little Rock school district became caught in the grip of forces beyond its control. The Capital Citizens' Council mounted a challenge to the desegregation plan, asking the board to stop the scheduled start date of fall 1957 and rallying others to support them. Concerned about the Council's actions, Superintendent Blossom requested a commitment from the Little Rock chief of police to support the school board's desegregation plan but failed to secure it. Similarly, a federal judge refused when Blossom requested that he make a public pronouncement on the consequences of blocking Court-ordered desegregation, and Governor Faubus refused Blossom's request for a public statement that he would retain order and not allow interference with the desegregation plan. Faubus instead released a public opinion poll showing a significant majority of Arkansas citizens opposed integration.[42] A representative of the Eisenhower administration came to Arkansas at the governor's request and indicated that the president did not want to be involved and would not be responsible for maintaining order.[43]

Nevertheless, the Little Rock School Board proceeded with plans for desegregation as required by the federal district court, and nine black students prepared to enroll at Central High for the fall term. On September 2, 1957, Governor Faubus declared a state of emergency and ordered the Arkansas National Guard to Central High School. This was the first time in history that a state had used troops to defy a decision by the U.S. Supreme Court, and the school authorities petitioned the federal district court for instructions. The school term started the next day, but the black students were not in class due to the presence of the National Guard on the school grounds. The following day, when one black student, Elizabeth Eckford, tried to enter Central High, she was turned away by the National Guard, and a crowd of white protesters screamed racial epithets at her. The federal court responded to the school board's "Petition for Instruction" by ordering the school district to move forward with the plan for integration of Central High School.[44] For the next three weeks, the situation at Central High was at an impasse; the nine students stayed home, and the Guardsmen remained surrounding the school.

On September 10, Governor Faubus received a summons to appear in federal court on a contempt proceeding for defying a federal court order. Four days later, he met secretly with Eisenhower, who urged him to back down. Faubus then was ordered by a federal court on September 21 to cease interfering with desegregation, and he responded by withdrawing the National Guard from the high school grounds.[45] On September 23, eight of the black students walked into Central High School as city police held back the crowd, which began to riot once they realized the black students were in the building. Fearing for the students' safety, officials secreted them out of the school in the middle of the day. Following this incident, Eisenhower finally was roused to action; the president later explained his action in his memoirs, noting that defiance of federal court orders "could lead to a breakdown of law and order."[46] The president dispatched troops from the 101st Airborne to Little Rock and later federalized the Arkansas National Guard, who now were under orders not from the governor to prevent the black students from entering the high school but from their commander in chief to uphold the federal court's decision that the desegregation plan must proceed. With military helicopters circling overhead and soldiers ringing the school grounds, the nine black students and their white classmates began the first year of integrated education at Central High School on September 25, 1957.

The first day of integration was marred by a bomb threat, and the black students' experience at Central High was marred by jeers and taunting from white classmates. Fearing further violence, the school board petitioned the federal court for a postponement of their desegregation plan. The district court granted the petition, but was reversed on appeal by the Eighth Circuit Court of Appeals, setting the stage for the Supreme Court's consideration of the issue in *Cooper v. Aaron*. The state's position in the appeal was that the governor and legislature of a state were not required to follow all Supreme Court decisions, specifically those in the area of public education. The Supreme Court rejected that position and affirmed the judgment of the Court of Appeals, ruling that no state could nullify the constitutional right to attend public schools without discrimination. In the process, the Court reaffirmed *Brown* as the supreme law of the land.

The Court's decisions in the *Brown II* and *Cooper v. Aaron* cases offer a fascinating contrast in rhetorical strategies for legitimization. Although the Court's authority to interpret the Constitution is at stake in both cases, the Court adopts an accommodating posture in *Brown II*. In *Cooper*, the Court makes no pretense at accommodation to the South; its every rhetorical move operates to reestablish its authority to interpret the Constitution and to make clear the duty of states to be bound by and follow that interpretation.

Brown II

The potential of a challenge to the Court's authority was a central focus of the justices' deliberations in the second half of the *Brown* case, but the opinion's rhetorical strategies are directed at appeasement. The Court faced a variety of concerns, both from the justices and the executive branch. One concern was that states would resist desegregation; another was that the ruling would engender violence.[47] Members of the Court also were not anxious to expose the judiciary's lack of enforcement mechanism. During the Court's private conference discussions of the case, Justice Minton argued the Court's foremost goal should be to get desegregation started without revealing the Court's enforcement impotence. Justice Black argued for avoiding issuance of orders that the Court was powerless to enforce.[48] Other justices expressed hope that the Court could avoid the appearance of arbitrariness or "mere imposition of a distant will."[49] Unanimity was, in the justices' minds, essential once again in *Brown II;* indeed, the Court sacrificed other rhetorical opportunities to achieve this desired end. Thus, as in all judicial opinions, the final text is the result of many compromises that allowed the decision to become the opinion of a unanimous Court, resulting in a decision that, in the words of one critic, "reflected compromise and equivocation in virtually every line."[50]

The justices' unanimity was intended to serve as a statement of strength; other textual features, however, undercut any authoritative posture. First, the delay in issuing this portion of the decision, which addressed a remedy for plaintiffs, runs counter to the Court's attempt to speak with authority. If the justices meant to maximize the Court's authority to announce the principle and its implementation, they should not have bifurcated the decision. Second, what we know of the justices' deliberations confirms the text's message of appeasement rather than establishment of authority. During conference discussions, Justice Black supported his argument for brevity in the written opinion by noting that the Deep South was only beginning to display some respect for the Court's authority, and that progress would be halted by an overly long or heavy-handed opinion in *Brown II*.[51]

The opinion is, indeed, very short and anything but heavy handed. It begins with the strongest statement of the entire text, a reiteration of the law it had declared in the first half of the case: "These cases were decided on May 17, 1954. The opinions of that date, declaring the fundamental principle that racial discrimination in public education is unconstitutional, are incorporated herein by reference. All provisions of federal, state, or local law requiring or permitting such discrimination must yield to this principle."[52] That mild and uninspiring reiteration of *Brown I* essentially ends any rhetorical effort by the Court to establish a powerful institutional persona in this text. Instead, the opinion sets out a story of a patient Court that is very attendant to the needs of states and school districts and of its attempts to be understanding of the situations faced by the defendants and segregated schools throughout the South.

L. H. LaRue analyzes constitutional law as a branch of rhetoric and argues that for courts to be persuasive in their rendition of constitutional law, they tell stories that support that view, just as history tells stories. These stories are fictional not because they are not true, but because humans can never know the truth of the past absolutely and so are left to fill in the gaps. Further, in the telling, stories by necessity leave out many of the myriad details as well as characterize events in particular ways from particular points of view. It is these fictions, argues LaRue, that make stories persuasive. Although this is true in any arena of human activity, in constitutional law, where "caution, care, and meticulous attention to detail" are what is expected of, and by, the Court, resulting in often pedantic recitation of facts and precedents, "one should listen for that moment in legal discourse when a story is told" because it reveals the human reality of constitutional law.[53]

The Court's storytelling in *Brown II* is not difficult to locate; the short opinion is mostly story and very little citation of legal theory or precedent. Warren's opinion recounts the Court's invitation to "the Attorney General of the United States and the Attorneys General of all states requiring or permitting racial discrimination in public education" to present their views on the question of the appropriate remedy for plaintiffs, both by filing legal briefs and by participating in oral argument. The story paints the Court in an accommodating posture by praising these contributions as "informative and helpful," acknowledging the "good faith" steps some school districts had taken toward desegregation and characterizing the task before the Court as complex. The story's end, which is the decision on the timetable for desegregation, is foreshadowed in the third paragraph of the opinion when it references the "transition" that faces segregated public education.

The tone and language of this text is remarkably counter to that in *Brown I*. Rather than standing on its announced constitutional principle and demanding an immediate end to segregated education, which is the usual remedy that accompanies a judicial finding of unconstitutional action by the government, the Court states that "full implementation" of this constitutional principle "may require solution of varied local school problems," and it acknowledges that the locus of authority for solving educational problems is school authorities. The role the opinion sets for courts is to "consider" whether those individuals acted in "good faith," which is a remarkably deferential treatment of constitutional violators by the very institution that has announced it has the authority to determine both the existence of and remedy for such violations. The Court takes itself out of the supervision of desegregation by assigning that role to federal district courts located in the regions involved, thereby again setting itself in an appeasing relationship to segregated school districts.

The antiauthoritarian structure and tone of this opinion is heightened by language describing the timetable for desegregation. The much-maligned phrase "with all deliberate speed" is the strongest description in the opinion with regard to timing.[54] Its effect is further tempered by the previous paragraph that refers variously to the timing of desegregation. District courts are to require the defendants to "make a prompt and reasonable start toward full compliance" and to admit plaintiffs to public schools "as soon as practicable," a term used twice within the span of two paragraphs. Once a start is made, a court can allow "additional time" and can consider a whole list of problems that may make speedy desegregation unworkable—problems ranging from transportation to revision of school districts to revision of local laws and regulations. This list functions as a Court-sanctioned set of acceptable excuses for delay while masquerading as a statement of a federal district court's authority for continuing jurisdiction in desegregation cases. The effect of sanctioning delay is heightened by a reference to the plaintiffs' "personal interest," as opposed to their constitutional right, to be admitted to public schools. The *Brown II* decision is couched neither in the language of authority nor of constitutional mandate; the key issues articulated by the Court are "the public interest" and admonitions to defendants to be "effective" and to courts to assess the "adequacy" of plans for "transition to a racially nondiscriminatory school system."

The only other sentence in the brief opinion that involves any sense of the Court's authority confirms, by its wording, that this is not an authoritative statement by the Court but instead one of appeasement. The Court's obligation to address potential Southern resistance to *Brown I* is dispatched thusly: "But it should go without saying that the vitality of these constitutional principles cannot be allowed to yield simply because of disagreement with them." This is not a Court throwing down the gauntlet of authority but, instead, one self-consciously portraying itself as reasonable and accommodating in telling the story of the gradual process of desegregation it envisions; it is not a story of villains or heroes but instead of various partners working toward a constitutional goal of desegregated schools at a pace that is deemed by a local federal judge to be appropriate for individual school districts.

Much has been made of the differences between both decisions in *Brown* and other Supreme Court opinions, which rely on citation of precedent and dense legal language. Appellate court opinions are written for those in the legal profession, and as a result, their role in public discourse is minimal. At most, what enter the public discourse are parsimonious phrases or metaphors that operate as legal sound bites, such as "separate but equal" or "all deliberate speed" from *Brown*, or the "wall of separation" between church and state from cases involving the establishment clause of the First Amendment.[55] The *Brown* decisions were written, according to Chief Justice Earl Warren, for a public rather than a legal audience. In his memoirs, Warren states that he decided to make the *Brown I* opinion "short, readable by the lay public, nonrhetorical, unemotional and, above all, nonaccusatory."[56] These qualities lead some legal scholars to condemn its lack of either a theoretical or federalist point of view.[57] Although Chief Justice Warren, like others steeped in the language of legal discourse, does not successfully avoid it in either opinion, *Brown II* is not so overburdened with either citation to legal precedent or legal terminology that its meaning is unclear to a lay reader. The story format is easily accessible, although the particular story of patience and understanding it tells may have accomplished little other than inviting Southern delay.

One reading of *Brown II* is that Southern reaction to *Brown I* cowed the justices into a retreat from the "high ground of constitutional principle" to the implementation principle of "deliberate speed."[58] Others credit *Brown II* with giving Southern states the opportunity to stall or even evade the mandate to desegregate, seeing in the accommodating language of *Brown II* a signal that enforcement would not be vigorous.[59] Furthermore, the assignment of federal district courts to supervise desegregation similarly may have signaled less-than-vigorous enforcement. Many Southern federal district court judges had political connections to the Southern senators who later would sign the "Southern Manifesto."[60] A Mississippi attorney is cited as saying, "We couldn't ask for anything better than to have our local, native Mississippi federal judges consider suits in good faith and act accordingly." Referring to the "as soon as feasible" language in *Brown II*, he continues: "Our local judges know the local situation and it may be 100 years before it's feasible."[61] Critics argue that the decision is a paradox as "its words summoned forth the South's nobler instincts, even as its implications indulged its darker, more violent side,"[62] and that its policy of gradualism was responsible for the tokenism in its wake.[63]

More favorable readings include the claim that the decision bought time for popular support for desegregation to coalesce[64] and that the Court felt trapped between conventional legal doctrine, which put legal authority for operating schools in the hands of state officials, allowing a moral evil to triumph, and the prospect of overstepping their institutional authority in order to declare unconstitutional a law they deemed immoral, thereby stepping on the wrong side of the "government of laws"/"government of men" dichotomy.[65] Similarly, the *Brown II* decision is praised for expressing "the very ideal on which our moral condemnation of the racial caste system is based—that social relations should not rest on force but on mutual respect among equals."[66] In any event, with the second half of the *Brown* decision, the Court had launched what one commentator calls "the erratic career of the 'all deliberate speed' formula." [67] This would remain the law of the land until 1969 when, weary of the South's delay, the Court finally ordered all schools districts to "operate now and hereafter only unitary schools."[68]

Despite the lack of authority in *Brown II*, the two-part *Brown* decision was not as impotent as some commentators paint it, nor as Justices Minton and Black had feared. A biographer of Justice Brennan describes the impact of the bifurcated decision on both constitutional law and the Court's role: "the Warren Court put political authorities on notice that tradition and history would no longer carry sufficient weight to immunize from judicial scrutiny" either state laws or practices that restrained individual liberties.[69] Notice proved to be insufficient, however; in its next school desegregation case, the Court would have to reassert its authority to interpret the Constitution as well as the correlative duty of states to abide by that interpretation. Although the justices had been cognizant of public opinion and self-conscious in their use of rhetorical strategies when drafting both the *Brown I* and *Brown II* decisions, the Court's rhetorical skill was demonstrated much more clearly in the 1958 case, *Cooper v. Aaron.*[70]

Cooper v. Aaron

The written opinion of the Supreme Court in Cooper begins, "Opinion of the Court by THE CHIEF JUSTICE, MR. JUSTICE BLACK, MR. JUSTICE FRANKFURTER, MR. JUSTICE DOUGLAS, MR. JUSTICE BUIRTON, MR. JUSTICE CLARK, MR. JUSTICE HARLAN, MR. JUSTICE BRENNAN, AND MR. JUSTICE WHITTAKER." This list of all nine justices, in order of seniority after the Chief Justice, as authors of the Court's opinion is only the most startling breach of the Court's usual procedures in a case in which the justices' every strategy seems chosen to legitimize its authority and the authority of its decision in *Brown*.

Although not unprecedented, the speed with which the *Cooper v. Aaron* case made its way from the first filing in federal district court to the Supreme Court's announcement of the decision is rare enough to be rhetorically powerful in its own right. Cases usually take at least two years from the first filing in a trial court to an appellate decision, and when the U.S. Supreme Court agrees to review a case, the timeline is even longer. In *Cooper*, the movement of the case from trial court hearing to Supreme Court decision was extraordinarily expedited. The federal district court's decision to grant the school board a delay in the implementation of their desegregation plan was handed down on June 20, 1958. That decision was appealed to the Eighth Circuit, which convened a special session on August 4 and, on August 18, reversed the district court's grant of a delay in the desegregation plan. On August 21, the Court of Appeals stayed the effective date of its own decision so the school board could petition the U.S. Supreme Court to review the decision. The Court's term begins each year on the first Monday in October, which in 1958 was October 6. However, the justices were summoned back to Washington from their summer break and agreed to call a special court term for only the third time in modern history.[71] They heard oral arguments on September 11. The following day, the Court issued a six-sentence *per curiam* ("by the court") unsigned opinion affirming the judgment of the Eighth Circuit Court of Appeals, thereby denying the School Board's petition for a delay of their desegregation plan. The Court announced that the purpose of its haste and the abrogation of its usual procedures was for the purpose of deciding the matter before the beginning of the school year, but it also operated to create a sense of resolve and served as a powerful response to such a direct challenge to its authority. Then, on September 29, the opinion starting with the names of all nine justices was announced and made part of the official decision of the case.

The unusual form of the decision was as powerful as the expedited procedure. When the Supreme Court first began hearing cases in the late 1700s, each individual justice wrote an opinion in every case. John Marshall, who became Chief Justice in 1801, changed that practice and created a tradition that continues to the present; one of the justices voting with the majority is the voice of the Court. That justice writes the opinion, and it begins "Opinion: MR. JUSTICE HARLAN [or whomever] delivered the opinion of the Court. . . ." Although the author of the opinion is indicated, the Court, also by long-standing convention, speaks in the first person plural rather than singular in the majority decision. Laura Ray argues that the Court "thus deliberately submerged the idea of a personal voice in the fiction of a collective voice" that speaks for the institution.[72] Also by long-standing convention, majority opinions refer to past actions by "the Court," focusing further on the timeless institutional voice. Any authoritative statement made by the Court in *Cooper v. Aaron* had to come within the context of these conventions. So, although the vote was unanimous, the Court became a unanimous upper-case chorus of authority only by taking the additional, unprecedented, and never again repeated step of beginning, "Opinion of the Court by THE CHIEF JUSTICE, MR. JUSTICE BLACK, MR. JUSTICE FRANKFURTER . . . " and so on. Each of the nine justices also signed the opinion in a similar collective show of institutional will.[73] The effect of the Court's rhetorical strategy is to create a black-robed jurisprudential wall of authority with no cracks and brooking no insubordination.

One threatened crack was averted in another unusual procedure. Although the other justices tried to convince him not to do it, Justice Frankfurter was determined to file a concurring opinion, which is the prerogative of a justice voting with the majority who wants to express his or her individual assessment of a case. The other justices were successful, however, in convincing Frankfurter to take the unusual step of delaying the release of his concurring opinion until October 6, so as not to mar the unblemished unanimity in the case when the decision was announced in open court.

The text of *Cooper v. Aaron* makes much of the Court's unanimity, present and past. A form of the term unanimous is used ten times, referring not only to the justices' united stand in the present case, but also in the prior Court cases cited as precedents for the decision in this case. For example, in citing *Marbury v. Madison*, the opinion notes, "Chief Justice Marshall, speaking for a unanimous Court. . . ."[74] In addition to variations on the word itself, the Court also uses language signaling its unanimity, such as "[t]his opinion of all of the members of the Court." Learned Hand argues that unanimity in a court creates a "monolithic solidarity on which the authority of a bench of judges so largely depends."[75] In *Cooper v. Aaron*, the justices understood the rhetorical effects of unanimity in maintaining the legitimacy of *Brown* and in meeting the frontal assault on its authority. By their repetition of the term and by reference to the unanimity of their brethren in the previous cases they use to support the decision in this case, the justices reinforce the image of the Court as a monolithic wall of authority. The image of Court authority is buttressed as well by the statement that membership on the Court has changed since the decision in *Brown II*, yet the three new justices "are at one with the Justices still on the Court" who participated in *Brown* and further that the *Brown* decision "is now unanimously reaffirmed."

Also reinforcing this wall-of-authority image is the Court's characterization of its own actions and the task before it. In addition to being unanimous, the Court describes its interpretation of the Constitution as "considered" and its actions in coming to that interpretation as "fully deliberated" upon. The Court uses the superlative form of the adjective and the first person plural pronoun in describing the task before it as of "highest importance to the maintenance of our federal system of government." The story of desegregation no longer features partners working diligently toward a constitutional goal as in *Brown II*; instead the Court sets itself as the authority that announces constitutional rights and obligations and sets school districts and states as institutions with a duty to honor and protect those rights. The issue before the Court, the opinion explains, is "the duty of desegregation." *Cooper v. Aaron* was decided quickly so that "the School Board might know, without doubt, its duty" prior to the opening of school. Further, state officials are "duty bound to devote every effort toward initiating desegregation."

The story told in *Cooper v. Aaron* is one of a state governor and legislature challenging the foundations of our federal system of government, and as with most good stories, this one builds to a crescendo by the end of the opinion. In the Court's story of Governor Faubus's and the Arkansas legislature's unwarranted actions, there is nothing of the reasonable and obliging approach in the *Brown II* story. The tone in *Cooper v. Aaron* is strident and unwavering from the first sentence, which characterizes what is at stake in the case as "of the highest importance to the maintenance of our federal system of government." The state actions and laws are characterized as "efforts to upset and nullify" the decision by the Court in *Brown*. The main villain is clear, as the state is portrayed as "flatly commanding" the legislature to "oppose" the law announced by the Court. These actions are characterized as completely without authority and unwarranted on every front, as they "had not been requested" by the school board and were "entirely unheralded." In the Court's story, the mayor of Little Rock believed the police force could handle the crowds and did not request the governor to send in the National Guard. Nor were Little Rock authorities consulted prior to the governor's action.

There is no ambiguity about agency in the story, as the state's action is characterized as the cause of all the problems now facing the school district. The Court quotes from the school board's petition for delay that the effect of the governor's action "was to harden the core of opposition to the Plan" and to "cause" individuals who had accepted the desegregation plan to be persuaded that the state of Arkansas had the power to nullify a Court decision. The Court says the governor's action caused the school board to ask the black students not to attend until the issue was resolved. Furthermore, the National Guard, ordered by the governor, was the agency preventing the school from obeying the Court's order to desegregate. As recounted in the Supreme Court's story, the district court, which ruled in favor of a delay in the desegregation plan, did so because it found "the School Board's plan had been obstructed by the Governor through the use of National Guard troops." In describing how the case came to the judicial system, the Court repeats the school board's position: "extreme public hostility" that was "engendered largely by the official attitudes and actions of the Governor and the Legislature" made it impossible to maintain the educational program at Central High with the black students in attendance. This story builds to its climax by a dramatic metaphoric claim that evokes memories of the previous century's armed struggle between South and North during the Civil War: "No state legislator or executive or judicial officer can war against the Constitution."

The school board's petition for delay in the desegregation plan is used to reinforce the image of state treachery. The Court quotes from that document, citing the effects of the Governor's action, which were to increase "hostility" to the plan and to make criticism of the plan "more bitter and unrestrained." Although it was the National Guard that prevented the nine students from entering the school, they were "acting pursuant to the Governor's order," and it was Faubus who "caused" the students not to be able to attend. Even the petition for delay is blamed on the governor, who "engendered" the "extreme public hostility" toward desegregation in Little Rock, which resulted in conditions at Central High School that school officials described as "chaos, bedlam and turmoil," including "repeated incidents of more or less serious violence."

The villainous status of state officials is not shared by the school board, who acknowledged their duty in a statement of policy that the Court quotes: "It is our responsibility to comply with Federal Constitutional Requirements and we intend to do so when the Supreme Court of the United States outlines the method to be followed." The Court says nothing about the board's timetable, which took full advantage of the *Brown II* allowance for gradualism. Instead, the board is portrayed in a positive light for creating a plan, discussing it with the community, and moving forward to enact it; the school board's actions are characterized as "an abundance of caution." The contrasting villainy of the governor is pictured in the failure of any state official to similarly consult local law enforcement officials. Furthermore, the black parents' lawsuit against the school board is dispatched by a recitation that the district court ruled in favor of the school board and that the review of that decision is not involved in the present case.

The Court sets the school board's actions in direct contrast to those of state officials in the next, significantly longer paragraph that details the amendment to the state constitution, which commanded opposition to the *Brown* decision and state laws that had been passed in keeping with that command, including a law "relieving school children from compulsory attendance at racially mixed schools." This paragraph operates as a litany of the state's volleys in its war against the Constitution and culminates with the image of school authorities attempting to desegregate Central High School, but being "met with drastic opposing action" in the form of the National Guard under the command of the governor.

Another notable aspect of the story told by the Court results from apparent regret concerning its rhetorical strategies in *Brown II*. A portion of the *Cooper* opinion is devoted to retelling that story, thereby recasting the *Brown II* decision in much stronger and more authoritarian terms than the original version. This retelling begins by repeating one of the two sentences in *Brown II* that speak to the Court's authority: "But it should go without saying that the vitality of these constitutional principles cannot be allowed to yield simply because of disagreement with them." What was at best a lukewarm statement of authority in *Brown II* now is surrounded by the strongest language in *Brown II* about timetable: "with all deliberate speed" and "a prompt and reasonable start toward full compliance." This language, which is scattered in the original opinion, is brought together by citation in *Cooper* as if the Court's obliging posture in the previous case can be recast in stronger terms by omission of its overall tone of patience and partnership. The Court inserts a new inference into the *Brown II* story, suggesting that in many locations, "immediate general admission" of black children would be required by that decision—a mandate nowhere stated in the first version of the story. Another addition to the *Brown II* story is to the list of factors that may warrant delay in a desegregation timetable; the Court now explains that the list "excludes hostility to racial desegregation," as if that exclusion were present in the original version of the story, which it was not. The supervisory duty of federal district courts also is made clearer in *Cooper*, as they are to "scrutinize" plans to make sure they "pointed toward the earliest practicable completion of desegregation." The Court, however, does not admit to recasting *Brown II*; instead, it insists that in the prior decision, "[i]t was made plain that delay in any guise . . . could not be countenanced." This new version of the story also defines "good faith," which was used without explanation in *Brown II*: "only a prompt start, diligently and earnestly pursued[,] . . . constitute[s] good faith." The Court claims this too "was made plain" in the previous decision. Finally, what in *Brown II* was a "personal interest" of black students in attending public school now is cast with much more force: "The right of a student not to be segregated on racial grounds in schools so maintained is indeed so fundamental and pervasive" that it was reached "unanimously" by the Court in *Brown I.*

One sense in which the stories in *Brown II* and *Cooper v. Aaron* are consistent is the Court's willingness to give credence to those who make good faith efforts to comply with constitutional mandate. Although the *Cooper* decision notes that the Court has "accepted without reservation" the school board's claim that "they displayed entire good faith" as well as the district court's findings that all students at the high school "suffered and will continue to suffer if the conditions which prevailed last year are permitted to continue," what allows the Court to demand that desegregation continue is that the conditions are "directly traceable" to the villains: the state legislators and members of the state executive branch, "in their official capacities" to resist *Brown*, thereby causing "violent resistance" in Little Rock. The Court recites yet another sentence from the school board's petition: "The legislative, executive, and judicial departments of the state government opposed the desegregation of Little Rock schools by enacting laws, calling out troops, making statements vilifying federal law and federal courts, and failing to utilize state law enforcement agencies and judicial processes to maintain public peace." This recitation makes clear that in rejecting the board's petition, the Court is not rejecting the board's good faith; it merely is refusing to tolerate state resistance to its decisions.

At this point in the story told in *Cooper*, the Court draws a line in the constitutional sand, asserting its authority in clear and convincing fashion: "The constitutional rights of respondents are not to be sacrificed or yielded to the violence and disorder which have followed upon the actions of the Governor and Legislature." Then, in the opinion's first citation of legal precedent, other than *Brown* or previous decisions of lower courts regarding desegregation in Little Rock, the Court cites an earlier desegregation case, *Buchanan v. Warley*, for the proposition that preservation of the public peace, while a laudable goal, is not the most important concern.[76] Put in its own words, the Court announces: "Thus law and order are not here to be preserved by depriving the Negro children of their constitutional rights."

This introduces the final four paragraphs of the case, in which the Court moves away from telling the story of Little Rock and retelling the story of *Brown II* to a more recognizable Supreme Court argument based on precedent established in prior cases. By this means, the Court weaves its legal argument that the Fourteenth Amendment prohibition against denying equal protection of the laws has no meaning if state agents can refuse to recognize the Court's authority. The Court proclaims, "the constitutional rights of children not to be discriminated against in school admission on grounds of race or color . . . can neither be nullified openly and directly" by state officials "nor nullified indirectly by them through evasive schemes," thus responding to the South's calls for massive resistance to *Brown* and the right of interposition. To make this argument, the Court uses a syllogism composed of "basic constitutional propositions which are settled doctrine." The first proposition is the Supremacy Clause from Article VI of the Constitution, which makes the Constitution the "supreme Law of the Land." The second proposition the Court finds in its own "unanimous" decision in *Marbury v. Madison*: it is "emphatically the province and duty of the judicial department to say what the law is." The Court supports this proposition, which being self-announced is the most controversial, by reference both to the proposition's long standing and unwavering adherence to it: "that principle has ever since been respected by this Court and the Country as a permanent and indispensable feature of our constitutional system." Based on these two premises, the Court concludes that its decision in *Brown* is the "supreme Law of the Land."

Having established its authority, the Court turns to the duty of states. Citing Article VI, the Court argues that states are bound to follow its decisions, "any Thing in the Constitution or Laws of any State to the Contrary notwithstanding." To reinforce this duty of state officials to abide by its decisions, the Court cites the oath that state officials must take "pursuant to Art. VI, cl. 3, 'to support this Constitution'" as well as citing an 1858 case, which was "unanimous": The framers of the Constitution, in their "anxiety to preserve it" and "to guard against resistance to or evasion of its authority, on the part of a State" required states' obedience to constitutional mandate.[77] Quoting from another unanimous decision from 1809, the Court says, "the constitution itself becomes a solemn mockery" if state legislatures "may, at will, annul the judgments of the courts of the United States."[78] Thus, in the section of the *Cooper* opinion most similar to other Supreme Court opinions, with reasoning in the form of legal argument based on citation of precedent, the ultimate issue the Court addresses is its own authority to interpret the Constitution and states' duty to abide by that interpretation.

Finally, in the last paragraph of the decision, the Court explicitly addresses the Southern states' claim that the responsibility for public education belongs to the state, thereby freeing them from any obligation to follow Supreme Court rulings on that topic. The claim is dispatched with little fanfare and even less analysis; the Court simply plays its trump card, asserting the Constitution's creation of equal justice under law and, in particular, the Fourteenth Amendment's requirements of equal protection and due process of law.[79] The only other argument it uses is that it seriously considered this issue in *Brown*, the extent of its consideration indicated by the fact that issues in the case were "briefed and twice argued."

In sum, the *Cooper* opinion is devoted to rewriting the story told in *Brown II*, telling the story of villainous actions of state officials and good faith efforts by the school board during the crisis at Central High School, as well as reestablishing its own authority to interpret the Constitution. In its final sentence, the Court makes absolutely clear the status of its story relative to others told about desegregation: "Our constitutional ideal of equal justice under law is thus made a living truth."

Commentary on *Cooper v. Aaron* generally focuses on its final paragraphs in which it sets out the deductive claim for its own authority. As Robert Burt describes those paragraphs, the Court "enunciated the most emphatic demand for unquestioning obedience in its entire jurisprudence"[80]—a demand that has been a lightning rod for criticism. Critics of the *Cooper* decision claim that *Marbury v. Madison* does not say what the opinion in *Cooper* claims it says[81] and that the Court claimed too much power for itself.[82] One commentator goes so far as to call for a "general repudiation of the dicta in *Cooper v. Aaron*," replacing it with an "understanding that judicial opinions are, at least from the perspective of nonjudicial actors, merely explanations for judgments."[83] Another criticism is that *Cooper* was a case with a "larger-than-life script" but "limited immediate impact"; although the Court's decision helped to reestablish the Court's authority, it did not solve the Little Rock crisis. Since he could not avoid desegregation of public schools by interposition or by participating in massive resistance to *Brown*, Governor Faubus responded to the *Cooper v. Aaron* decision by shutting down public high schools in Little Rock during the 1958-1959 school year, reopening the following year only in response to a federal court ruling that the action was unconstitutional.[84] However, the fact that the governor eventually responded to a federal court is indication that the *Cooper* decision was not without impact.

Another Retrospective

David Garrow, speaking about the *Brown* decision, suggests that the "professorial urge for interpretive novelty" can lead to "revisionist interpretations" that he labels "rhetorical excesses."[85] In the years following *Brown II* and *Cooper v. Aaron*, there has been no paucity of legal analysis about the two decisions. These cases have received critical analysis that ranges from praise to damnation, based on what the Court said or should have said, as well as on what it accomplished or failed to accomplish. One important perspective that has been less discussed than some others is the international audience for *Brown* and *Cooper*, one that was highly critical of U.S. racial law and politics. Mary Dudziak analyzes *Brown*'s worldwide significance: "In announcing that democratic principles embodied in the American Constitution were inconsistent with racial segregation, the Supreme Court had salvaged democracy as a system of government that might appeal to peoples of color across the globe"; and she notes the U.S. Information Agency used *Brown* in propaganda distributed throughout the world. However, when images of the National Guard preventing Elizabeth Eckford from entering Central High School were broadcast around the world, an American political crisis became a foreign affairs crisis that was quelled only by Eisenhower's eventual intervention and the Court's decision in *Cooper v. Aaron*, which the *London Times* referred to as a "shining opinion." Dudziak claims that, despite the Court's failure to immediately desegregate schools in Little Rock, the opinion in *Cooper* "played an essential role in the construction of an image of democracy" for the world; the "imprimatur of constitutionalism was firmly placed on the side of equality," and the "supremacy of the federal government's voice in the articulation of the fundamental values of the nation was underscored."[86]

This is an image that endured in the United States, as well. The two opinions analyzed in this chapter played an important role in the construction of the image of equal protection under the Constitution arising out of their very different rhetorical strategies of legitimization. In *Brown II*, the Court uses a rhetoric of partnership and patience to establish its legitimacy in an atmosphere that is highly charged and ripe for resistance; in *Cooper v. Aaron*, patience has evaporated, and the Court marshals the strongest strategies it has available in order to declare its authority and the corresponding duties of other governmental agencies. In the process, the Court tells two very different stories of equal protection. One features a proposal for a well-meaning partnership to achieve equal rights, while the other is a strongly worded declaration of inalienable and nonnegotiable rights and responsibilities. Both are central to a story that Americans like to tell about themselves.

Jack Balkin refers to that story as the "Great Progressive Narrative," in which the United States is portrayed as "continually striving for democratic ideals." Although American history has featured terrible injustices, in this narrative the Constitution is a shining reflection of "America's deepest ideals," which we finally achieved after "historical struggle and acts of great political courage."[87] The *Brown* decisions have become the most important in the history of the Supreme Court precisely because of the role they play in this national narrative, and although the opinion itself largely has dropped from public consciousness, *Cooper v. Aaron* played a crucial role in creating the story of progress toward the ideal of equal justice in American democracy. However, it is *Brown* that stars in the American narrative, and the stature of the case grows with each passing decade, thanks in part to the seemingly mandatory spate of retrospective analyses that appear on every ten-year anniversary, each giving a slightly different spin as it strives for interpretive novelty. Like all good stories, this narrative improves with each telling. Even in the legal community, where critics and novel interpretations of the *Brown* decisions and *Cooper v. Aaron* abound, *Brown*'s role in the constitutional canon is secure.[88] The case is central to any legal argument on civil rights, no matter what position that argument takes.

A critical analysis of this blizzard of words that has been written about these decisions, however, reveals a surprising irony, for discourse about this narrative's central character, the *Brown* case, and its long-forgotten sidekick, *Cooper v. Aaron*, unknowingly exposes a fraudulent feature of the national progressive narrative about constitutional rights. J. Harvie Wilkinson III articulates the problem in a discussion about affirmative action:

> We ought never to forget that the debate on race and education in the years since *Brown* has been roughest of all on black pride. Every white initiative aimed at integration has demeaned and patronized in its own unwitting way. Integration itself was a way to improve blacks through contact with whites; busing came to involve a black chase and white escape; affirmative action alleged a need for favored treatment and a double standard.[89]

Although Wilkinson is arguing against special treatment, his perspective is an unwitting critique of the civil rights story. Patting themselves on the back for progress toward the democratic ideal of equal protection under the law, white Americans ignore the racism inherent in their telling of the progressive narrative about Americans' battle for equal rights. In addition to marshalling rhetorical strategies designed to give legitimacy to the Court in its self-proclaimed role as interpreter of the Constitution, *Brown II* and *Cooper v. Aaron* play into this narrative, for neither opinion displays any awareness of the implicit but equally important issue of legitimacy underlying equal protection—the ways in which the law and discourse about the law talk about race. In both of these cases, the

Court portrays itself as solving racial inequality, and therein lies the fraud. "Imagining racism as a fixable aberration," argues Derrick Bell, "obfuscates the way in which racism functions as an ideological lens through which Americans perceive themselves, their nation, and their nation's Other." Bell's version of the American narrative is only beginning to be told and appreciated, and it is an interpretive novelty that is long overdue. It certainly is a version that is absent from the Court's civil rights decisions in the 1950s—cases that position "the law as that which fixes racism rather than as that which participates in its consolidation."[90] Until the latter perspective is considered more broadly, the Great Progressive Narrative will remain more fairy tale than truth.

Notes

1. James Boyd White, *Acts of Hope: Creating Authority in Literature, Law, and Politics* (Chicago: University of Chicago Press, 1994), xi. He defines rhetoric as "the central art by which community and culture are established, maintained, and transformed." James Boyd White, "Law as Rhetoric, Rhetoric as Law: The Arts of Cultural and Communal Life," *University of Chicago Law Review* 52 (1985): 684.

2. This issue is discussed in Stanley Fish's response to Owen Fiss's characterization of interpretation. Stanley Fish, "Fish v. Fiss" in *Doing What Comes Naturally: Change, Rhetoric, and the Practice of Theory in Literary and Legal Studies* (Durham, NC: Duke University Press, 1989), 132-140.

3. *Brown v. Board of Education*, 347 U.S. 483 (1954).

4. Learned Hand, *The Bill of Rights: The Oliver Wendell Holmes Lectures* (Cambridge, MA: Harvard University Press, 1958), 4.

5. *Marbury v. Madison*, 5 U.S. 137, 177-178 (1803). Learned Hand argues that the judicial branch of government was "undoubtedly the best 'Department' in which to vest such a power," because federal judges, "by the independence of their tenure . . . were least likely to be influenced by diverting pressure," a reference to their lifetime appointments. Hand, 29.

6. Alexander M. Bickel, *Politics and the Warren Court* (New York: Harper & Row, 1965), 77.

7. Morton J. Horwitz, *The Warren Court and the Pursuit of Justice: A Critical Issue* (New York: Hill and Wang, 1998), xi.

8. "Bloodstains on White Marble Steps," *Daily News*, 18 May 1954, cited in *Brown v. Board of Education: A Brief History with Documents*, ed. Waldo E. Martin, Jr. (Boston: Bedford/St. Martin's, 1998), 204.

9. David R. Goldfield, *Black, White, and Southern: Race Relations and Southern Culture 1940 to the Present* (Baton Rouge: Louisiana State University Press, 1990), 75.

10. *Congressional Record*, 83rd Congress, 2nd sess., 1954, 100, pt. 9: 11525.

11. Francis M. Wilhoit, *The Politics of Massive Resistance* (New York: George Braziller, 1973), 31.

12. According to Numan Bartley, the successful candidate in the nine-person primary race for the Democratic nomination in the Georgia gubernatorial race said, "The meddlers, demagogues, race baiters and Communists are determined to destroy every vestige of states' rights." Numan V. Bartley, *The Rise of Massive Resistance: Race and Politics in the South during the 1950s* (Baton Rouge: Louisiana State University Press, 1969), 68, citing the *New York Times*, May 18, 1954.

13. Bartley, 81.

14. Kenneth O'Reilly, *Nixon's Piano: Presidents and Racial Politics from Washington to Clinton* (New York: Free Press, 1995), 170-171. See also, Wilhoit, 43-44.

15. Michal R. Belknap, *Federal Law and Southern Order: Racial Violence and Constitutional Conflict in the Post-*Brown *South* (Athens: University of Georgia Press, 1987), x. Plessy v. Ferguson, 163 U.S. 537 (1896).

16. Most schools that desegregated were, according to Wilhoit, in "peripheral areas: Arkansas (Charleston and Fayetteville), Delaware (Wilmington), Kansas, Maryland (Baltimore to a small extent), Missouri (nine school districts), New Mexico, Oklahoma (only at the college and parochial school levels), West Virginia (in 25 of the state's 55 counties), and the District of Columbia" (41).

17. Tony Freyer, The *Little Rock Crisis: A Constitutional Interpretation* (Westport, CT: Greenwood, 1984), 7-8.

18. Richard Kluger, *Simple Justice: The History of* Brown v. Board of Education *and Black America's Struggle for Equality* (New York: Alfred A. Knopf, 1980), 727.

19. *Brown v. Board of Education*, 349 U.S. 294, 301 (1955).

20. Robert P. Green, Jr. argues that the "Court's vagueness concerning implementation, combined with the expected intransigence of the white South, postponed meaningful desegregation for years." "Introduction: 1955-1998: Equality and Reaction," in *Equal Protection and the African American Constitutional Experience: A Documentary History*, ed. Robert P. Green, Jr. (Westport, CT: Greenwood, 2000), 247.

21. Freyer, 63. He argues that "the doctrine of interposition deflected attention away from questions of moral principle and equal justice, emphasizing instead a legalistic abstraction" (73).

22. "The Right of Interposition," *Richmond News Leader*, 22 November 1955; "Interposition, Now!" *Richmond News Leader*, 29 November 1955.

23. Bartley, 130-131.

24. Daisy Bates, *The Long Shadow of Little Rock: A Memoir* (New York: David McKay, 1962), 47-48.

25. Darlene Clark Hine, William C. Hine, and Stanley Harrold, *Since 1863*, vol. 2 of *The African-American Odyssey* (Upper Saddle River, NJ: Prentice Hall, 2000), 503.

26. Wilhoit, 45-51.

27. The *Brown* decision did not explicitly overrule *Plessy*; however, in 1957, a federal district court stated that *Brown* had overruled *Plessy*. *Simkins v. City of Greensboro*, 149 F. Supp. 562, 564 (M.D.N.C. 1957). A Supreme Court decision, written by Justice Black, made the same claim in 1970. *Oregon v. Mitchell*, 400 U.S. 112, 133 (1970).

28. *Congressional Record*, 84th Cong., 2nd sess., 1956, 102, pt. 4: 4460. The "Manifesto" was not the only threat to the Court's authority. In addition to *Brown*, Court decisions broadening federal power had created an anti-Court alliance among Southern Democrats and conservative Republicans, further challenging the Court's authority. Bartley, 290-291.

29. Benjamin Muse, *Ten Years of Prelude: The Story of Integration Since the Supreme Court's 1954 Decision* (New York: Viking, 1964), 66.

30. Carl Tobias, "Public School Desegregation in Virginia during the Post-*Brown* Decade," *William and Mary Law Review* 37 (Summer 1996): 1268.

31. J. Harvie Wilkinson III, *From* Brown *to* Bakke*: The Supreme Court and School Desegregation: 1954-1978* (New York: Oxford University Press, 1979), 79.

32. Bartley, 251. Local government was relatively free of corruption, and the influence of Republican business leaders kept the city from one-party politics. Freyer, 18. Among the causes commentators cite for the crisis are a breakdown of community leadership, including a lame-duck mayor and city council, an ineffective police chief who opposed integration, and meddling by the governor of Georgia. Wilhoit, 177-178.

33. Freyer, 21.

34. Bartley, 251-255. Superintendent Bloosom was not enthusiastic about desegregation, but neither he nor the school board ever suggested defiance to *Brown*. Bartley, 253, 255. See also, Judith A. Hagley, "Massive Resistance: The Rhetoric and the Reality," *New Mexico Law Review* 27 (Winter 1997): 202.

35. Freyer, 17.

36. Bates, 51-52.

37. Arkansas Constitution, Amendment 44. This amendment finally was ruled void *ab initio* as unconstitutional in 1989, after two members of the Arkansas Legislature filed suit to invalidate it. Governor Bill Clinton conceded that the Amendment violated the Supremacy Clause, and both the House and Senate of the Arkansas Legislature passed identical resolutions requesting the attorney general to admit its unconstitutionality. In a brief opinion, the federal court

noted the "intemperate text" of the Amendment "represents a reckless defiance of the rule of law" and "flagrantly challenges" principles that "are the bedrock on which this republic was founded." *Dietz v. Arkansas*, 709 F. Supp. 902, 904-905 (E.D. Ark. 1989).

38. Bartley, 257.

39. Juan Williams, *Eyes on the Prize: America's Civil Rights Years, 1954-1965* (New York: Penguin, 1987), 93. Williams calls Governor Faubus an "old-fashioned southern politician who tried to tell the people what they wanted to hear" and who "was always running for office," as the term of office for the Arkansas governor was two years.

40. Freyer, 75, 81.

41. *Aaron v. Cooper*, 143 F. Supp. 855, 866 (E.D. Ark. 1956).

42. Bartley, 259-260.

43. Belknap, 44-46.

44. *Aaron v. Cooper*, 156 F. Supp. 220 (E.D. Ark. 1957).

45. 156 F. Supp. at 227.

46. Dwight D. Eisenhower, *The White House Years: Waging Peace, 1956-1961* (Garden City, NY: Doubleday, 1965), 171.

47. Horwitz, 29-30.

48. Mary Frances Berry, *Stability, Security, and Continuity: Mr. Justice Burton and Decision Making in the Supreme Court 1945-1958* (Westport, CT: Greenwood, 1978), 160.

49. Cited in Kluger, 739.

50. Dennis J. Hutchinson, "Unanimity and Desegregation: Decision-making in the Supreme Court, 1948-1958," *Georgetown Law Journal*, 68 (October 1979): 56.

51. Kluger, 738-741.

52. *Brown II*, 298.

53. L. H. LaRue, *Constitutional Law as Fiction: Narrative in the Rhetoric of Authority* (University Park: Pennsylvania State University Press, 1995), ix-x, 2, 10-11.

54. The term apparently came from Justice Frankfurther, who had used the phrase in two opinions he had written in the 1940s. He borrowed the phrase from Justice Oliver Wendell Holmes, who used it in a 1918 case. In that decision, Holmes claimed the term came from English Chancery, but after considerable research in later years, Frankfurter was unable to authenticate its source. Richard Kluger argues Holmes may have misremembered where he took it and suggests it may have come from lines in Francis Thompson's 1893 poem, "The Hound of Heaven." Kluger, 742-743.

55. This phrase comes from *Reynolds v. United States*, 98 U.S. 145, 164 (1879); however, it is Justice Black's use of the term in the majority opinion in *Everson v. Board of Education*, 330 U.S. 1, 18 (1947) that brought the metaphor

into wider acknowledgment. For a discussion of legal metaphor, see Haig Bosmajian, *Metaphor and Reason in Judicial Opinions* (Carbondale: Southern Illinois University Press, 1992).

56. Kluger, 711.

57. See, for example, Hagley, 179.

58. This was the expressed view of Justice Hugo Black. "Black Believes Warren Phrase Slowed Integration," *New York Times*, 4 December 1968.

59. Tobias, 1268.

60. Horwitz, 29.

61 Reed Sarratt, *The Ordeal of Desegregation: The First Decade* (New York: Harper & Row, 1966), 200.

62. Wilkinson, 65.

63. Walter Gellhorn, ""A Decade of Desegregation—Retrospect and Prospect," *Utah Law Review* 9 (1964): 6.

64. Jennifer E. Spreng, "Scenes from the Southside: A Desegregation Drama in Five Acts," *University of Arkansas Little Rock Law Journal* 19 (Spring 1997): 336.

65. Robert A. Burt, "*Brown's* Reflection," *Yale Law Journal* 103 (1994): 1491.

66. Burt, 1494.

67. Wilhoit, 23.

68. *Alexander v. Holmes County Board of Education*, 396 U.S. 19, 20 (1969).

69. David E. Marion, *The Jurisprudence of Justice William J. Brennan, Jr.: The Law and Politics of "Libertarian Dignity"* (Lanham, MD: Rowman & Littlefield, 1997), 16-17. Not all commentators praise *Brown*. Learned Hand argued in a Harvard lecture that the Court used judicial review to enlarge the Bill of Rights, overruling state law based on "its own reappraisal of the relative values at stake." Hand, 54.

70. *Cooper v. Aaron*, 358 U.S. 1 (1958).

71. Freyer, 148.

72. Laura Krugman Ray, "The Road to *Bush v. Gore*: The History of the Supreme Court's Use of the *Per Curiam* Opinion," *Nebraska Law Review* 79 (2000): 518. Ray notes that Justice Breyer's inadvertent use of the pronoun "I" in a majority opinion not only was noticed but, once pointed out, corrected by the justice. She also suggests that Justice Reed's eventual capitulation in *Brown I* "stands as one of the last triumphs of an earlier model that placed consensus above individualism" and sacrificed "personal conviction for institutional solidarity" (534).

73. Horwitz, 31.

74. 358 U.S. at 16, emphasis added.

75. Hand, 72.

76. *Buchanan v. Warley*, 245 U.S. 60 (1917).

77. *Abelman v. Booth*, 62 U.S. 506 (1858). The *Cooper* court indicates the case was decided in 1859 and uses the original citation, 21 Howard 506.

78. *United States v. Peters*, 9 U.S. 115 (1809). The Court uses the original citation, 5 Cranch 115.

79. The Court cites as precedent for the due process claim a civil rights case, *Bolling v. Sharpe*, 347 U.S. 497 (1954).

80. Robert A. Burt, "Constitutional Law and the Teaching of Parables," *Yale Law Journal* 93 (January 1984): 472. He argues that the Court seeks to persuade by mystification by citing very old cases, which mystify a lay audience with "a parade of historic figures" and "a flurry of mysterious citations" and a legal audience by citing obscure cases that are either currently discredited or would be decided differently today (473). Specifically, one of the cases cited by the Court struck down New Deal legislation prior to the Court's abrupt about-face on the topic that followed President Roosevelt's Court-packing threat, and another was authored by Chief Justice Taney, who also wrote the most maligned decision ever issued by the Court, the *Dred Scott* case, *Scott v. Sandford*, 60 U.S. 393 (1856).

81. Thomas W. Merrill, "Judicial Opinions as Binding Law and as Explanations for Judgments," *Cardozo Law Review* 15 (1993): 52.

82. Michael Stokes Paulsen, "The Most Dangerous Branch: Executive Power to Say What the Law Is," *Georgetown Law Journal* 83 (1994): 297-298. See also, Merrill, 52-53.

83. Merrill, 79.

84. Wilkinson, 94. That case was *Aaron v. McKinley*, 173 F. Supp. 944 (E.D. Ark. 1959),

85. David J. Garrow, "Hopelessly Hollow History: Revisionist Devaluing of *Brown v. Board of Education*," *Virginia Law Review* 80 (February 1994): 151.

86 Mary L. Dudziak, "The Little Rock Crisis and Foreign Affairs: Race, Resistance, and the Image of American Democracy," *Southern California Law Review* 70 (September 1997): 1643, 1645, 1709, 1712.

87. Jack M. Balkin, "*Brown* as Icon," in *What "Brown v. Board of Education" Should Have Said: The Nation's Top Legal Experts Rewrite America's Landmark Civil Rights Decision*, ed. Jack M. Balkin (New York: New York University Press, 2001), 5.

88. Brad Snyder, "How the Conservatives Canonized *Brown v. Board of Education*," *Rutgers Law Review* 52 (2000): 384.

89. Wilkinson, 296.

90. Derrick A. Bell, "(dissenting)," in *What* Brown v. Board of Education *Should Have Said*, 198-199.

Works Cited

Abbott, Watkins M. "Segregation of the Public Schools of Virginia." *Congressional Record.* 84th Congress, 2nd sess. 18 January 1956. Vol. 102, pt. 1: 851.

Aleinikoff, T. Alexander. "Re-reading Justice Harlan's Dissent in *Plessy v. Ferguson*: Freedom, Antiracism, and Citizenship." *University of Illinois Law Review* (1992): 961-997.

Almond, J. Lindsay. "Inaugural Address." *Congressional Record.* 85th Congress, 2nd sess. 13 January 1958. Vol. 104, pt. 1: 286.

———. "Virginia Won't Weaken." *Congressional Record.* 86th Congress, 1st sess. 21 January 1959. Vol. 105, appendix: A365.

Amar, Akhil Reed. "The Bill of Rights and the Fourteenth Amendment." *Yale Law Journal* 101 (1992): 1193-1284.

———. "The Bill of Rights as a Constitution." *Yale Law Journal* 100 (1991): 1131-1210.

———. "The Fifteenth Amendment and 'Political Rights.'" *Cardozo Law Review* 17 (1996): 2225-2229.

Baker, J. Newton. "The Segregation of White and Colored Passengers on Interstate Trains." *The Yale Law Journal* 19 (1910): 445.

Baker, Lee. *From Savage to Negro: Anthropology and the Construction of Race 1896-1954.* Berkeley: University of California Press, 1998.

Balkin, Jack M. "Brown as Icon." In *What* Brown v. Board of Education *Should Have Said: The Nation's Top Legal Experts Rewrite America's Landmark Civil Rights Decision.* Edited by Jack M. Balkin, 3-28. New York: New York University Press, 2001.

Balkin, Jack M. and Sanford Levinson. "The Canons of Constitutional Law." *Harvard Law Review* 111 (1998): 963-1024.

Baron, Jane B. "Law, Literature, and the Problems of Interdisciplinarity." *Yale Law Journal* 108 (1999): 1059-1085.

Bartanen, Kristine M. "The Rhetoric of Dissent in Justice O'Connor's *Akron* Opinion." *Southern Speech Communication Journal* 52 (Spring 1987): 240-262.

Bartley, Numan V. *The Rise of Massive Resistance: Race and Politics in the South during the 1950s*. Baton Rouge: Louisiana State University Press, 1969.

Bates, Daisy. *The Long Shadow of Little Rock: A Memoir*. New York: David McKay, 1962.

Beagle, Ben and Ozzie Osborne. *J. Lindsay Almond: Virginia's Reluctant Rebel*. Roanoke, Va.: Full Court Press, Inc., 1984.

Becker, George J. "Albion W. Tourgée: A Pioneer in Social Criticism." *American Literature* 19 (1947): 59-72.

Belknap, Michal R. *Federal Law and Southern Order: Racial Violence and Constitutional Conflict in the Post-*Brown *South*. Athens: University of Georgia Press, 1987.

Bell, Carlyn C. *Revolution, Romanticism, and the Afro-Creole Protest Tradition in Louisiana, 1718-1868*. Baton Rouge: Louisiana State University Press, 1997.

Bell, Derrick A. "(dissenting)." In *What* Brown v. Board of Education *Should Have Said: The Nation's Top Legal Experts Rewrite America's Landmark Civil Rights Decision*. Edited by Jack M. Balkin, 185-200. New York: New York University Press, 2001.

Benoit, William L. "Argumentation in *Miranda v. Arizona*." *Communication Studies* 42 (Summer 1991): 129-140.

———. "Attorney Argumentation and Supreme Court Opinions." *Argumentation and Advocacy* 26 (Summer 1989): 22-38.

Bernstein, Barton J. "Plessy v. Ferguson: Conservative Sociological Jurisprudence." *Journal of Negro History* 48 (1963): 196-205.

Berry, Mary Frances. *Stability, Security, and Continuity: Mr, Justice Burton and Decision Making in the Supreme Court 1945-1958*. Westport, CT: Greenwood, 1978.

Bickel, Alexander M. *The Morality of Consent*. New Haven, CT: Yale University Press, 1975.

———. *Politics and the Warren Court*. New York: Harper & Row, 1965.

"Black Believes Warren Phrase Slowed Integration." *New York Times*, 4 December 1968.

Blaustein, Albert P. and Andrew H. Field. "Overruling Opinions in the Supreme Court." *Michigan Law Review* 57 (1958): 151-196.

Blight, David W. *Race and Reunion: The Civil War in American Memory*. Cambridge, MA: Harvard University Press, 2001.

Bosmajian, Haig. *Metaphor and Reason in Judicial Opinions*. Carbondale: Southern Illinois University Press, 1992.

Braden, Waldo W. Introduction to *Oratory in the New South*, ed. Waldo W. Braden. Baton Rouge: Louisiana State University Press, 1979.

Brennan, William J., Jr. "In Defense of Dissents." *Hastings Law Journal* 37 (1986): 427-438.

Breshears, David. "One Step Forward, Two Steps Back: The Meaning of Equality and the Cultural Politics of Memory in *Regents of the University of California v. Bakke*." *Journal of Law & Society* 3 (2002): 67-90.

"Brief for Appellants in Nos. 1, 2, and 4 and for Respondents in No. 10 on Reargument, *Brown v. Board of Education*, 347 U.S. 483 (1954)." In *Landmark Briefs and Arguments of the Supreme Court of the United States: Constitutional Law*. Vol. 49. Edited by Philip B. Kurland and Gerhard Casper. Washington, D.C.: University Publications of America, 1975.

Bruschke, John. "A Critical Analysis of Objectivity in the Legal Sphere." *Argumentation & Advocacy* 30 (Spring 1994): 220-235.

Bryant, Donald C. "Rhetoric: Its Functions and Its Scope." *Quarterly Journal of Speech* 39 (December 1953): 401-424.

Burt, Robert A. "*Brown's* Reflection." *Yale Law Journal* 103 (1994): 1483-1494.

———. "Constitutional Law and the Teaching of Parables." *Yale Law Journal* 93 (January 1984): 455-502.

Cahn, Edmond. "Jurisprudence." *New York University Law Review* 30 (1955): 150.

Cardozo, Benjamin N. *The Nature of the Judicial Process*. New Haven, CT: Yale University Press, 1921.

———. *Selected Writings of Benjamin Nathan Cardozo*. Edited by Margaret E. Hall. New York: Fallon, 1947.

Carle, Susan D. "Race, Class, and Legal Ethics in the Early NAACP (1910-1920)." *Law and History Review* (Spring 2002). (Online at www.historycooperative.org/journals/lhr/20.1/carle.html; downloaded 20 June 2003).

Carlson, A. Cheree. "John Quincy Adams' 'Amistad Address': Eloquence in a Generic Hybrid." *Western Journal of Speech Communication* 49 (Winter 1985): 14-26.

Chamberlain, D. H. "Reconstruction and the Negro." *The North American Review* 128 (February 1879): 173.

Chin, Gabriel J. "The First Justice Harlan by the Numbers: Just How Great Was 'The Great Dissenter?'" *Akron Law Review* 32 (1999): 629-647.

———. "The *Plessy* Myth: Justice Harlan and the Chinese Cases." *Iowa Law Review* 82 (1996): 151-182.

"The Civil Rights Bill." *The Nation* 481 (17 September 1874): 180-181.

Clark, Hunter R. *Justice Brennan: The Great Conciliator*. New York: Birch Lane, 1995.

Clark, Kenneth B. "The Effects of Prejudice and Discrimination." In *Personality in the Making*. Edited by Helen Witmer and Ruth Kotinsky, 136. New York: Harper and Brothers, 1952.

Clark, Kenneth B. and Mamie P. Clark. "Racial Identification and Preferences in Negro Children." In *Readings in Social Psychology*. Edited by Theodore

Newcomb and Eugene Hartley, 602-611. New York: Henry Holt and Company.

(Cleveland) Gazette, 27 October 1883-30 May 1896.

Cobb, James C. "Segregating the New South: The Origins and Legacy of *Plessy v. Ferguson*." *Georgia State University Law Review* 12 (1996): 1017-1036.

Cole, Melissa, "The Color-Blind Constitution, Civil Rights-Talk, and a Multicultural Discourse for a Post-Reparations World." *New York University Review of Law & Social Change* 25 (1999): 127-180.

Cole, Thomas. *The Origins of Rhetoric in Ancient Greece*. Baltimore: Johns Hopkins University Press, 1991.

Congressional Record. 83rd Cong., 2nd sess., 1954. Vol. 100, pt. 9.

Congressional Record, 84th Cong., 2nd sess., 1956. Vol. 102, pt. 4.

Cooper, N. Lee. "The Harlan Standard." *American Bar Association Journal* 83 (June 1997): 8.

Crable, Richard E. "Models of Argumentation and Judicial Judgment." *Journal of the American Forensics Association* 12 (1976): 113-120

Cravens, Hamilton. *The Triumph of Evolution*. Philadelphia: University of Pennsylvania Press, 1978.

Crenshaw, Carrie. "Colorblind Rhetoric." *Southern Communication Journal* 63 (Spring 1998): 244-256.

———. "The Normality of Man and Female Otherness: (Re)Producing Patriarchal Lines of Argument in the Law and the News." *Argumentation and Advocacy* 32 (Spring 1996): 170-184.

Dabney, Virginius. "Address to National Association of Secondary School Principals," 26 February 1957. *Congressional Record*. 85th Congress, 1st sess. 8 March 1957. Vol. 103, pt. 3: 3349.

Day, John Cocchi. "Retelling the Story of Affirmative Action: Reflections on a Decade of Federal Jurisprudence in the Public Workplace." *California Law Review* 89 (2001): 59-127.

"Declaration of Constitutional Principles." *Congressional Record*. 84th Congress, 2nd sess. 12 March 1956. Vol. 102, pt. 4: 4460.

Degler, Carl N. *In Search of Human Nature*. New York: Oxford University Press, 1991.

Desdunes, R. L. "Was It a Measure of Revenge?" *The (New Orleans) Crusader*, 19 July 1890: 1.

Dickens, Milton and Ruth E. Schwartz. "Oral Argument Before the Supreme Court: *Marshall v. Davis* in the School Segregation Cases." *Quarterly Journal of Speech* 57 (1971): 32-42.

Douglass, Frederick. "Colored National Convention At New Orleans," *The (New York) Independent*. 2 May 1872: editorial page.

Dubois, W. E. B. "Forethought," from *The Souls of Black Folk*. In *W. E. B. Dubois: Writings*, 359-364. New York: Library of America, 1986.

Dudziak, Mary. "The Little Rock Crisis and Foreign Affairs: Race, Resistance, and the Image of American Democracy." *Southern California Law Review* 70 (September 1997): 1641-1716.

Duncan, John C., Jr. "The American 'Legal' Dilemma: Colorblind I/Colorblind II—The Rules Have Changes: A Semantic Apothegmatic Permutation." *Virginia Journal of Social Policy and the Law* 7 (2000): 315-453.

Dure, Leon. "Statement to Commission on Education." 6 March 1959. Leon Dure Papers (no. 9751), Manuscripts Department, University of Virginia Library, Charlottesville, VA.

Eisenhower, Dwight D. *The White House Years: Waging Peace, 1956-1961*. Garden City, New York: Doubleday, 1965.

Ellison, Ralph. "An American Dilemma: A Review." In *The Death of White Sociology*. Edited by Joyce Ladner, 94. New York: Random House, 1973.

Elry, James W., Jr. *The Crisis of Conservative Virginia: The Byrd Organization and the Politics of Massive Resistance*. Knoxville: University of Tennessee Press, 1976.

Fish, Stanley. "Fish v. Fiss." In *Doing What Comes Naturally: Change, Rhetoric, and the Practice of Theory in Literary and Legal Studies*. Edited by Stanley Fish, 120-140. Durham, NC: Duke University Press, 1989.

Fjelstad, Per. "Legal Judgment and Cultural Motivation: Enthymematic Form in *Marbury v. Madison*." *Southern Communication Journal* 60 (Fall 1994): 22-32.

Flanders, Robert G., Jr. "The Utility of Separate Judicial Opinions in Appellate Courts of Last Resort: Why Dissents Are Valuable." *Roger Williams University Law Review* 4 (1999): 401-424.

Frankenberg, Erica, Chungmei Lee, and Gary Orfield. "A Multiracial Society with Segregated Schools: Are We Losing the Dream?" Cambridge, MA: The (Harvard) Civil Rights Project, January 2003. (www.civilrightsproject.harvard.edu; downloaded 9 July 2003).

Fredrickson, George. *The Black Image in the White Mind: The Debate on Afro-American Character and Destiny 1817-1914*. New York: Harper & Row, 1971.

Freyer, Tony. *The Little Rock Crisis: A Constitutional Interpretation*. Westport, CT: Greenwood, 1984.

Garrow, David J. "Hopelessly Hollow History: Revisionist Devaluing of *Brown v. Board of Education*." *Virginia Law Review* 80 (February 1994): 151-160.

Gates, Robbins L. *The Making of Massive Resistance: Virginia's Politics of Public School Desegregation, 1954-1956*. Chapel Hill: The University of North Carolina Press, 1962.

Gellhorn, Walter. "A Decade of Desegregation—Retrospect and Prospect." *Utah Law Review* 9 (1964): 3-17.

Gilmore, Glenda E. *Gender and Jim Crow: Women and the Politics of White Supremacy in North Carolina, 1896-1920*. Chapel Hill: University of North Carolina Press, 1996.

Goings, Kenneth W. *The Defeat of John J. Parker*. Bloomington, IN: Indiana University Press, 1990.

Goldberg, Steven. *Culture Clash: Law and Science in America*. New York: New York University Press, 1994.

Goldfield, David R. *Black, White, and Southern: Race Relations and Southern Culture 1940 to the Present*. Baton Rouge: Louisiana State University Press, 1990.

Gordon, James W. "Religion and the First Justice Harlan: A Case Study in Late Nineteenth Century Presbyterian Constitutionalism." *Marquette Law Review* 85 (2001): 317-422.

Gotanda, Neil. "A Critique of 'Our Constitution Is Color-Blind.'" *Stanford Law Review* 44 (1991): 1-68.

Gould, Stephen J. *The Mismeasure of Man*. New York: Norton, 1981.

Graglia, Lino. *Disaster by Decree: The Supreme Court Decisions on Race and the Schools*. New York: Cornell University Press, 1976.

Green, Robert P., Jr. "Introduction: 1955-1998: Equality and Reaction." In *Equal Protection and the African American Constitutional Experience: A Documentary History*. Edited by Robert P. Green, Jr., 247-252. Westport, CT: Greenwood, 2000.

Grey, Thomas C. "The Constitution as Scripture." *Stanford Law Review* 37 (1984): 1-25.

Griffin, Leland M. "The Rhetoric of Historical Movements." *Quarterly Journal of Speech* 38 (1952): 184-188.

Gunther, Gerald. *Constitutional Law*, 11th ed. Mineola, NY: Foundation Press, 1985.

Hagan, Michael R. "*Roe v. Wade*: The Rhetoric of Fetal Life." *Central States Speech Journal* 27 (1976): 192-199.

Hagley, Judith A. "Massive Resistance: The Rhetoric and the Reality." *New Mexico Law Review* 27 (Winter 1997): 167-221.

Hand, Learned. *The Bill of Rights: The Oliver Wendell Holmes Lectures*. Cambridge, MA: Harvard University Press, 1958.

Harrison, Burr P. "Address to the American Carpet Institute," 23 October 1958. *Congressional Record*. 86th Congress, 1st sess. 15 January 1959. Vol. 105, pt. 1: 755.

———. "The Unsteady Liberals of Morningside Heights." *Congressional Record*. 85th Congress, 1st sess. 26 June 1957. Vol. 103, appendix: A5143.

Hasian, Marouf, Jr. "The Aesthetics of Legal Rhetoric: The Ambiguities of 'Race' in *Adarand v. Pena* and the Beginning of the End of 'Affirmative Action.'" *Howard Journal of Communication* 8 (January 1997): 113-127.

———. *Colonial Legacies in Post Colonial Contexts: A Critical Rhetorical Examination of Legal Histories*. New York: Peter Lang Publications, 2002.

———. "Critical Legal Rhetorics: The Theory and Practice of Law in a Post-modern World." *Southern Communication Journal* 60 (Fall 1994): 44-56.

———. "The Domestication of Legal Argumentation: A Case Study of the Formalism of the Legal Realists." *Communication Quarterly* 46 (Fall 1998): 430-445.

———. "Holocaust Denial Debates: The Symbolic Significance of *Irving v. Penguin & Lipstadt*." *Communication Studies* 53 (Summer 2002): 129-145.

———. "Judicial Rhetoric in a Fragmentary World: 'Character,' and Storytelling in the Leo Frank Case." *Communication Monographs* 64 (September 1997): 250-269.

———. *Legal Memories and Cultural Amnesias in Anglo-American Rhetorical Culture*. Boulder, CO: Westview Press, 2000.

———. "Narrative and the Invention of Legal Science: Oliver Wendell Holmes, Jr. and 'The Path of the Law.'" *Journal of Communication Studies* 13 (1994): 27-40.

Hasian, Marouf, Jr. and Geoff Klinger. "Sarah Roberts and the Early History of the 'Separate but Equal' Doctrine: A Study in Rhetoric, Law, and Social Change." *Communication Studies* 53 (Fall 2002): 269-283.

Hasian, Marouf, Jr. and J. Michael D'Agostine. "'The Case of the Midnight Judges' and Multiple Audience Discourse: Chief Justice Marshall and *Marbury v. Madison*." *Southern Communication Journal* 59 (Winter 1994): 89-96.

Hasian, Marouf, Jr. and Trevor Parry-Giles. "'A Stranger to Its Laws': Freedom, Civil Rights, and the Legal Ambiguity of *Romer v. Evans* (1996)." *Argumentation and Advocacy* 34 (Summer 1997): 27-42.

Hasian, Marouf, Jr., Celeste Michelle Condit, and John Louis Lucaites. "The Rhetorical Boundaries of 'The Law': A Consideration of the Rhetorical Culture of Legal Practice and the Case of the 'Separate but Equal' Doctrine." *Quarterly Journal of Speech* 82 (November 1996): 323-342.

Hine, Darlene Clark, William C. Hine, and Stanley Harrold. *The African American Odyssey*. 2 Vols. Upper Saddle River, NJ: Prentice Hall, 2000.

Hohmann, Hanns. "Judicial Legitimacy and Legal Interpretation in the Debate Between *Brutus* and *Publius*." *Southern Communication Journal* 60 (Fall 1994): 75-86.

Horwitz, Morton J. *The Transformation of American Law 1870-1960: The Crisis of Legal Orthodoxy*. New York: Oxford University Press, 1992.

———. *The Warren Court and the Pursuit of Justice: A Critical Issue*. New York: Hill and Wang, 1998.

Hunsaker, David M. "The Rhetoric of *Brown v. Board of Education*: Paradigm for Contemporary Social Protest." *Southern Speech Communication Journal* 43 (1978): 91-109.

Hutchinson, Dennis J. "Unanimity and Desegregation: Decision-making in the Supreme Court, 1948-1958." *Georgetown Law Journal* 68 (October 1979): 1-87.

"Impressions and Expressions." *Emporia Independent Messenger*, 8 July 1954. Reprinted in *Congressional Record.* 83rd Congress, 2nd sess. 15 July 1954. Vol. 100, appendix: A5101.

(Indianapolis) Freeman, 31 May 1890-27 June 1896.

"Integration and Moral Standards." *Virginia Methodist Advocate.* Reprinted in *Congressional Record.* 85th Congress, 2nd sess. 18 July 1958. Vol. 104, appendix: A6456.

"Interposition, Now!" In *Interposition: Editorials and Editorial Page Presentations.* Richmond, VA: Richmond News Leader, 1959: 18.

Jackson, John, Jr. *Social Scientists for Social Justice: Making the Case Against Segregation.* New York: NYU Press, 2001.

Jackson, Percival E. *Dissent in the Supreme Court.* Norman: University of Oklahoma Press, 1969.

Jackson, Walter W. *Gunnar Myrdal and America's Conscience.* Chapel Hill: University of North Carolina Press, 1990.

(Jackson, Mississippi) Daily News, 18 May 1954.

Jefferies, John C., Jr. *Justice Lewis F. Powell, Jr.: A Biography.* New York: Scribner's, 1994.

Johnson, John. *American Legal Culture, 1908-1940.* New Haven, CT: Greenwood Press, 1981.

Jones, Nathaniel R. "The Harlan Dissent: The Road Not Taken—An American Tragedy." *Georgia State University Law Review* 12 (1996): 952-972.

Jones, Stephen B. "Justification in Judicial Opinions: A Case Study." *Journal of the American Forensics Association* 12 (1976): 121-127.

"Justice Harlan Concurring." *New York Times* 23 May 1954, section IV: 10.

Kennedy, Randall. "Race Relations Law in the Canon of Legal Academia." *Fordham Law Review* 68 (2000): 1985-2010.

"Kentucky Resolutions, November 16, 1789." In *Great Issues in American History: From the Revolution to the Civil War 1765-1865.* Edited by Richard Hofstadter, 177. New York: Vintage Books, 1958.

Keppel, Ben. *The Work of Democracy: Ralph Bunche, Kenneth B. Clark, Lorraine Hansbury, and the Cultural Politics of Race.* Cambridge, MA: Harvard University Press, 1995.

Kilpatrick, James J. "Kilpatrick to Luther Hodges, 21 December 1955." James J. Kilpatrick Papers (no. 6626-b). Manuscripts Department, University of Virginia Library, Charlottesville, VA.

———. *The Southern Case for School Segregation.* New York: The Crowell-Collier Publishing Company, 1962.

———. *The Sovereign States: Notes of a Citizen of Virginia.* Chicago: Henry Regnery Company, 1957.

Klarman, Michael J. "The Plessy Era." *1998 Supreme Court Review* (1999): 327-336.

Klinger, Geoffrey D. "Law as 'Communicative Praxis': Toward a Rhetorical Jurisprudence." *Argumentation & Advocacy* 30 (Spring 1994): 236-247.

Kluger, Richard. *Simple Justice: The History of Brown v. Board of Education and Black America's Struggle for Equality*. New York: Vintage Books, 1975.

Kolsky, Meredith. "Justice William Johnson and the History of the Supreme Court Dissent." *Georgetown Law Review* 83 (1995): 2069-2098.

Krishnakumar, Anita S. "On the Evolution of the Canonical Dissent." *Rutgers Law Review* 52 (2000): 781-826.

Kurland, Phillip B. and Gerhard Caspar, *Landmark Briefs and Arguments of the Supreme Court of the United States, Constitutional Law*. Arlington, VA: University Publications of America, 1975.

Kuusisto, Riikka. "Heroic Tale, Game, and Business Deal? Western Metaphors in Action in Kosovo." *Quarterly Journal of Speech* 88 (2002): 50-68.

LaRue, L. H. *Constitutional Law as Fiction: Narrative in the Rhetoric of Authority*. University Park: Pennsylvania State University Press, 1995.

Latham, Frank B. *The Great Dissenter: John Marshall Harlan*. New York: Cowles, 1970.

LaValley, Joseph C., II. "The Calculus of Dissent: A Study of Appellate Division." *Albany Law Review* 64 (2001): 1405-1427.

Lawrence, Charles. "'One More River to Cross:' Recognizing the Real Injury of Brown: A Prerequisite to Shaping New Remedies." In *Shades of Brown: New Perspectives on School Desegregation*. Edited by Derrick Bell, 51. New York: Columbia University, 1980.

Levi, Edward H. *An Introduction to Legal Reasoning*. Chicago: University of Chicago Press, 1949.

Levine, Samuel J. "Unenumerated Constitutional Rights and Unenumerated Biblical Obligations: A Preliminary Study in Comparative Hermeneutics." *Constitutional Commentary* 15 (1998): 511-527.

Levinson, Sanford. *Constitutional Faith*. Princeton, N.J.: Princeton University Press, 1988.

Levison, Gayle Lewis. "The Rhetoric of the Oral Argument in '*The Regents of California v. Bakke*.'" *Western Journal of Speech Communication* 43 (Fall 1979): 271-277.

Lewis, William. "Of Innocence, Exclusion, and the Burning of Flags: The Romantic Realism of the Law." *Southern Communication Journal* 60 (Fall 1994): 4-21.

Llewellyn, Karl N. "Some Realism about Realism." In *Jurisprudence: Realism in Theory and Practice*. Chicago: University of Chicago Press, 1962. Reprinted from *Harvard Law Review* 44 (1931): 1222-1264.

Lofgren, Charles A. *The Plessy Case: A Legal-Historical Interpretation.* New York: Oxford University Press, 1987.

Lucaites, John Louis. "Between Rhetoric and 'The Law': Power, Legitimacy, and Social Change." *Quarterly Journal of Speech* 76 (1990): 435-449.

Lucaites, John Louis and William Weithoff. "Rhetoric and Law: History, Criticism and 'Praxis.'" *Southern Communication Journal* 60 (Fall 1994): 1-3.

Lucaites, John Louis and William Weithoff, eds. "A Sampler for Legal Rhetoricians and Rhetorical Lawyers." Special Issue of *Legal Studies Forum* 17 (1994): 341-436.

Lundin, Marquez. "The Call for a Color-blind Law." *Columbia Journal of Law and Social Problems* 30 (1997): 407-458.

Makau, Josina M. "The Supreme Court and Reasonableness." *Quarterly Journal of Speech* 70 (1984): 379-396.

Makau, Josina M. and David Lawrence. "Administrative Judicial Rhetoric: The Supreme Court's New Thesis of Political Morality." *Argumentation & Advocacy* 30 (Spring 1994): 191-205.

Maltz, Earl M. "Only Partially Color-Blind: John Marshall Harlan's View of Race and the Constitution." *Georgia State University Law Review* 12 (1996): 973-1016.

Mangis, Daniel E. "Today's Dissents and Tomorrow's Law: A Generic Analysis of U.S. Supreme Court Dissenting Opinions in Equal Protection Clause Cases, 1872-2002." Paper presented at the annual meeting of the National Communication Association. New Orleans, Louisiana. November 2002.

Margold, Nathan. "Preliminary Report to the Joint Committee Supervising the Expenditure of the 1930 Appropriation by the American Fund for Public Service to the N.A.A.C.P." Records of the NAACP. Group I (1909-1939), Series C, Box 200. Library of Congress.

Marion, David E. *The Jurisprudence of Justice William J. Brennan, Jr.: The Law and Politics of "Libertarian Dignity."* Lanham, MD: Rowman & Littlefield, 1997.

McDorman, Todd F. "Challenging Constitutional Authority: African American Responses to *Scott v. Sandford*." *Quarterly Journal of Speech* 83 (May 1997): 192-209.

McIntosh, Simeon C. R. "Reading *Dred Scott*, *Plessy*, and *Brown*: Toward a Constitutional Hermeneutics." *Howard Law Journal* 38 (1994): 53-78.

Medley, Keith Weldon. "The Sad Story of How 'Separate' but 'Equal' Was Born." *Smithsonian* 24 (February 1994): 108-109.

Merrill, Thomas W. "Judicial Opinions as Binding Law and as Explanations for Judgments." *Cardozo Law Review* 15 (1993): 43-79.

Mills, Gary B. "Book Review: Revolution, Romanticism, and the Afro-Creole Tradition in Louisiana," *The American Historical Review* 104 (1999): 1303.

Mody, Sanjay. "Note: *Brown* Footnote Eleven in Historical Context." *Stanford Law Review* 53 (2002): 801.

Motley, Constance Baker. "In Memory of Thurgood Marshall." *New York University Law Review* 68 (1993): 208-211.

Muse, Benjamin. *Ten Years of Prelude: The Story of Integration Since the Supreme Court's 1954 Decision*. New York: Viking, 1964.

Myrdal, Gunnar. *The American Dilemma: The Negro Problem and Modern Democracy*. 1944. Reprint, New York: Harper & Row, 1962.

Nelson, John S., Allan Megill, and Donald N. McCloskey, eds. *The Rhetoric of the Human Sciences: Language and Argument in Scholarship and Public Affairs*. Madison: University of Wisconsin Press, 1984.

(New Orleans) Crusader, 19 July 1890.

(New Orleans) Daily Picayune, 10 July 1890-19 May 1896.

New York Daily Tribune, 1 March 1866.

(New York) Independent, 26 May 1896.

New York Times, 29 November 1879.

Newell, Sara E. and Richard D. Rieke. "A Practical Reasoning Approach to Legal Doctrine." *Journal of the American Forensic Association* 22 (Spring 1986): 212-222.

Newport News Daily Press, 16 February 1959.

Novick, Sheldon M. *Honorable Justice: The Life of Oliver Wendell Holmes*. Boston: Little, Brown and Co., 1989.

Oberst, Paul. "The Strange Career of *Plessy v. Ferguson*." *Arizona Law Review* 15 (1973): 389-418.

O'Brien, Molly Townes. "Justice John Marshall Harlan as Prophet: The *Plessy* Dissenter's Color-Blind Constitution." *William & Mary Bill of Rights Journal* 6 (1998): 753-775.

Olsen, Otto H. *The Carpetbagger's Crusade: A Life of Albion Winegar Tourgée*. Baltimore: John Hopkins University Press, 1965.

———. *The Thin Disguise: Plessy v. Ferguson, A Documentary Presentation*. New York: Humanities Press, 1967.

O'Reilly, Kenneth. *Nixon's Piano: Presidents and Racial Politics from Washington to Clinton*. New York: Free Press, 1995.

O'Rourke, Sean Patrick. "Cultivating the 'Higher Law' in American Jurisprudence: John Quincy Adams, Neo-classical Rhetoric, and the 'Amistad' Case." *Southern Communication Journal* 60 (Fall 1994): 33-43.

Oxford Companion to the Supreme Court of the United States. Edited by Kermit L. Hall. New York: Oxford University Press, 1992.

Parry-Giles, Trevor. "Property Rights, Human Rights and American Jurisprudence: The Rejection of John J. Parker's Nomination to the Supreme Court." *Southern Communication Journal* 60 (Fall 1994): 57-67.

Parson's Weekly Blade, 30 May 1896.

Paulsen, Michael Stokes. "The Most Dangerous Branch: Executive Power to Say What the Law Is." *Georgetown Law Journal* 83 (1994): 217-345.

Perelman, Chaim. *The Idea of Justice and the Problem of Argument*. Trans. John Petrie. New York: Humanities Press, 1963.

———. *The Realm of Rhetoric*. Trans. William Kluback. Notre Dame, IN: University of Notre Dame Press, 1982.

Perelman, Chaim and Lucie Olbrechts-Tyteca. *The New Rhetoric: A Treatise on Argumentation*. Trans. John Wilkinson and Purcell Weaver. Notre Dame, IN: University of Notre Dame Press, 1969.

Primus, Richard A. "Canon, Anti-Canon, and Judicial Dissent." *Duke Law Journal* 48 (1998): 243-303.

Prosise, Theodore O. and Craig R. Smith. "The Supreme Court's Ruling in *Bush v. Gore*: A Rhetoric of Inconsistency." *Rhetoric & Public Affairs* 4 (Winter 2001): 605-632.

Purcell, Edward A., Jr. *The Crisis of Democratic Theory: Scientific Naturalism and the Problem of Value*. Lexington: University of Kentucky Press, 1973.

Rabin, David A. "Gottlieb's Model of Rule-Guided Reasoning: An Analysis of *Griswold v. Connecticut*." *Journal of the American Forensics Association* 15 (1978): 77-99

Ray, Laura Krugman. "Justice Brennan and the Jurisprudence of Dissent." *Temple Law Review* 61 (1988): 307-352.

———. "Judicial Personality: Rhetoric and Emotion in Supreme Court Opinions." *Washington & Lee Law Review* 59 (2002): 193-234.

———. "The Road to *Bush v. Gore*: The History of the Supreme Court's Use of the *Per Curiam* Opinion." *Nebraska Law Review* 79 (2000): 517-576.

Reid, Karla Scoon. "Va. Expresses 'Regret' for Closures Aimed at Resisting Desegregation." *Education Week* 19 February 2003: 17.

Republic Courier, 27 January 1900.

Richmond Dispatch, 12 January 1900.

Richmond News Leader, 21 November 1955-20 January 1959.

Richmond Times-Dispatch, 18 May 1954-20 January 1959.

Rieke, Richard D. and Randall K. Stutman. *Communication in Legal Advocacy*. Columbia: University of South Carolina Press, 1990.

Ritter, Kurt W. "American Political Rhetoric and the Jeremiad Tradition: Presidential Nomination Acceptance Addresses, 1960-1976." *Southern Speech Communication Journal* 31 (1980): 153-171.

Robertson, A. Willis. "Freedom of Association." *Congressional Record.* 84th Congress, 2nd sess. 5 March 1956. Vol. 102, pt. 3: 3964.

———. "The Origin and Meaning of Virginia's Declaration of Rights." 4 July 1961. *Congressional Record.* 87th Congress, 1st sess. 7 July 1962. Vol. 107, pt. 9: 12010.

Robinson, Amy. "Forms of Appearance of Value: Homer Plessy and the Politics of Privacy." In *Performance and Cultural Politics*. Edited by Elin Diamond, 237-261. New York: Routledge, 1996.

Rodgers, Raymond S. "Absolutism and Natural Law Argument: William O. Douglas on Freedom of Expression." *Southern Speech Communication Journal* 48 (1982): 22-37.

———. "Generic Tendencies in Majority and Non-Majority Supreme Court Opinions: The Case of Justice Douglas." *Communication Quarterly* 30 (1982): 232-236.

Rosen, Jeffrey. "The Color-Blind Court." *American University Law Review* 45 (1996): 791-801.

Rountree, Clarke. "Instantiating 'The Law' and Its Dissents in *Korematsu v. United States*: A Dramatistic Analysis of Judicial Discourse, " *Quarterly Journal of Speech* 87 (February 2001): 1-24.

———. "On the Rhetorical Analysis of Judicial Discourse and More: A Response to Lewis." *Southern Communication Journal* 61 (Winter 1995): 166-173.

Rountree, J. Clarke, III. "Building up to War: Bush's 'Administrative Rhetoric' in the Persian Gulf Conflict." *The Speech Communication Annual* 10 (Spring 1996): 5-19.

———. "Judicial Invention in Cases Contributing to the Development of Corporate Criminal Liability: A Multi-Dimensional Dramatistic Analysis." Ph.D. diss., University of Iowa, 1988.

———. "Prospective Argument: Constraining and Licensing Future Arguments." In *Argument and Critical Practices*. Edited by Joseph W. Wenzel, 207-213. Proceedings of the Fifth SCA/AFA Conference on Argumentation. Annandale, VA: Speech Communication Association, 1987.

———. "Prospective Argument, Part II: Laying the Ground for Future Argument." In *Argument in Controversy*. Edited by Donn W. Parson, 58-63. Proceedings of the Seventh SCA/AFA Conference on Argumentation. Annandale, VA: Speech Communication Association, 1991.

———. "Reversing *Roe v. Wade* through the Courts: The Rhetorical Strategy of *Americans United for Life*." Paper presented to the National Convention of the Speech Communication Association, San Francisco, November 1989.

Rountree, J. Clarke, III and Robert Strikwerda. "'I Shot an Arrow in the Air . . . ': The Rhetorical Trajectories of Knowledge Production." Paper presented to the National Convention of the Speech Communication Association, San Antonio, November 1995.

Sarratt, Reed. *The Ordeal of Desegregation: The First Decade*. New York: Harper & Row, 1966.

Scallen, Eileen A. "Classical Rhetoric, Practical Reasoning, and the Law of Evidence." *American University Law Review* (Summer 1995): 1717-1815.

———. "Judgment, Justification and Junctions in The Rhetorical Criticism of Legal Texts." *Southern Communication Journal* 60 (Fall 1994): 68-74.

Schmidt, Benno C. "Principle and Prejudice: The Supreme Court and Race in the Progressive Era. Part I: The Heyday of Jim Crow." *Columbia Law Review* 82 (1982): 444-524.

Schwarze, Steve. "Rhetorical Traction: Definitions and Institutional Arguments in Judicial Opinions about Wilderness Access." *Argumentation & Advocacy* 38 (Winter 2002): 131-150.

Schwartz, Bernard. "REMARK: Chief Justice Earl Warren: Super Chief in Action." *Tulsa Law Journal* 33 (Winter 1997): 477-503.

———. *Super Chief: Earl Warren and His Supreme Court—A Judicial Biography*. New York: New York University Press, 1983.

Scott, Daryl Michael. *Contempt and Pity: Social Policy and the Image of the Damaged Black Psyche, 1880-1996*. Chapel Hill: University of North Carolina Press, 1997.

Shreve, Gene R. "Rhetoric, Pragmatism and the Interdisciplinary Turn in Legal Criticism: A Study of Altruistic Judicial Argument." *American Journal of Comparative Law* 46 (1998): 41-67.

Simon, John. *The Antagonists: Hugo Black, Felix Frankfurter, and Civil Liberties in Modern America.* New York: Simon and Schuster, 1989.

Smith, Howard Worth. "Our Federal Constitution and Our Supreme Court." *Congressional Record*. 86th Congress, 1st sess. 27 January 1959. Vol. 105, pt. 1: 1221.

Smith, Steven D. "Believing Like a Lawyer." *Boston College Law Review* 40 (1999): 1041-1137.

Snyder, Brad. "How the Conservatives Canonized *Brown v. Board of Education*." *Rutgers Law Review* 52 (2000): 383-494.

Southern, David A. *Gunnar Myrdal and Black-White Relations*. Baton Rouge: Louisiana State University Press, 1987.

"Speech of Hon. Henry Demas, on the Separate Car Bill, Delivered in the Senate, at Baton Rouge, La, July 8, '90," *The (New Orleans) Crusader* 19 July 1890: 4.

Spreng, Jennifer E. "Scenes from the Southside: A Desegregation Drama in Five Acts." *University of Arkansas Little Rock Law Journal* 19 (Spring 1997): 327-412.

Srader, Doyle. "Spanning Ideological Chasms: The Response to Conceptual Segregation in 'Bowers v. Hardwick.'" *Argumentation & Advocacy* 30 (Spring 1994): 206-219.

Stack, Kevin M. "The Practice of Dissent in the Supreme Court." *Yale Law Journal* 105 (1996): 2235-2259.

Stampp, Kenneth. *The Peculiar Institution*. New York: Vintage Books, 1956.

Steiner, Henry J. *Moral Argument and Social Vision in the Courts*. Madison: University of Wisconsin Press, 1987.

Strasser, Mark. "*Plessy*, *Brown* and HBCUs: On the Imposition of Stigma and the Court's Mechanical Equal Protection Jurisprudence." *Washburn Law Journal* 40 (2000): 48-69.

Strother, David B. "Polemics and the Reversal of the 'Separate but Equal' Doctrine." *Quarterly Journal of Speech* 49 (1963): 50-56.

Sundquist, Eric J. "Mark Twain and Homer Plessy." *Representations* 24 (Fall 1988): 105

Taylor, R. C. "The Demise of Race Distinctions in Graduate Education." *Duke Bar Journal* 1 (June 1951): 141.

Thomas, Brook. "*Plessy v. Ferguson* and the Literary Imagination." *Cardozo Studies in Law and Literature* 9 (1997): 45-62.

Thomas, Clarence. "Toward a 'Plain Reading' of the Constitution—The Declaration of Independence in Constitutional Interpretation." *Howard Law Journal* 30 (1987): 983-995.

Tobias, Carl. "Public School Desegregation in Virginia during the Post-*Brown* Decade." *William and Mary Law Review*, 37 (Summer 1996): 1261-1306.

Toulmin, Stephen. *The Uses of Argument.* Cambridge: Cambridge University Press, 1958.

Tourgée, Albion W. *Bricks without Straw.* New York: Fords, Howard & Hulbert, 1880.

Trevigne, Paul. "The World Will Move." *The (New Orleans) Crusader* 19 July 1890: 1.

Tuck, William M. "Address at Longwood College," 5 January 1956. *Congressional Record.* 84th Congress, 2nd sess. 18 January 1956. Vol. 102, pt. 1: 851.

Tucker, William. *The Science and Politics of Racial Research.* Urbana: University of Illinois Press, 1994.

Turner, Kathleen J. "Rhetorical History as a Social Construction." In *Doing Rhetorical History: Concepts and Cases.* Edited by Kathleen J. Turner, 1-15. Tuscaloosa: University of Alabama Press, 1998.

Tushnet, Mark V. *Making Civil Rights Law: Thurgood Marshall and the Supreme Court, 1936-1961.* New York: Oxford University Press, 1994.

———. *NAACP's Legal Strategy, Against Segregated Education.* Chapel Hill: University of North Carolina Press, 1987.

Ulrich, Walter. "The Creation of a Legacy: Brandeis' Concurring Opinion in *Whitney v. California.*" *Southern Speech Communication Journal* 50 (Winter 1985): 143-155.

Unger, Robert Mangabeira. *The Critical Legal Studies Movement.* Cambridge, MA: Harvard University Press, 1983.

"Virginia Resolutions, December 24, 1798." In *Great Issues in American History: From the Revolution to the Civil War 1765-1865.* Edited by Richard Hofstadter, 183. New York: Vintage Books, 1958.

Warren, Earl. *The Memoirs of Earl Warren.* New York: Doubleday, 1977.

Weiss, Gail. "Sex-Selective Abortion: A Relational Approach." *Hypatia* 12 (Winter 1995): 202-217.

Welke, Barbara Y. "Beyond *Plessy*: Space, Status, and Race in the Era of Jim Crow." *Utah Law Review* 267 (2000): 267-299.

Wetlaufer, Gerald B. "Rhetoric and Its Denial in Legal Discourse." *Virginia Law Review* 76 (1990): 1545-1597

White, James Boyd. *Acts of Hope: Creating Authority in Literature, Law, and Politics*. Chicago: University of Chicago Press, 1994.

———. *Heracles' Bow: Essays on the Rhetoric and Poetics of Law*. Madison: University of Wisconsin Press, 1985.

———. "The Judicial Opinion and the Poem: Ways of Reading, Ways of Life." *Michigan Law Review* 82 (1984): 1669-1699.

———. "Law as Rhetoric, Rhetoric as Law: The Arts of Cultural and Communal Life." *University of Chicago Law Review* 52 (1985): 684-702.

———. *When Words Lose Their Meaning: Constitutions and Reconstitutions of Language, Character, and Community*. Chicago: University of Chicago Press, 1984.

White, William S. "Ruling to Figure in '54 Campaign." *New York Times*, 18 May 1954: A20.

Wilhoit, Francis M. *The Politics of Massive Resistance*. New York: George Braziller, 1973.

Williams, Juan. *Thurgood Marshall: American Revolutionary*. New York: Random House, 1998.

Wilson, Kirt H. *The Reconstruction Desegregation Debate: The Politics of Equality and the Rhetoric of Place, 1870-1875*. East Lansing: Michigan State University Press, 2002.

Woodward, Vann C. *The Strange Career of Jim Crow*, 2nd ed. New York: Oxford University Press, 1966.

Wright, Warren E. "Judicial Rhetoric: A Field for Research." *Speech Monographs* 31 (1964): 64-72.

Yarbrough, Tinsley E. *Judicial Enigma: The First Justice Harlan*. New York: Oxford Press, 1995.

Yudof, Mark. "School Desegregation: Legal Realism, Reasoned Elaboration, and Social Science Research in the Supreme Court." *Law and Contemporary Problems*, 42 (1978): 57-110.

Zarefsky, David. "A Skeptical View of Movement Studies," *Central States Speech Journal* 31 (Winter 1980): 245-254.

Cases Cited

Aaron v. Cooper, 143 F. Supp. 855 (E.D. Ark. 1956).
Aaron v. Cooper, 156 F. Supp. 220 (E.D. Ark. 1957).
Aaron v. McKinley, 173 F. Supp. 944 (E.D. Ark. 1959).
Abelman v. Booth, 62 U.S. 506 (1858).
Alexander v. Holmes County Board of Education, 396 U.S. 19 (1969).
Bluford v. Canada, 32 F. Supp. 707 (1940).
Bolling v. Sharpe, 347 U.S. 497 (1954).
Brown v. Board of Education, 346 U.S. 483 (1954).
Brown v. Board of Education, 349 U.S. 294 (1955).
Buchanan v. Warley, 245 U.S. 60 (1917).
Civil Rights Cases, 109 U.S. 3 (1883).
Cooper v. Aaron, 358 U.S. 1 (1958).
Council v. Western & A.R.R. 1 I.C.C. 339 (1887).
Davis v. County School Board of Prince Edward County, 347 U.S. 483 (1954).
Dietz v. Arkansas, 709 F. Supp. 902 (E.D. Ark. 1989).
Everson v. Board of Education, 330 U.S. 1 (1947).
Fisher v. Hurst, Chief Justice, et al., 333 U.S. 147 (1948).
Gilbert v. Minnesota, 254 U.S. 325.
Grovey v. Townsend, 295 U.S. 45 (1935).
Hall v. De Cuir, 95 U.S. 485 (1878).
Heard v. Georgia R.R., 1 I.C.C. 428 (1888).
Heard v. Georgia R.R., 3 I.C.C. 111 (1889).
Korematsu v. United States, 323 U.S. 214 (1944).
Marbury v. Madison, 5 U.S. (1 Cranch) 137 (1803).
McCabe v. Atchison, Topeka & Sante Fe Railway Company, 235 U.S. 151 (1914).
McLaurin v. Oklahoma State Regents for Higher Education, 339 U.S. 637 (1950).
McLaurin v. Oklahoma State Regents for Higher Education et al., 87 F. Supp. 526 (W.D. Okla. 1948).
Missouri ex rel. Gaines v. Canada, 308 U.S. 337 (1938).
Missouri v. Jenkins, 515 U.S. 70 (1995).
Nixon v. Condon, 286 U.S. 73 (1932).

Nixon v. Herndon, 273 U.S. 536 (1927).
Oregon v. Mitchell, 400 U.S. 112 (1970).
Pearson v. Murray, 169 Md. 478 (1936).
Plessy v. Ferguson, 163 U.S. 537 (1896).
Powell v. Alabama, 287 U.S. 45 (1932).
Reynolds v. United States, 98 U.S. 145 (1878).
Scott v. Sandford, 60 U.S. 393 (1856).
Simkins v. City of Greensboro, 149 F. Supp. 562 (M.D.N.C. 1957).
Sipuel v. Board of Regents of Oklahoma et al., 199 Okla. 36 (1947).
Sipuel v. University of Oklahoma, 332 U.S. 631 (1948).
Slaughterhouse Cases, 83 U.S. (16 Wall.) 36 (1873).
Smith v. Allwright, 321 U.S. 649 (1944).
State ex rel. Bluford v. Canada, 348 Mo. 298 (1941).
State ex rel. Michael et al. v. Witham et al., 179 Tenn. 250 (1942).
Strauder v. West Virginia, 100 U.S. 303 (1880).
Sweatt v. Painter, 339 U.S. 629 (1950).
United States v. Buntin, 10 F. 730 (S.D. Ohio 1882).
United States v. Peters, 9 U.S. (5 Cranch) 115 (1809).
Wrighten v. University of South Carolina, 72 F. Supp. 948 (E.D.S.C. 1947).
Yick Wo vs. Hopkins, 118 U.S. 356 (1886).

Index

About the Contributors

Ann E. Burnette is Associate Professor in the Department of Communication Studies at Texas State University, San Marcos, where she conducts research and teaches classes in political communication and American public address. She has published research on presidential crisis rhetoric, the gender gap in U.S. politics, and historical social movements.

David Droge is Associate Professor in the Department of Communication Studies at the University of Puget Sound. He is coeditor of *Voices of Strong Democracy*, a volume in the American Association for Higher Education series on service learning in the academic disciplines. His current research interests focus on the ways science has been used to both support and refute claims regarding racial differences.

Ann M. Gill is Professor in the Department of Speech Communication and Associate Dean of the College of Liberal Arts at Colorado State University. Her previous scholarship includes analyses of rhetorical strategies in legal discourse and explication of First Amendment issues.

Marouf Hasian Jr. is Professor in the Department of Communication at the University of Utah. He is the author of *The Rhetoric of Eugenics in Anglo-American Thought* (1996). He is currently working on a book that explores how various national and international communities have reacted to Holocaust trials.

Daniel Mangis is a commercial trial attorney in Austin, Texas. He is presently completing his doctorate in communication studies from the University of Texas at Austin. His dissertation proposes a rhetoric-based model for legal reporting. Aside from legal rhetoric, he also studies the communicative functions of trademarks, cultural property, and alternative dispute resolution systems.

Clarke Rountree is Associate Professor and Chair of the Department of Communication Arts at the University of Alabama in Huntsville. His previous work has studied justification in U.S. Supreme Court opinions, the development of corporate criminal law by appellate courts, and the construction of motives in political and religious discourse. He is currently completing a book on the U.S. Supreme Court decision in *Bush v. Gore*.